1987

ARTHURIAN STUDIES IV

*The Character of King Arthur
in Medieval Literature*

ARTHURIAN STUDIES

I

ASPECTS OF MALORY
Edited by Toshiyuki Takamiya and Derek Brewer

II

THE ALLITERATIVE MORTE ARTHURE
A Reassessment of the Poem
Edited by Karl Heinz Göller

III

THE ARTHURIAN BIBLIOGRAPHY
I Author Listing
Edited by Cedric E. Pickford and Rex Last

V

PERCEVAL
The Story of the Grail
Chretien de Troyes

Translated by Nigel Bryant

VI

THE ARTHURIAN BIBLIOGRAPHY
II Index
Edited by Cedric E. Pickford and Rex Last

ISSN 0261–9814

The
Character of King Arthur
in Medieval Literature

ROSEMARY MORRIS

D. S. BREWER · ROWMAN & LITTLEFIELD

© 1982 Rosemary Morris

First published 1982
by D. S. Brewer, 240 Hills Road, Cambridge
an imprint of Boydell & Brewer Ltd
PO Box 9, Woodbridge, Suffolk IP12 3DF
and Rowman & Littlefield
81 Adams Drive, Totowa, NJ 07512, U.S.A.

Reprinted 1985

British Library Cataloguing in Publication Data

Morris, Rosemary
    The character of King Arthur in medieval literature.
    (Arthurian studies, ISSN 0261-9814; 4)
    1. Arthur, *King*   2. Literature, Medieval —
    History and criticism
    I. Title   II. Series
    398'.352   DA152.5.A7

    ISBN 0 85991 088 1

Library of Congress Cataloging in Publication Data

Morris, Rosemary
    The character of King Arthur in medieval literature.
    (Arthurian studies, ISSN 0261-9814; 4)
    Includes bibliographies and index.
    1. Arthurian romances — History and criticism.
    I. Title   II. Series
    PN686.A7M67   809'.93351   82-3712

    ISBN 0 8476 7118 6   AACR2

Printed in Great Britain by
St Edmundsbury Press, Bury St Edmunds, Suffolk

CONTENTS

A NOTE ON THE TEXTS

This study is based on literary works in Latin, Welsh, English, French, Spanish and Portuguese, from earliest times until approximately 1500. I have occasionally referred to Italian sources when they seemed particularly relevant to the discussion. All generalisations are intended to apply only to the linguistic field just defined. Quotations from Welsh texts are translated in the notes.

Numerous works are covered, and for various reasons they are not discussed in strict chronological order. I have assumed an extensive Arthurian knowledge in the reader. The relationships of all the basic texts are discussed in *Arthurian Literature in the Middle Ages*, edited by R. S. Loomis,[1] which I take as read. In dealing with the chronicle tradition I have been guided by R. H. Fletcher's *The Arthurian Material in the Chronicles*.[2]

Several major texts are currently being re-edited, notably the prose *Lancelot* and the prose *Tristan*. For the first I use volume III of Sommer's Vulgate, together with the six volumes of Micha's critical edition.[3] For the second, I use the two volumes of René Curtis's new edition, and the selection edited by J. Blanchard under the title *Les Deux Captivités Tristan*. These I supplement with Löseth's analysis. The notes indicate which is being cited at any one time.[4] For the Boron *Merlin* I use Gaston Paris' edition, the so-called 'Huth Merlin'.[5] For *Palamède* I use Lathuillière's analysis, entitled *Guiron le Courtois;*[6] I continue to prefer the former title. For the *Prophécies de Merlin* I use British Library MS Additional 25434, as L. A. Paton's edition does not contain the 'adventurous' material.[7] For Manessier's continuation of *Perceval*, the only one not yet published by Roach, I supplement Potvin's edition with National Library of Scotland MS Advocates 19-1-5.[8]

There is some confusion at present over the titles of major French prose romances. I use the following titles:

Vulgate (Cycle): for the works in Volumes I-IV of Sommer.
Lancelot-Graal: the ensemble of LP, Vulgate *Quest*, Vulgate *Mort*.
Boron Merlin: the presumed prose rendering of Robert de Boron's *Merlin*, ending on page 146 of Huth.
Vulgate *Merlin* (hereafter VM): for the continuation to the above in Volume II of Sommer.
Post-Vulgate (Cycle): for the ensemble of works discussed in Fanni.
Bogdanow's *The Romance of the Grail* (hereafter RG).[9]
Post Vulgate *Quest*: pending F. Bogdanow's edition of this, I have used the Spanish *Demanda del sancto grial* (cited as *Demanda*), controlling it with the Portuguese translation.[10]

Note on the Prose Lancelot

There has long been dispute over the composition of the various redactions of LP. The publication of Micha's edition is bound to facilitate and renew this controversy. Dr Elspeth Kennedy believes that the original romance, represented by Micha's MSS KR, ended after the False Guinevere episode and ought to be considered as a self-contained work. Others disagree.[11] The existence of two separate redactions of the rest of the romance has been demonstrated by Micha, but he refuses to decide which is the earlier. Since both these questions are so vexed, I have considered each version on its own merits, but assessing arguments for priority when these are relevant to my discussion.

Notes

1. Oxford, 1959. Hereafter ALMA.
2. Harvard University Notes and Studies in Philology, 10. Reprint: Burt Franklin Bibliographical Series, 10 (New York, 1958).
3. *Arthurian Romances*, ed. H. O. Sommer, 7 vols (Washington, 1908-13), vol. III; *Lancelot*, ed. A. Micha, 6 vols, TLF 247, 249, 262, 278, 283, 286 (1978-80). Hereafter LP.
4. *Le Tristan en Prose*, ed. R. Curtis, 2 vols (vol. I, Munich, 1963; II, Leyden, 1976). *Les Deux captivités Tristan*, ed. J. Blanchard, BFRB 15 (Paris, 1976). E. Löseth: *Le Roman en prose de Tristan* (Paris, 1891). The romance is hereafter referred to as TP.
5. *Merlin*, ed. G. Paris and J. Ulrich, 2 vols, SATF (Paris, 1886). Hereafter cited as Huth I, II.
6. R. Lathuillière, *Guiron le Courtois*, PRF 86 (Geneva, 1966).
7. *Les Prophécies de Merlin*, ed. L. A. Paton (New York and London, 1927).
8. *Continuations of the Old French Perceval*, ed. W. Roach, 4 vols to date (Philadelphia, 1965-71); *Perceval le Gallois*, ed. A. Potvin, 6 vols (Mons, 1865-71), vol. 6.
9. Manchester, 1965.
10. Spanish: *Libros de caballerias*, ed. A. Bonilla, 2 vols (Madrid, 1907), vol. 1. Portuguese: *A Demanda do santo Graal*, ed. A. Magne, 3 vols (Rio de Janeiro, 1944).
11. E. Kennedy: 'The Two Versions of the False Guinevere episode in the Old French Prose Lancelot', R 77 (1956), 94-104. Dr Kennedy has also permitted me to consult material from her forthcoming book on the *Lancelot*. For the opposing view see A. Micha: 'Les épisodes du voyage en Sorelois et de la fausse Guenièvre', R 76 (1955), 334-41, 'Le Départ en Sorelois', Mélanges Delbouille, vol. II (Gembloux, 1964), 495-507.
12. See his articles in R 81 (1960), 145-87; 84 (1963), 28-60; 85 (1964), 293-317, 478-504; 86 (1965), 330-59; 87 (1966), 194-233.

INTRODUCTION

Two approaches to the Arthurian material are available to the student. One is to trace the chosen theme from work to work through the language areas involved. This, however, can easily result in fragmentation, especially in the case of Arthur himself, who passes so easily from one language area to another that a language-by-language approach inevitably produces confusion. Medieval Arthurian material, like medieval social organisation, cuts across linguistic and geographical boundaries, so that (for instance) an English chronicler has more in common with a French chronicler than with an English ballad-writer. That is not to say that national boundaries are irrelevant to Arthur, for they are often intensely significant; but they do not condition his legend. The material can also cut across temporal boundaries. Changing literary, linguistic and social conditions are of course mirrored in the development, but an up-to-the-minute fourteenth-century romancer can co-exist with a chronicler who tells the story as Geoffrey, or even Nennius, knew it. It is thus unproductive to pursue Arthur on fixed routes through time and space.

The alternative method is to analyse all the elements which contribute to the development of the chosen theme, so as to reveal exactly how various authors reacted to the challenge of the material, and co-operated to produce a convincing whole. This approach suits the figure of Arthur very well, since all medieval Arthurian writers believed themselves to be describing an identifiable historical figure, and expressed their criticisms of the evidence for that figure by rewriting it.[1]

The present study therefore seeks to analyse Arthur's development by examining his 'literary biography', but, unlike a genuine biographer, I use Arthur to find out about the sources rather than vice versa. The 'biographical' approach has a further advantage in that, by reviewing a sequence of themes, it helps one to keep an open mind on the question of their relative significance. It is, of course, vital to give careful consideration to the outside influences which helped to shape medieval literary texts; but this approach can also narrow the mind, since the more one pursues a single theme, the more one tends to find it everywhere. The reflection of contemporary events is a prime case. One could make out a splendid case for the influence of Henry V's conquest of France on the HRB Roman expedition. Henry was challenged in his own court by an insolent message; his counsellors urged him to take up the challenge, which he joyfully did; he crossed the Channel, landing at Harfleur, swept through Northern France, fought a great battle and was hailed as king, but died before he could be crowned. All this Geoffrey's Arthur does — in the 1130s. Countless other false parallels could be invented. They warn us to be suspicious of historical parallels even when the chronology permits them; to beware, too, of dating fictional works by the historical resemblances which we may seem to detect in them. The arm of coincidence is very long. Even when a historical reference is undoubted, we must ask why it is there. Is the author out to flatter a patron? write a propaganda or allegory? simply cast about for inspiration? Or is the reference made unconsciously? Does it reflect the author's own experience? Such questions are hard to decide; but there must always be more to a reference than the satisfaction its detection gives to a critic.

The same applies, *mutatis mutandis*, to influences of every class, including the literary. Fully to appreciate any work of medieval literature would require a complete understanding of every aspect of the author's time and place, and even then it would be hard precisely to evaluate the author's personal contribution, especially as the majority are anonymous or – like Chrétien and Malory – little more than names. Such complete awareness is impossible; but the open mind may at least be sensitive to some of the multifarious echoes which play round Arthur's place in a work.

The biographical approach may have its own myopia, however. Concentration on a single figure may cause overestimation of his importance, either overall or in individual works. It is undeniable that Arthur is absent from vast tracts of verse and prose romance, and even from considerable areas of chronicle, such as the skirmishes in the Roman war. Even the post-Vulgate, which has been claimed to centre on Arthur,[2] often removes far from him, and itself repeatedly claims to be the romance of the Grail. But even when Arthur is absent for long periods, he is not insignificant. The name 'Arthur' comports a world, and any author who uses it means to evoke something of that world. The common pool of ideas is so rich that he can hardly fail. Thus, when we refer to verse romances, we do not forget that their bulk is devoted to adventures away from court; but we do not consider that Arthur's admittedly rare appearances can be discounted. In the verse as elsewhere, Arthur's appearances are important individually, but much more so collectively. They contribute to the overall picture we seek. In its turn, that picture lends its weight to each appearance. Arthur is more important than any other figure. His world can survive without Lancelot or Guinevere or even Gawain, but remove him and there is nothing. Concentration on him does not, therefore, involve distortion of the legend; on the contrary, it holds the key to the force which gives that legend its coherence.

The 'biographical' approach might also mislead by suggesting that qualities which are actually common in medieval characters are unique to the subject under discussion. In order to avoid this I have borne two acknowledged parallel figures, Finn and Alexander, continually in mind as controls, and have specified the comparison where it is particularly illuminating, as in relation to the birth-tale and Arthur as hunter. In fact, the Arthurian, Alexandrian and Fenian worlds are alike in innumerable ways, both because their creators shared in numerous heroic beliefs and because of direct borrowing from one tradition by another. In any case, all individuality results from particular combinations of human traits; otherwise no individual, fictional or real, could ever be described or understood.

Whatever Arthur borrows from other heroes becomes part of himself.

A third risk of the biographical approach is that of excessive involvement with the subject, which produces angry reaction to unfavourable presentation to him in a particular work — as if all authors were not free to present the 'truth' of a literary character as seemed best to them. Jessie Weston's annoyance over the late French degradation of Gawain, J. Markale's scorn over the 'degenerate' continental Arthur,[3] are examples of such involvement. To avoid it, one must seek reasons for the authors' attitudes, submitting one's own prejudices to theirs. Such involvement with a medieval character is, however, significant in itself. It proves that the authors present him with sufficient conviction and basic consensus to persuade even a modern reader, bred in a largely alien tradition, of his reality and importance. This becomes all the more striking if we remember that historical biographers undergo similar involvement — witness the debates over Napoleon's character or Hitler's. The debates of Arthur's medieval 'biographers' are just as intense, and carry an infectious conviction.

Talk of historical biographies brings us to the 'historical' Arthur. I shall have little to say about him, for the simple reason that nothing can be said with certainty. More important is the fact that medieval authors believed in Arthur's historicity. The dividing line between 'historical' and 'poetic' truth was, of course, not rigidly drawn in the Middle Ages; but even the most inventive authors were convinced that they were describing a 'real' person, and the conviction conditioned their approach.

If it is impossible to reconstitute the 'real' history of Arthur, can one reconstitute his 'original' *fictional* biography? It was for long suspected that the Welsh created a complete tale, now lost, of Arthur's life, and that its *disjecta membra* were scattered through existent Welsh and continental literature, like echoes of the Big Bang. J. Markale has recently tried to reassemble them, with hilarious results.[4] It is now more generally agreed that the Welsh material is not wreckage, but raw material which has the unrealised potential to accrete into a legend.[5] Arthur's first biography is Geoffrey's, and that does not require 'reconstitution'. It is impossible to overstate the importance of Geoffrey to Arthur's literary development. This fact will bear reiteration, for Celticists still maintain the non-essentiality of HRB. The uneven and inconsistent fashion in which Finn's vague and contradictory 'biography' developed shows what the Celts would have done with Arthur had he been left to them. There is no lost biography of Arthur. Nevertheless I have included some of the early material in the biographical scheme, because even at this stage Arthur was beginning to acquire recognisable characteristics.

I have generally avoided all questions of ultimate origins, save in cases like the birthtale, where the significance of the story depends greatly on the nature of its sources, since the origins of, (for example) Excalibur, the Round Table, or the name 'Arthur' have already been the subject of endless investigation. Much of it has divided critics into pro- and anti-Celtic camps, with the inevitable consequence of factionalism. Now, as I hope to show, things function in our texts according to the authors' own intention, and if an author 'falsifies' a Celtic meaning, this does not prevent the object from functioning perfectly in its new setting. Even where misunderstandings cause confusion in an author's mind — as seems to happen in Marie's *Yonec* — modern explanations can do nothing to alleviate the confusion or improve the *sen* of the work. Certainly the objects associated with Arthur are clearly understood by each author on his own terms, and some authors make deliberate modifications so as to adjust an object to a new level of meaning. Most especially does this apply to Arthur himself; the question of his ultimate literary — or mythic — origins is a fascinating puzzle rather than the key to his entire development. Moreover it is unanswerable. Arthur has been 'explained' as an Irish prince, a Celtic deity, a bear-god, a linguistic misrepresentation and (inevitably) the sun. Each explanation is as unsatisfactory as it is ingenious, and none of them explains why Arthur, rather than a dozen other legendary figures, should attract attention, as he undeniably does even pre-Geoffrey. The present study does not attempt the useless task of solving the mystery, but seeks to analyse the ensuing phenomenon of Arthur's adoption as a prime literary symbol of the Middle Ages.

This question, however, leads on to another important point. Critics often speak of Arthur's legend as if it 'just growed', like a living thing, without human agency. This is the less surprising as medieval authors often thought in the same way, speaking of a story's 'branches', and using phrases like 'or dist li contes', which imply that the story itself is an active, autonomous agency. This, of course, helps them to deny the charge of originality, but it also convinces them, and through them the reader, that the Arthurian secondary world has an objective reality which can be discovered, and analysed from various angles, rather than invented *ex nihilo*. The truth is, of course, that the legend can grow only when an author takes it up, and from Nennius onward — as we shall see — every stage in the growth of Arthur's biography can be pinpointed. Nevertheless the legend is at every stage common property, with no copyright and no prize for originality. Each author is an independent agent, but cannot work without his predecessors: he is a dwarf standing on the shoulders of a cumulative giant. The present study attempts to gauge the importance of individual contributions great and small. Some are excellent in themselves; some are not, but stimulate fruitful development; some are neither, but are interesting for their very bizarreness, which demonstrates an author's independence of mind, or simple isolation. This variety often makes it dangerous to take a single author as representative of a group, though it can often be done with the chroniclers, and with most Spanish translators, who reproduce their originals very accurately — an advantage, perhaps, where the original is lost, but a disappointment to the seeker after topicalia and local references. Even works which do belong to a group can exhibit microcosmic variations of great interest; particularly notable, for instance, are those introduced by the ingenious chronicler William of Rennes, who really deserves a study to himself.

In general, however, each work must be considered on its merits. Most authors think carefully about their work, and react sharply against what displeases them in the source. *Sen* changes more readily than *matiere*; but both are essentially fluid. Ideas which displease a majority of authors will wither even if backed by a powerful author. On the whole, the 'winners' are those which — like

Boron's accession-story or Lancelot's love for Guinevere — produce a more powerful narrative, despite the fact that their inventors often lack narrative skill. This survival is, however, often a chancy affair, firstly because authors cannot rely on an universal canon of public good taste, and secondly because of the hazards of manuscript survival. Some atrocious works may have perished — though it is hard to imagine anything more atrocious than the *Chevalier a l'espee* — but the narrow escape of *Sir Gawain and the Green Knight* and the alliterative *Mort* indicates that excellent works, too, may have perished in the hazards of eight centuries. Yet the *Mort* elbowed its way into Malory alongside the popular *Lancelot-Graal*, and the aberrant story of Arthur's fight with a monster cat interests enough minor authors to survive for an amazingly long period. Arthurian literature, unlike oral literature, develops artificially, because writing is artificial, and despite all the critical talk of 'oral tradition', we can know the medieval Arthuriana only through its written traces.

I have then, laid under contribution works of all types, irrespective of genre, language and literary merit. However, these works do undoubtedly fall into three distinct genres — chronicle, verse romance and prose romance — about which generalisations are possible. The key to the distinction lies in attitudes towards the fundamental 'truth' of HRB. Chroniclers modify it, but never reject it; verse-romancers make it almost irrelevant by rejecting the idea of objective, historical time. Prose romancers accept it, but only as the barest bones of a truth which their own 'discoveries' elucidate. That truth is the truth about a whole world, many-layered, complex, neither consistent nor finite. They are doublethinkers, able to believe their own inventions; indeed, doublethinking is one of the salient characteristics of the medieval romancer, though the term is not, of course, pejorative in this connection. Of the three 'genres', the prose romance is the most dynamic; but all three remain vital to Arthur's development. We have to do not so much with three Arthurs, as with three views of the same Arthurian world; and the very contrasts in perspective eventually contribute to the enduring solidity of that world.

Dynamic the prose romances may be, but they do not monopolise Arthurian excellence. Indeed, the most perfect work in medieval Arthurian literature, *Sir Gawain*, has little to say about Arthur. Even more notable for our purposes is the fact that the most interesting and intelligent single account of Arthur is arguably that of *Perlesvaus*. *Perlesvaus*, however, is an Arthurian dead end, within which all enquiries, however enthralling, eventually run up against a blank wall. The reason for this lies, paradoxically, in the author's very originality and inventiveness. He defies the canonical HRB, and his narrative is so tightly organised that it cannot easily be adapted by later authors. In Arthurian matters, intrinsic excellence is no guarantee of success. In any case, no work combines all the best features of Arthur's story, for although the Vulgate and post-Vulgate together cover most of them, they are swamped by extraneous material. In the former, moreover, the multiplicity of authors precludes biographical or artistic consistency, while in the latter, the brilliant inventions and subtle reasoning of the beginning eventually degenerate into an inept farrago which (once again) seems to argue a change of authors.

Where brilliance fails, dullness and unoriginality may, perversely, succeed. Thus the proliferation and persistence of the HRB-based chronicles keep the HRB story available to almost every medieval reader. It is even more fundamental to Arthur than pseudo-Callimachus to Alexander, providing a solid support which outlasts the vagaries of authors like Jean d'Outremeuse or Rauf de Boun, and perhaps bolstering Arthur's reputation when romancers attack it. Similarly, the proliferation of verse romances, while it has almost no effect on the mainstream development, contributes enormously to the secondary world. Chrétien can claim to be the virtual creator of that world, and he lays down laws for it, and for the presentation of Arthur himself, which are faithfully followed by all his successors in the genre — as well as being a major inspiration to the prose writers. To the very end of our period, indeed, Arthur's court is everywhere still constructed on Chrétienesque lines. However, while Chrétien's dominating genius must always command our attention, it is unfair to dismiss all his verse-romance successors as 'dull' and 'unoriginal'. The later ones, such as *Yder*, *Floriant* and *Rigomer*, say far more of Arthur than Chrétien does, and make lively and effective contributions to his overall portrayal. Many of these romances are overdue for the rehabilitation which they will receive as the field of Chrétien studies becomes exhausted. Moreover, the study of Arthur's role in them provides a good key to their general quality, for if they can overcome conventionality in presenting the king, its stultifying effects will be little felt elsewhere. In fact, if dull works can help Arthur, it is also true that a bold consideration of Arthur may help to relieve a work from dullness. Our consideration of the material reveals not only that all Arthurian works basically refer to the same world, but also that none is wholly valueless in the struggle to keep that world alive.

The importance of individual contribution, of varying quality, highlights another important feature which emerges many times from our study. The legend was never codified by a single genius, and diffuseness is of its essence: for every unifying factor there is one of fragmentation. This diffuseness means that many opportunities to improve Arthur's story were missed, either temporarily or permanently. The Arthurian world grew so intricate that it was impossible to present *all* its reality. The very fertility of the romancers' invention was their undoing. Indeed, the whole legend might well have perished if Malory had not cut away so much of the dead wood, and it is to Malory more than to any other writer that we owe the survival of the legend over the succeeding centuries.[6]

Another conspicuous result of the legend's diffuseness is the persistence of beliefs in the teeth of most of the evidence, beliefs like Arthur's birth in Tintagel, Arthur's reputation for justice, and his ownership of the Table and Excalibur. Authors become confused amidst all the complexities, and eventually Arthur himself acquires autonomy from them, so that aspects of his development defy all conscious attempts at modification and pass into a peculiar literary, and popular, subconscious, where indeed they dwell to this day.

Autonomy is, indeed, a very important feature of Arthur's whole world. Again and again we find that the Arthurian 'secondary world'[7] is conservative and true to itself, many of its contemporary references and borrowings being superficial or even accidental. The Arthurian legend is 'anachronistic' in the truest sense of the word: it is timeless. It did not, and does not, survive because it reflects medieval civilisation. If it were only a medieval curio it would perish, as indeed it almost did in the Renaissance and after, when readers noticed only its medievalism and not its universality. Its present enormous public popularity in Britain owes a good deal to Malory, but is not confined to him. There is great interest in the 'historical' Arthur, as was shown during the Cadbury excavations, but the legendary figure, also, has featured both on television and in the new 'popular' books which have appeared at a rate of one every year since 1975. Modern enthusiasts seek three things from Arthur: assurance of his historicity, in support of which they will swallow the most incredible conjectures, because it gives them a link with an enthrallingly barbaric British past; a link with a little-understood world of 'Celtic magic', which combines in their minds with the Grail, Stonehenge, early spacemen and other modern substitutes for religious speculation; and, finally, a contact with the mythic universals, such as religion once provided. In fact, modern readers seek from the legend much the same things as did the original readers; and it is, above all, the perennial themes of passion, guilty love, fated doom and mysterious death which most fix the reader's attention in either epoch. These themes can never be irrelevant to the human condition, but only when their superficial clothing is thought attractive can their fascination be appreciated. The modern clap-trap of Glastonbury 'mysteries' and souvenirs of Tintagel serves that purpose as well as did the medieval paraphernalia of knightly orders and tournament scorecards. Both can point the mind which cries out for enlightenment towards the deeper truths expressed by the legend. The present study has sought to show how the medieval authors forged and expressed those truths, and how far their particular outlook helped or hindered in their clarification. Arthur is not solely the affair of scholars, as his present cult (a significant word) shows; but it is for scholarship to explain why the twentieth century finds in Arthur an alleviation for its malaise.

I

ANTECEDENTS

Despite the infinite variety within the medieval presentation of Arthur, it is possible to discuss him as one figure. For medieval writers, freedom in the treatment of sources does not preclude respect for them, and every treatment of Arthur has links with the aggregate of material. The broad lines of the chronological development of Arthurian material are so well-known that this study will not discuss them in detail. Rather is it concerned to trace some of the complex interlinkages in the material, which often traverse time and space to reveal a curious and enlightening marriage of minds. My chronological order will be not that of literary history, but as far as possible that of Arthur's own life: his literary biography. There is no 'fact' in it which was not at some time disputed by a medieval writer; but from text to text there is always a line to follow.

Let me begin, like a true biographer, by investigating Arthur's antecedents. I do not mean the historical conditions which produced the 'real' Arthur, if such a man existed: I mean the background to his career as it was imagined, and as it evolved, in the minds of medieval writers.

Not all medieval writers on Arthur were concerned about his antecedents. In fact, none, at any time or in any genre, seems to have sat down with the sole purpose of writing Arthur's biography. But there were many who contributed in some way to the provision of a past and a context for Arthur, many who tried to reveal or recreate something of what they took to be the 'real' Arthur. They, like modern historical biographers, weighed up evidence: they considered the work of their predecessors, modified it, added to it or rejected it. They, like modern biographers, were often tempted to supplement the evidence by drawing on their own imaginations: and since, to many of them, beauty was truth, they were far less inhibited about this than any modern historian. Their attitude tended to be constructive whereas that of modern historical criticism — especially, as it happens, where the 'real' Arthur is concerned — tends to be destructive. They built on each other's work to produce a whole which was far greater than the sum of its parts. That is why the literary Arthur, in all his manifestations, is so much more rewarding as a field of study than the historical one.

Our material, taken as a whole, gives us a choice of four contexts for the establishing of Arthur's antecedents. These are:

(i)   The Saxon wars and the loss of Britain
(ii) World history
(iii) Grail history
(iv) Romance history

To these categories some Celticists would doubtless wish to add 'mythic' history. They would draw on Welsh and Irish evidence, and on supposed Celtic elements in the continental material, to establish Arthur as a hero or god of Celtic mythology. However, such antecedents − even if they can be proved − have no place in the medieval authors' conscious explaining of Arthur. This applies to Welsh writers on him as much as to all the others. None of them is in the least concerned to provide any recognisable past for Arthur. They toss his name into the eternal present of a broken-down legendary tradition. Elements of the tradition may coalesce anew to make a recognisable figure of Arthur; they do not indicate that such a figure existed beforehand.

Let us now consider the categories one by one. They do not, of course, supersede one another in the literature in tidy chronological order, though the Saxon war context was undoubtedly the first to emerge, and the 'romantic' context the last. All four still exist, side by side, to the close of our period. It is always in this cumulative − as opposed to supersessive − way that Arthurian development proceeds. Each category can influence the others; but the distinctions remain clear, and important.

The first category begins where Arthurian evidence is traditionally held to begin: with Gildas.[1] Gildas, as everyone knows, does not mention Arthur. Nor does Gildas' work, if we read it without the benefit of hindsight, leave an obvious gap into which Arthur ought to be fitted. The famous passage about the battle of Badon, read in that way, presents no problems: it is obvious that the British commander must be Ambrosius, whose career Gildas has already begun to trace with enthusiastic praise.[2] In spite of this, however, we cannot at once dismiss Gildas with the remark that his 'whole relation to the Arthurian story is accidental'.[3] Gildas' work was used, knowingly or unknowingly, by so many later writers that his peculiar attitudes became fossilised in Arthurian literature. He was so used because, between his time and Nennius',[4] the name of Arthur, culled from who knows what obscure context, had attracted enough attention to begin wresting stories from other figures. He wrested the battle of Badon from Ambrosius: and ever after, anyone who read Gildas with the Arthur-Badon connection in mind would be likely to assume that Gildas' confusingly expressed passage could be forced to yield a context for Arthur. This is exactly what most medieval readers of Gildas, like most modern ones, did. A notable medieval exception is Higden. When using Gildas he automatically assumes that Ambrosius was the commander at Badon. A few lines later, while using Nennius, he meekly restores that role to Arthur.[5] Higden himself is unprejudiced, as a historian ought to be; but the prejudice of other readers was to have more effect on the development of Arthur's legend.

Gildas, then, was laid under contribution by the constructors of Arthur's first set of antecedents. What materials did he supply? Gildas' impassioned scorn for British degeneracy and his loathing for the pagan Saxons overlay a relatively coherent view of British history: of the interaction of Celt, Roman, Pict and Scot, of the coming of the Saxons, and of God's plan for the 'Praesens Israel'.[6] The story goes as far as Gildas' present: recently, the 'superbus tyrannus' has let in the Saxons and the British have deservedly suffered untold miseries, but at the moment, after an indecisive struggle, an uneasy peace reigns. These recent events are, naturally, overwhelmingly important to Gildas, for they are his present reality. Little less important, however, is the Roman past: it embraces all that is worthwhile in British history, and in *romanitas* dwells all that is best in worldly existence.[7] The sense of urgency and actuality in the Saxon struggle is never lost by British and Welsh writers, for whom Norman oppression in time renews the sting of Saxon conquest. For non-British writers, the Saxon theme has not such personal urgency; but it persists in altered form. As for the Roman past, it long continues to be an essential part of Arthur's antecedents, although later authors do not all share Gildas' fervid admiration for *romanitas*. A brave British commander, in sympathy with Roman ideals and dedicated to combating the Saxon menace: such must Arthur be if he is to chime in with Gildas' views, and those views do indeed help to shape Arthur.

No one can deny that there is an Arthur in the *Historia Brittonum*, although his appearance there will probably never be satisfactorily accounted for. Nennius provides him with a reasonably coherent set of antecedents, but his attachment to them is somewhat loose. His famous list of battles is, as it were, embedded in an account of Saxon activities which are not profoundly affected by the interpolation of Arthur's victories. Arthur seems to be a contemporary of Octa, son of Hengest: this ought to put him in the late fifth century, one generation after the *Adventus Saxonum*. This *Adventus* now comports the full story of Vortigern, which prefaces to Arthur (without linking it directly to him) an exciting context of Saxon war, treachery, universal human passions, and, with the story of Ambrosius, magic.[8] Ambrosius' curious transformation from commander to prophet eliminates the only great British commander before Arthur, save for Vortimer[9] — and Vortimer's career is brief. Now, in Nennius the Vortigern story is far more interesting than what is said of Arthur, and appears far more likely to enthral and inspire a later author. Indeed, Arthur only comes to overshadow it, in HRB, by receiving into his own story the most appealing features of Vortigern's, which he adds to his successes as anti-Saxon warrior. His story does not replace Vortigern's, however: the latter long remains an essential element in Arthur's antecedents, in 'World' and 'Grail', as well as 'Saxon' history.

Nennius interweaves the story of Vortigern with that of St Germanus. The presence of the saint gives the entire context a religious colouring, which vanishes almost entirely if one disentangles the saint's legend from that of the *Adventus Saxonum*. It is curious that this should be so, because Gildas interprets the *Adventus* as an outrage against Christianity (Gildas, p.53). With this background one would expect Nennius to bring out the religious aspect of Vortigern's own story, especially as in Nennius his receiving of the Saxons is compounded with his coupling with a pagan woman. One phrase expresses moral disapproval: 'intravit Sathanas in corde Guorthigerni, ut amaret puellam' (Nennius, p.176), but there is no further emphasis. Germanus does, indeed, reproach Vortigern for a sinful marriage, but it is not the marriage to Hengest's daughter, and belongs to Germanus' own story.[10] Now Geoffrey of Monmouth, in using the Vortigern story, omits everything to do with Germanus, but heavily emphasises the Christian-versus-pagan elements of the Saxon struggle, and expresses horror at Vortigern's betrayal of Christianity.[11] Geoffrey, in fact, combines *matiere* and *sen* from both Gildas and Nennius in order to give the Saxon struggle, which colours Arthur's antecedents, the greatest possible interest even to non-British readers. He edits his predecessors' contributions. Nennius himself sees Arthur as a Christian warrior (p.195), but it is Geoffrey who brings out the continuity of the struggle. The religious element proves a powerful magnet for constructors of Arthur's Grail antecedents, who care nothing for British history as such. The seeds of Grail history are thus present in Gildas' work itself.

Nennius also describes the Roman past, but he is no apostle of *romanitas*. For him, Roman history is important only insofar as it affects Britain.[12] Nennius' rambling sentences and mountainous inaccuracies make his account of the Roman period seem myopic in the extreme, but his attitude is the pointer for Geoffrey's ingenious presentation of a Rome dependent on Britain for leadership and regeneration, but also her rival; and that Rome is essential both to Arthur's past and to his present in HRB. Geoffrey exactly reverses Gildas' view of Rome; Nennius is the half-way house.

It is not entirely thanks to Nennius, or even to Geoffrey, that the Romano-British interaction remains in so many works a vital part of Arthur's story. All Christian historical vision since Augustine, and all secular history since Sallust, had been deeply or exclusively concerned with the Roman experience.[13] This means that an Arthurian writer of any western nation, at any time during the Middle Ages, is likely to be pre-disposed to take seriously anything which touches on Rome's past. Rome is also likely to be important to any such writer in his own day. There was still a Roman Empire; Rome was still the centre of the Christian world; and in the opinion of many it was still the ultimate source of political power, whether this derived from the emperor or the pope. Any writer on Arthur is therefore likely to be interested and inspired by the immediacy of Rome in his present and his past, and this is particularly true of world historians. It is therefore in Nennius that we find the first seeds of Arthur's integration into world history.

Nennius has yet more to contribute. Behind the Romans, he takes us into the realm of origin stories. Curiosity about racial origins was a feature of the literacy climate in both Nennius' and Geoffrey's day.[14] Within the Arthurian material, however, it is not in the least confined to those periods. The urge to seek completeness is operative in Arthurian literature throughout the medieval centuries. It does not always lead back to Troy, popular though this origin was in Geoffrey's time,[15] and persistent afterwards by reason of his authority. Nor is it always exclusively dedicated towards putting Arthur in context: that is not true even in Nennius and Geoffrey themselves. In some works, Arthur is indeed the culmination of a long period of history. In others, particularly in the great world histories, it is the long period which counts, and Arthur is only a tiny part of the whole. Nevertheless, it is important that he should be in contact over the centuries with the very beginnings of European civilisation.

Nennius begins his work, as do Gildas, Bede and Geoffrey, with a description of Britain (pp.151-2). This may be taken to launch the one great constant in the presentation of Arthur: he is a British figure. Early Welsh references may confine him to a single corner of Britain; Geoffrey and others give him the dominion of half Europe, or of the world. The concept of Britain varies hugely from author to author: sometimes we get the precision of an ordnance survey map, sometimes the vagueness of a fairy tale, but the link between Arthur and Britain is never broken. However Arthur's antecedents are constructed, wherever the author begins his tale, he must always come to Britain before he can find Arthur.

Saxons, Vortigern, Romans, origins, geographical context: such is Nennius' legacy for the study of Arthur's antecedents. This legacy is more important to the overall legend than is the famous list of battles. Each element influences the presentation not only of Arthur's past, but also of his own career.

Inevitably, we have already, in anticipation, begun to talk about Geoffrey of Monmouth, the Great Divide of Arthurian literature. The development of that literature is very largely a matter of authors' asking the right questions, and Geoffrey asked more of them than any other writer. Few writers after Geoffrey went back to his original sources; most would have been startled and disappointed if they had. Geoffrey himself expresses astonishment at the scantiness of materials available on his period.[16] How little there actually was is plain from the work of Geoffrey's contemporaries, Henry of Huntingdon and William of Malmesbury. All three were rational, intelligent, critical writers; all three had the same materials available to them.[17] But Henry and William are, from the Arthurian viewpoint, writers who did not ask the right questions. For their own purposes they have no need to: their interest is in the recent past, and from that perspective Arthur is very unimportant to them. They do try to situate him in this wider context, but confine him to a small section. In that they try at all, they do represent an advance over Nennius. For Henry, Arthur belongs to a period of remorseless Saxon advance: his successes barely check it.[18] This is exactly what can be deduced from an unprejudiced reading of Nennius. William[19] is slightly more inventive. He harmonises the accounts of Gildas and Nennius, and gives a calm evaluation of Arthur's career on that basis. He tidies up the context by making Arthur a contemporary of Ambrosius, who succeeds Vortigern as king: both are reasonable deductions from the available material. Arthur bravely defends his country against the Saxons, but wins no definitive victory: another plausible deduction. William, who has heard the survival legend,[20] is plainly trying to discount such fictions and give the last word on the 'real' Arthur, summarising all that can ever be known of him. He uses his material at least as well as many modern historians of the period, but his account is an Arthurian dead end. In Arthurian matters, fiction is infinitely preferable to truth.

Geoffrey himself scarcely needs further praise for his superb shaping of the riches which his imagination and learning manufacture from his scrappy sources. His balanced tracing of the rise and fall of a nation; his integration of human passions into politics; his controlled alertness to contemporary issues: all of this is too well-known to require further exposition, as is the vast extent of the debt owed by later writers to HRB. We must remember, however, that Geoffrey did not write the entire HRB solely in order to create a context for Arthur. It has been rightly said that the hero of HRB is Britain.[22] Arthur is treated in more detail than any other monarch, and appealed most to Geoffrey's contemporaries, as he does to us.[23] Geoffrey's *ex nihilo* creation of a complete biography for Arthur is an ineffably important achievement, and that biography is the most appealing story in the work. Arthur encapsulates all the qualities of previous good kings, with the additional attraction of magic. We should not, however, allow Arthur's triumphs to distract us from the fortunes of the true hero. When Arthur arises, Britain has already entered on an irrevocable decline. The high point of British success is Brennius' conquest of Rome; the most important character – to Britain – is arguably Brutus, who creates the British nation out of nothing. It is Brutus, not Arthur, who gives his name to the whole HRB-derived chronicle genre. The great downturn in Britain's fortunes comes with Maximus' removal of all the best elements in the population. After that, Britain, even under Arthur, can never stand alone. Therefore when the Saxons arrive, well before Arthur, their eventual victory is already assured. Geoffrey's overall vision is as pessimistic as Gildas', despite his deeply-felt pride in the British achievement. For him, Arthur is still part of the tale of the loss of Britain.[24] This shadow of loss hangs over vast areas of the later material. From a strictly Arthurian viewpoint, of course, HRB does contain a thorough codification of Arthur's antecedents, both near and remote, which is scarcely less important than the biography itself. As regards the immediate past, Arthur's role in the Saxon struggle is firmly attached to that of his predecessors in Gildas and Nennius. The invention of relationships is an important means to this end. It must have been tempting to make Arthur into Ambrosius' son; but learned contemporaries of Geoffrey might have protested at such an unwarranted assumption from the source-material. Instead, Geoffrey introduces a new figure: Uther, who is made Ambrosius' brother.[25] Arthur is thus connected to Ambrosius by the privileged uncle-nephew link. The two never meet, but the Saxon struggle is nonetheless a family affair. It has something of the flavour of a dynastic struggle, the House of Constantine versus the House of Hengest, with the traitor Vortigern and his loyal son Vortimer spreadeagled in the middle. The family network also gives Arthur a close connection with the enthralling Vortigern story. The family relationship also, of course, sets Arthur in the huge descent of the British royal house and its collective destiny.

The next most important link between Arthur and the immediate past is the person of Merlin.[26] Although – an important point in view of developments later in the literature – Arthur and Merlin never meet in HRB, Merlin links Arthur to Uther, Ambrosius and Vortigern by a strand of magic. In HRB, Merlin is not the directing force of the action: that is a later development. He obeys the orders of the kings, save when he acts before Vortigern to save his own life. Merlin's importance in HRB is of another kind. He is a repository of mysterious power. When he is present, the boundaries of human experience may at any moment be enlarged, for the benefit or the perdition of his interlocutors. He represents the intervention of the incalculable, the supernatural, in human affairs: and that is what gives Arthur's immediate antecedents their peculiar fascination.

Merlin's most significant role in HRB is, arguably, not his intervention in the action, but his character of prophet. To the medieval mind, history and prophecy were closely linked.[27] It was believed that a thorough knowledge of past and present, coupled with supernatural — normally divine — inspiration, really could enable a man to read the future. Merlin's prophecies, situated as they are at the linking-point of Vortigern's story and Ambrosius', link Vortigern, the Saxons and the House of Constantine in a chain of ominous mystic half-revelation which encompasses the whole HRB, both past and future, and stretches on to the reader's own day. One does not need to interpret the prophecies in order to sense their importance. Through them, history reaches beyond the complications of day-to-day events, beyond the pattern of early British history, and becomes an adumbration of divine purpose. It is the prophecies, not the 'magic', which qualify Merlin for the vital role he is to play in the Grail romances; it is the prophecies which make Arthur's HRB antecedents thrilling even to those who are not moved by the Saxon wars.

Saxon war, magic, passion and prophecy are the attractive components of Arthur's immediate HRB past. For Grail writers, this is all that is required from HRB: at this point, Arthur's Grail antecedents split off from his Saxon War antecedents. There are, however, many writers — chiefly chroniclers — who follow Geoffrey much further back. Such writers find that the remoter past, too, is closely connected with Arthur. Maximus' expedition determines the nature of the Britain and the Europe which Arthur is to tackle. Maximus himself capitalises on the relationship between Britain and Rome. To Geoffrey, the Roman period is still vital, but Britain is the conqueror of Rome rather than *vice versa*. Caesar's invasion is not a spontaneous aggresssion, but an attempt to avenge the success of Brennius (HRB 306): an attempt which barely succeeds, and which makes Rome dependent on Britain rather than dominant over her. Arthur's own Roman war is but an attempt to reclaim what he considers to be already his (HRB 462-3). Thus the climax of Arthur's career, and his downfall, depend entirely on the Roman past.

Earlier HRB events are less obviously connected with Arthur, but the remorseless recurrence of behaviour-patterns reminds us that all belong to one story.[28] The elaborate origin story is more directly relevant, not only as an adumbration of British character and success, but also for the even remoter links which it establishes. Brutus' story begins at the end of Aeneas', Aeneas' at the end of Troy's. Arthur is thus connected, via Brutus, to a whole world of classical knowledge and story. Something of the fame of the antique heroes must surely accrue to the new character, Arthur, the seeds of whose glory are sown at the time of Achilles.[29] They are all part of one story: a fact which is recognised with particular clarity by the compilers of Welsh manuscripts which preface Dares Phrygius to the *Brut*.[30]

HRB's opening description of Britain reminds us afresh of the symbiosis between Arthur and his homeland. Geoffrey's Britons are always conscious of the world outside, but they stand and fall by, and in, Britain. It is in a deep sense theirs and no other race's, for they took in from non-humans (HRB 294), something which no subsequent invader can claim. The giants themselves are important to some followers of Geoffrey, who consider their origins part of the story of Britain and of Arthur.[31] Arthur, himself a giant-killer,[32] has at least an ideological link with the British giants, and with their mighty enemy Corineus, who is as much an adumbration of Arthur as Brutus is.

The HRB Arthur, then, grows out of the whole work and carries the full weight of its ideology. Obviously, Geoffrey's patterning is so elaborate that it would be hard to alter it without destroying it altogether. This is a positive advantage to the uninspired chronicler: everything is neatly set out for him, and he need make no effort to create a coherent story. Hence the endless summaries and reproductions of HRB which we find in monastic chronicles. But the solidity is also an advantage to the creative adaptor who desires a secure basis for his inventions. A Wace or a Layamon can invent freely, secure in the knowledge of the excellence of the story he tells. The same solidity is useful not only to chroniclers, but also to romancers of all periods who wish to situate Arthur, but have no wish to retell the whole HRB story, nor to invent a new one. Relying on knowledge of the popular HRB story in their audience, such romancers can evoke it by brief allusion. Thus, at a stroke, Chrétien can recall for us the whole vista of Geoffrey's history – without in the least disturbing the flow of his own narrative: '...toz li roiames de Logres,/ qui jadis fu la terre as ogres'.[33] Some two hundred years later, *Sir Gawain and the Green Knight*[34] can, with equal confidence, preface and conclude its narrative with an evocation of the whole course of British history from the destruction of Troy, impressing the reader with the prestigious depth of the roots whence Arthurian civilisation – and, ultimately, English civilisation – sprang.

Arthur's Saxon war context, and what lies behind it, can thus crop up in unexpected places. Such allusions are, however, relatively rare in the non-cyclic verse romances. For them, Arthur's reign is an eternal present: this is, indeed, the distinguishing mark of the verse-romance concept. Reference to remote events (as opposed to a vague and harmless 'long ago') can very easily shatter the golden bubble of continuous present, and, by reminding us of change in the past, warn us of the inevitability of change in the future. Prefatory references, like those of GGK or the Latin *Historia Meriadoci*,[35] cause less disturbance, and give a certain solidity to Arthur's sometimes fairytale world. More disturbing are references like those in Chrétien's *Perceval* to the troubles attendant on the end of Uther's reign (ll.462-8) and to Arthur's (dead?) mother (ll.8740ff).[36] Now in *Perceval* there is indeed a sense of change, following upon the appearance of the Grail. The references to the past trouble the present and the future, and presage the abandonment of verse-romance security – which, in the major prose Grail romances, does indeed take place. More typical of the verse romances are works like *Cligès* and *Bliocadran*,[37] which begin with the hero in his cradle, but show no sense of the historical changes which ought to take place as the hero's life proceeds.

Reproduction and brief allusion do not exhaust the variety of possible approaches to Arthur's Saxon war antecedents. Most important for Arthurian development is the approach of selective adaptation. This, however, leads to the introduction of HRB material into other categories of antecedents, which we shall deal with in their turn. There is one further approach which stays within the Saxon war category, but which rejects the HRB patterning altogether. The most notable exponent of this approach is William of Newburgh.[38] The scope of William's work is exactly the same as that of the chronicles of Henry of Huntingdon and William of Malmesbury. Like them, he was chiefly interested in recent events; like them, he felt it incumbent on him also to delve into the remote past, and to clarify what he found there. For William, however, it was not a case of drawing together small scraps of material, but of cutting through the *embarras de richesse* presented by HRB. William of Newburgh, like William of Malmesbury, has a suspicious nature. Both are little inclined to believe in fictions about Arthur: but whereas, for Malmesbury, 'fictions' mean oral survival-tales, for Newburgh they mean Geoffrey's story. For Newburgh, beauty definitely does not equal truth: in this he stands apart from the vast majority of Arthurian writers. He goes behind HRB, as few of its medieval readers do, and finds the original sources. Now most medieval writers, if they come across conflicting accounts, will attempt to harmonise them. For William of Newburgh, however, the more reliable source cancels out the lesser, and for the 'Arthurian' period he considers the most reliable source to be Bede. Having decided that Geoffrey's work is unreliable, William then sets out to demolish it. Thus far, he has proceeded very much as a modern historian would. We must, however, beware of assuming that he criticises Geoffrey from the same viewpoint as a modern historian. His scepticism is bounded by the intellectual climate of his own time. Thus, he challenges the story of Merlin's supernatural powers not on the basis of the non-existence of demons, but on the basis of what he considers to be a sounder estimation of demonic capabilities. He dismisses Arthur's giant not because there are no such things as giants, but because there have been none since biblical times. He challenges the authenticity of Merlin's prophecies not on the grounds that accurate prophecy of the future is impossible, but on the grounds that Merlin's prophecies have not come true. When castigating the inaccuracy of Geoffrey's 'facts', he relies more on scorn than on detailed refutation, or else voices his own opinion, supported by probability rather than fact, that the thing is impossible. William is a better literary than historical critic: he gives a shrewd estimation of Geoffrey's reasons for inventing such fictions. All in all he achieves, to his own satisfaction, the task of clearing the ground for more sober histories. He concentrates his attack on Arthur himself, evidently because he knows that Arthur is the most popular feature of the book; but in eliminating Arthur he automatically destroys the whole HRB context as well. He does not even substitute a supposedly historical residue: since Bede does not mention Arthur, there is no such residue anyway. It is not, however, surprising that William's remarks did not lead to a wildfire spread of incredulity. Like most people, he believes what he wants to believe. It would not be difficult to marshal arguments, equally sound within the twelfth-century context, in Geoffrey's favour. Trevisa and Thomas Gray produce some of them in later centuries.[39] Paradoxically, William's work, which achieved so little, is in itself a witness to the success of Geoffrey's patterning.

A different kind of rejection, still within the Saxon war context, is found in the work of the Scottish chroniclers, Boece and his successors.[40] They accept Geoffrey's material and his patterning of it, but reject his basic assumption: that the Britons, alone of the Five Races, have a right to the land. The Normans, for whom Geoffrey wrote, apparently did not consider themselves insulted by this premiss: even William of Newburgh writes in the interests of abstract truth, not of nationalistic prejudice. The continental French did consider themselves insulted by HRB, but reacted by completely reshaping the antecedents — as we shall shortly see. There is no early Saxon account of Arthur; if there were, we should expect a hostile denigration. Thomas Gray suggests that Bede's silence on Arthur could be explained by his hostility to a great British figure:[41] if Arthur were a historical person, this would be a perfectly reasonable explanation. Layamon's early Middle English account does not (as do later English works) think of Arthur as an honorary Englishman, but it excuses his Britishness on the grounds of his Christianity.

It is in the Scots that we find nationalistic prejudice most violently at work. Ironically they, too, see Arthur as an honorary Englishman,[42] and therefore attack Geoffrey for something he never meant to do.

Basically, the Scottish chroniclers view the events in HRB from a northern angle. To Geoffrey, and to all other Arthurian writers, the northerners — the Picts and the Scots — are as indistinguishable as mustard and cress. They have little to do with the mainstream of British history, being at most a tiresome, albeit persistent, distraction. The Scots reverse this view. The Picts and Scots are clearly distinguished nations, each with their own affairs and policies; the British and the Saxons are the distraction, and, save for the paganness of the Saxons, there is little to choose between two wicked nations. Geoffrey himself (drawing on Gildas) gives the Scots their handle for the castigation of British wickedness. HRB accepts the view that the British lost the dominion of Britain because (all the best elements having gone to Brittany) they were no longer worthy to hold it. All the Scots have to do is to develop the idea of British unworthiness. Since the British are wicked, any northern attack on the south is justified: and these attacks are strung together with a consistent motivation. The inversion of Geoffrey's *sen* is carried out with vigour and ingenuity. Thus, it is Vortigern himself who murders Constans; his uncouth Pictish mercenaries become noble innocents, framed and then unjustly executed by the British king. It is to avenge this outrage that the northerners invade Britain, forcing Vortigern to compound his crime by calling in the Saxons. Geoffrey himself does not whitewash Vortigern; but the Scots give an entirely new slant on his crimes. Later, Hengest pours poison in the ears of Vortigern, distorting the northerners' legitimate territorial claims against the Saxon settlers. These claims are the eternal bone of contention between south and north (as they were in the chroniclers' own times).[43] Ambrosius and Vortimer are still 'good' Britons — because they respect the northerners and humbly accept their indispensable help against the Saxons. The Britons alone cannot resist the Saxons: after the death of Ambrosius, Uther is forced to patch up a peace with Octa — whom in HRB he easily defeated and imprisoned. The Britons, always fundamentally corrupt, use the peace to indulge in vice of which Uther's seduction of Ygerne is merely symptomatic. Uther ends his life in shameful defeat.[44] It is against such a background that Arthur appears, and in such a way that he himself is to conduct his relations with Saxon, Pict and Scot. The defeat and loss which, in HRB, hangs over the Arthurian period but is suspended in a last blaze of glory, is in the Scottish chronicles a permanent, ever-active feature. The Scottish purpose, in describing Arthur's antecedents, is to doom him from the start to failure, degradation and corruption. Their ingenuity proves that it is not necessary to reject Geoffrey in order to cut Arthur down to size. A propagandist is always most successful when he speaks his enemies' language.

For the vast majority of medieval readers, however, HRB was the basic account of the 'historical' Arthur. It could be adapted or rejected, but never suppressed. Our first category of antecedents, as codified by Geoffrey, is therefore the basis of all the others.

Our second category is that of world history. It is the least important from a strictly Arthur-centred point of view, but it does represent a particular use of the figure. It also helps to ensure Arthur's integration into the world of international medieval learning. Alfonso el Sabio's *General Estoria* was one of the first works to introduce Arthur into Spain; Gottfried of Viterbo was the first Italian to give literary treatment to Arthur in his *Pantheon*.[45] As an example of the world chronicle, let us take the popular *Polychronicon* of Higden. Higden, unlike some such chroniclers, is no mere compiler. He attempts to harmonise and rationalise his materials. Now, Arthur, even in his HRB clothing, is necessarily only a tiny element in the massive sweep of world events from the Creation to the present day. In addition, however, Higden's assembling of material for the 'Arthurian' period, material both British and otherwise, leads him to distrust Geoffrey. For him as for William of Newburgh, the more reliable sources cancel out the lesser. The lesser, as far as Arthur is concerned, are HRB and the romances; the more reliable are Gildas, Nennius and Bede. These Higden attempts to harmonise, and in doing so he creates a completely new context for Arthur. With a little juggling of possible dates, Higden settles that Arthur was a contemporary of Cerdic of Wessex; and he virtually confines Arthur's activities to an unsuccessful local struggle against that monarch. From a world conqueror, Arthur shrinks to a tiny thorn in the Saxons' side, less important than he was in Nennius or William of Malmesbury. All his tightly-constructed HRB antecedents are dissipated amidst the mass of worldwide reportage, so that although his clearly situated he is almost as isolated as he is in Nennius (ll. 328-36). Higden's debunking of Arthur had more success than William of Newburgh's. It was notably influential when it was read by Boece, who uses Higden's anti-HRB arguments as fuel for his own attacks on Arthur's glory. The HRB-based chronicle of Hales, the mixed compilations of Thomas Gray and John of Glastonbury — to name no more — also use Higden.[46] Thus the idea of Arthur's insignificance when set in the context of world history crossed over into other antecedent-categories, influencing authors, assisting them, and often perplexing them. *Polychronicon* is a standing challenge to HRB.

The third category is that of 'Grail antecedents'. This, like the world-history view, involves a complete change of perspective. Unlike world history of the Higden kind, however, it does not induce a complete abandonment of HRB, which the Grail writers — and first and foremost Robert de Boron — accept as the repository of basic Arthurian truth. There is much in HRB which is attractive to a pious writer. The figure of Merlin is, as we have seen, a suitable grappling-hook for someone wishing to attach supernatural wonders to HRB's secular story. Geoffrey also pays close attention to the conversion of the Britons, and gives details of British ecclesiastical organisation. Bishops play an important part in the story. The horror of Saxon paganism, and of Vortigern's sufferance of it, is emphasised. Arthur himself is a Christian warrior at Badon and at Siesia.[47] Several imitators of Geoffrey bring out the religious elements, but without departing from his basic pattern. Notable examples are the 'Variant Version' — and Wace, through whom the HRB reached French vernacular writers.[48] All such imitators are, however, bound eventually to submit *religio* to *natio*. The Grail writers set out to do the reverse. They are not interested in Britain and British Christianity, nor in Arthur, for their own sake. Their hero is the Grail: Britain is important as the receptacle of the Grail, and Arthur as the Augustus during whose reign the new Messiah, the Grail knight, will appear. If the Grail is to be traced back to its ultimate, non-British origin, a large part of the HRB past becomes an irrelevant distraction, and must be jettisoned. It then becomes necessary to graft the new Grail history on to what is to be retained of HRB.

To the medieval mind, all historiography began with the Bible.[49] Later events were part of the same history of salvation. World histories always begin with biblical events. Nennius and Geoffrey themselves had established chronological correspondences with biblical history. Therefore, the Arthur of HRB-based chronicles and of world histories already stands in an historical tradition leading back to the Bible. Robert de Boron simply follows a different strand of that tradition. His *Joseph*[50] is a new Acts of the Apostles. Joseph and his relatives, like Christ's apostles, come forth from Judea soon after the Ascension, to spread God's word among the Gentiles. Like Acts, *Joseph* follows straight on from the Gospels, which in turn grow out of Old Testament history. Joseph's voyage to Britain thus establishes a direct link between that country and the Holy Land, and Arthur is linked not to Brutus and Troy, but to Christ.

Once in Britain, Boron's 'apostles' cannot exist *in vacuo*. If Boron is to work his way from Joseph to Arthur, he must re-tell British history. Joseph's wanderings are indeed, parallel to Brutus', though one is led by God and the other by a pagan goddess. The two events are, however, not contemporaneous. According to Geoffrey, Christ was born in the reign of Cunobelinus (HRB 320), some fifty-three generations after Brutus. Is Robert to integrate his story of Joseph's kin in Britain with Geoffrey's complex account of the eighteen-odd generations between Cunobelinus and Arthur? It is impossible. There is no room for Joseph in Geoffrey's unequivocal tale of the Britons' conversion under Lucius. Nor will the chronology fit: there are only two generations between Joseph and Perceval in *Joseph*.[51]

Faced with such irreconcilable contradictions, Boron gave up. We do not possess his account of the Grail-bearers' adventures in Britain: quite likely he never got round to writing it.[52] He in fact latched on to HRB at a later point, where Merlin was waiting to welcome him. By tracing Merlin's story back to his own starting-point, the Crucifixion, he was able to confirm the vital link between his material and HRB's. Even so, in the prose *Merlin* the join is glaringly obvious: '. . . Et Engleterre n'avoit adont eut encore rois crestiien, ne des rois qu'i avoient esté devant ne me tient a retraire fors tant que a ceste conte amonte.' (Huth I.35) For readers acquainted with Wace — and many of Boron's original readers were doubtless in that position — the first statement is untrue. Nonetheless, the join has been made, for better or for worse. At least the vague reference to former kings may induce the informed (but not too well-informed) reader to remember the HRB procession of kings and feel himself on firm historical ground.

Once Boron is inside Geoffrey's story, he becomes to some extent a prisoner of its powerful structure. He elaborates and modifies enormously, of course, but the familiar events are there in the familiar order. The most profound change is the emphasis given to Merlin's direction of events,[53] and the growing awareness that he is steering them towards the foundation of the second Round Table and the birth of Arthur. He does so because both occurrences are vital for the achievement of the Grail. Through him, sacred history infiltrates secular history. Through Boron, sacred history monopolises the structuring of Arthur's antecedents.

A more satisfactory way of restructuring Arthur's past is found by the author of *Perlesvaus*,[54] who begins determinedly *in medias res*, and explains Arthur's connection with the Grail in ideological, not historical, terms. He thus achieves what very few prose romancers can bear to attempt: a sacrifice of completeness to clarity. Boron's flounderings highlight the wisdom of the *Perlesvaus* author's decision. It is plain, however, that it is only Boron's work which encourages future development along the same lines. Such development did take place. The prose *Estoire*[55] tells the full story of the Grail-bearers' adventures in Britain. It worries not a jot about the HRB data, taking Boron as its guide. The result is an alternative prehistory of Arthurian Britain, which, like *Polychronicon*, is a standing challenge to HRB. The challenge is quite serious, because the *Estoire* shares, however undeservedly, in the popularity of the Vulgate Cycle to which it prudently attaches itself.

In other sections of that same cycle, however, there is yet another set of antecedents for Arthur, which again jettisons most of HRB's data: that provided by LP. Here we enter on our fourth category, that of 'romance antecedents'. The author of the first part of LP is a realist. He does not, like a verse romancer, see Britain as a land of magic; he sees it as a political entity, and he sees it as France's enemy across the Channel — just as the later Scottish authors see it as Scotland's enemy across the Humber. It is, nevertheless, this realist who begins the creation of what I call Arthur's romance antecedents. He explains the context for Arthur in his opening paragraphs, and describes it from a French viewpoint which at once implicitly challenges HRB's Britain-centredness. The author explains that the current situation in France is the result of Uther's recent warlike activities there. The naming of Uther and Hoel indicates an awareness of HRB; but Uther's continental adventures find no mention in that work, any more than do the names of Ban, Bohors or Claudas. An Uther with time to go raiding on the continent is more like a prefiguration of Arthur than like the embattled Uther of HRB. In a few sentences, the LP author loosens the grip of HRB on Arthur's antecedents more thoroughly than Boron ever does. The remote past, with all its power to shape Arthur's destiny, disappears from view. Arthur can look only to his father: and his father is so like his (Arthur's) HRB self that it seems that time, between Uther and Arthur, virtually stands still. Something of the eternal present of the verse romance lays its grip on LP. Arthur's past and present coalesce and confuse one another.

Both the Boron *Merlin* and LP gained great prestige in the French literary circles. Since each dealt with a different stage in the history of Arthurian Britain, it was natural that the thirteenth-century literary ambience, with its passion for completeness and comprehensiveness, should encourage the forging of a link between the two. However, attempts to do this inevitably comported a clash of antecedents similar to the clash between *Joseph* and HRB. Boron's account of Uther leaves no room for his raiding as told in LP: doubtless that is why no manuscript exists in which the Boron *Merlin* is followed directly by LP. The join could be eased over by the insertion of vast amounts of additional material, as is done in the Vulgate *Merlin* and in the *Livre d'Artus*;[56] but even so the linking authors become entangled in innumerable contradictions, some of which we shall have occasion to examine in later chapters. Basically, Boron and LP have totally irreconcilable viewpoints.

The attachment of LP to the Boron *Merlin* did not totally inhibit the development of Arthur's romance antecedents, though it prevented them from collecting into a complete, separate work. Instead, followers of LP trace back its allusions to the past piecemeal. They take advantage of the very looseness of the Boron-LP join to weave new themes, in a way never permitted by the tightly-knit structure of HRB. The early TP provides a good example of the procedure. Tristan's ancestors insinuate themselves into Arthur's Grail antecedents by relating themselves to the Grail family, and into his romance antecedents by connecting themselves with the French past, whose importance for Arthur's career LP had irrevocably established. Not only does this process vindicate Tristan's own claim to importance in the Arthurian present: it also enlarges the scope of the romance past. Tristan's ancestors in the past have adventures similar to the Arthurian adventures of LP and the verse romances. The adventurous world which such romances hold to be unique to Arthur's reign thus escapes from Arthur's exclusive control. The *Livre d'Artus* similarly refers to an adventure, the 'Ile Tournoiant', which was set up in Uther's time and is to be achieved in Arthur's. TP itself also has more general references to conditions in Uther's reign, such as the information that Ban and Bohors were frequent and honoured visitors to his court. This strongly suggests that Uther's court was similar to Arthur's, which also has an honoured French guest in Ban's son Lancelot.

The idea that Uther's time was similar to Arthur's, faintly adumbrated at the beginning of LP, confirmed in TP and echoed in the *Livre d'Artus*, is codified in

Rusticiano's compilation[57] and in *Palamède*. These works do not set out deliberately to tell the story of Uther's reign, but they carry the TP technique (the allusions to relics of the past, and characters' reminiscences of it) to such a pitch that we continually lose sight of the Arthurian present. Uther's court becomes quite indistinguishable from Arthur's. At least once in *Palamède*, the same story is told of Uther in one manuscript and of Arthur in another.[58] Many of the characters survive from Uther's reign into Arthur's, and carry on exactly as before. Not only HRB and Grail history, but even LP history, are almost completely lost sight of. Arthur's romance past, fully developed, is simply a backward extension of his present. He shapes the past rather than *vice versa*. There is, of course, no reason why this Arthurianisation of the past, having extended to Uther, should not extend even further back. It was, after all, no new idea that *chevalerie* had existed in ancient times.[59] Such extensions were practised: *Perceforest* is a notable example of an Arthurian-type romance in a setting remote in time from the Arthurian period. Such works, however, are not claimed as Arthurian, whereas *Palamède* is. Some close connection with the magic name of Arthur, and all the trappings which generations of authors attach to that name, is still needed if the work is to partake of the unfailing Arthurian enchantment. It is easier to appreciate Arthur without a past — as the verse romancers present him — than a past without Arthur.

From LP onwards, Arthur's romance antecedents also have another connotation. Early in LP, a hermit challenges Arthur's knights to equal Uther's knights, who conquered France. Evidently the author's belief is that Arthur's knights are inferior. In Rusticiano and *Palamède* this belief is continually reiterated. The authors cannot bear to have their favourite heroes, who belong in Uther's time, outdone by the new generation. Tristan and Lancelot are grudgingly allowed to equal their sires, but all others are subordinated. The inferiority of Arthur's generation is expressed outright many times, most notably in Rusticiano's popular 'Ancient Knight' adventure.[60] Now, all the French prose cycles show a tendency to limit Arthur's power and prestige, for they use him as a text to criticise contemporary notions of kingship. Here, we see that limitation backdated to Arthur's past. The universal human sentiment that the past was better than the present gives their attack conviction. Arthur's romance antecedents threaten to rob him of his glory, if not his very self. They undermine the whole edifice to such an extent that not even French authors can maintain it for ever: it is surely no coincidence that there are no major re-workings of Arthur's story in French after *Palamède*.

It is plain that none of our last three categories of antecedents has the coherence, the force and the fascination of Geoffrey's. It is not, therefore, surprising that the HRB account keeps its popularity and influence throughout the Middle Ages. Neither is it surprising that authors, still seeking for comprehensiveness, attempted the impossible task of reconciling the HRB antecedents with one or more of the later categories. Naturally, the result is always either simple juxtaposition or total confusion. In John of Glastonbury we find juxtaposition. He touches on Grail antecedents when he traces Arthur's ancestry back to Joseph of Arimathaea, goes on to situate him according to

Higden's data, and describes his continental conquests in genuine HRB fashion.[61] Some attempt is made to mould all the borrowings into a coherent story, but their conflicting implications are not discussed. In Thomas Gray we find confusion, with attempts at clarification. Gray locates Arthur according to HRB data, but attempts to rationalise the extent of his success against the Saxons so as to conform to Higden's authority. He then goes on to include elements from the Boron *Merlin* and the post-Vulgate, with their Grail and romance-antecedent connotations. Finally, he embarks on a discussion of Arthur's historicity in which he refers to the attitude of Bede and, apparently, of Nennius.[62] His discussion raises many intelligent arguments, but their intelligence is invalidated by the extensive credulity *vis-à-vis* Geoffrey, and the boundless credulity *vis-à-vis* the romances, which are exhibited in his own narrative. In Gray, a critical historian struggles against a hopeless romantic; the struggle does not make for consistency.

Finally, in Jean d'Outremeuse[63] we find not only total confusion, but enjoyment of it. He claims to be a world chronicler, and certainly he starts with remote origins (the siege of Troy), and thoroughly mixes events in various places – completely without the control and discrimination attempted by a Higden. He is not, however, content to give Arthur a small corner in world history. He emphasises Arthur's prominence by including a summary – albeit a fantastically inaccurate one – of all his HRB antecedents. Like the prose romancers, however, he has a predominantly French viewpoint, and does not hesitate to distort Arthur's story in order to clarify that of a French hero. Like the prose romancers also, Jean backdates the adventurous period to a long way before Arthur's own reign. This mixture of three categories – HRB, world history and romance – is overlarded generously with the products of Jean's own imagination, which completes the chaos. The painstaking work of generations of Arthurian writers is mangled and abused.

With Jean d'Outremeuse we virtually come round full circle. Arthur has his beginning in the mists of the Dark Ages, shot through with the dubious lights of shattered mythology, half-understood history and folkloric invention. In Jean's chronicle, he floats in a coloured mist of literary reminiscences, torn from their context and with their ideology obscured. No one medieval concept of Arthur could ever monopolise Arthurian literature. Arthur could outlive any prejudice and any intellectual fashion. The way was always open for the creation of new concepts, and the ruins of the old ones furnished material for the new. Jean's work is itself a potential quarry. That no Geoffrey ever came to exploit it was merely an unfortunate chance.

II

CONCEPTION AND BIRTH

Ideas on Arthur's antecedents may vary, but there is only one account of his parentage and engendering. Geoffrey's story is so bizarre, and yet so full of human interest, that it proved sufficient stimulus to Arthurian writers throughout the medieval centuries. It is variously developed, re-interpreted, occasionally suppressed, but never replaced.

So important is the HRB birthtale that some consideration of its origins seems to be in order. I do not wish to re-open in detail the long-term Celtic-versus-Classical controversy on the subject. Tatlock's trenchant discussion of the problem exposes the weakness of the Celticists' parallels.[1] Only those ubiquitous scape-goats, Oral Tradition and the Lost Story, can explain the discrepancies between the Celtic stories and Arthur's birthtale, and such conjectures are of little value. The Classicists, on the other hand, can cite two striking parallels: the births of Hercules and Alexander. Tatlock energetically advocates the former, but cannot disguise the fact that it was difficult of access in the twelfth century. The allusions in the *Metamorphoses* to which Tatlock refers[2] are comprehensible only to someone already familiar with the story. I quote them:

> (Jupiter) . . . Amphitryon fuerit, cum te, Tirynthia, cepit.
>> (VI. 112)
>> . . . nam, quo te iactas, Alcmena nate, creatum,
>> Iuppiter, aut falsus pater est aut crimine verus.
>> (IX. 23-4)
>> . . . nec cognoscenda remansit
>> Herculis effigies, nec quicquam ab imagine ductum
>> matris habet, tantumque Iovis vestigia servat.
>> (IX. 263-5)

Even Geoffrey, with his talent for creating a story out of the barest reference,[3] could not re-forge from these *Metamorphoses* references something so similar to the original story.

Of the other suggested sources, Vitalis of Blois' *Geta* belongs to the mid-twelfth century. A recent study gives a *terminus ante quem* of 1170-80, but is unable to give a precise *terminus post quem*.[4] It is doubtful whether Geoffrey, writing before 1136, would have had access to it. The two works exhibit no striking

24

verbal or narrative similarities. In *Geta*, the story is treated as comedy, and the actual birth of Hercules is not even mentioned.

It is Hyginus who furnishes the closest correspondence with Geoffrey's story.[5] In Hyginus' account, Amphitryon is away at the wars; Alcmena, deceived, receives the disguised imposter in her bed; the two are surprised by the news of Amphitryon's return (corresponding to Gorlois' death in Geoffrey); Alcmena is reassured; Hercules is engendered. The resemblance does suggest direct imitation on Geoffrey's part. Tatlock asserts that 'Hyginus was somewhat known to medievals'[6] but in fact traces of him are scanty. Only one manuscript survives, in fragments, and it certainly never came near England.[7] It is true that William of Rennes clearly saw the similarity of the two stories.[8] This, however, does not prove that 'writers later than Geoffrey had little trouble in recognising the parallel'.[9] William is only one writer, and is exceptionally learned in classical literature. The detail which William draws from the Hercules story — the lengthening of the night — is the one detail in Hyginus' account which finds no echo in HRB; we should have expected Geoffrey to capitalise on such a striking notion. Did William wish to indicate, by a sly allusion, that he had identified Geoffrey's source? Or was he independently struck by the parallel, which he used to increase the dramatic solemnity of the story? William's usage does prove that the story was available in the twelfth century, perhaps in some obscure florilegium. As for Geoffrey, it is almost certain that he used the legend, possible that he used Hyginus: more than that we cannot say. It is certain that no other medieval imitator of Geoffrey shows signs of recognising the Hercules parallel.

Tatlock also suggests a parallel with Alexander.[10] Now, it is unquestionable that Geoffrey had Alexander in mind when creating Arthur, though the similarity of their careers is more general than particular. But in the birth tale, only the fact of shape-shifting is the same; all the other circumstances are different. The Alexander story could not alone have inspired Geoffrey, but it might well have influenced his decision to use the Hercules story. (Indeed, the latter may have inspired the author of the original Alexander romance.)[11]

There is a third possible source of inspiration: the story of David and Bathsheba (II Samuel 11-12). It cannot, of course, be the sole source, for there is no shape-shifting and no deception of the wife. But the basic crime is the same. A king covets at first glance the wife of his most valued war-captain. The king begets a child on the wife; the king causes the husband's death in battle and weds the wife. Geoffrey himself was very probably struck by the similarity between this story and Hercules'. At least one early imitator recognised it: the moralising author of the Variant Version.[12] The similarity is significant, for the biblical story has a strong moral colouring. If Geoffrey had it in mind, then he would be forced to consider the moral implications of his own story. Moreover, any clerical reader of Geoffrey would be similarly struck. The moral condemnation involves son as well as father. In the biblical story, the son dies (II Samuel 12.38). Arthur does not; but many authors are to opine that he cannot escape the taint of his father's crime.

These moral indications must colour our answer to the question: 'Why did Geoffrey concoct such a birthtale for Arthur?' It is easy to say 'To make Arthur

25

more interesting'. This is true but inadequate, for the moral problem cannot be so lightly dismissed.[13] Helen Adolf suggests that the story in HRB, like that of Galahad in the Vulgate, is used to free the hero from 'tradux peccati', as if doubtful parentage were the same as no parentage.[14] But this is certainly not true of Galahad. The Vulgate author insists that he is conceived 'en pechié et en avoltire' (V. 110). The story in fact encapsulates the notion of original sin and its redemption by the Messiah. As for Geoffrey, he does not openly moralise, but he makes clear that Uther's is a cruel and guilty lust. The idea of original sin strikes us far more sharply through Uther's adultery than it would if Arthur were born in normal wedlock. Moreover, there is never any doubt, in HRB, as to who Arthur's father is, so the 'tradux peccati' cannot be avoided that way.

One could argue, with Hanning, that Uther's sin is redeemed by the good of Arthur's birth.[15] This is the case in the Galahad story; but in HRB Uther's sin is not a 'malum necessarium': a few hours' patience would have given him Ygerna in all legality, and the omniscient Merlin might be expected to know that. All in all, Geoffrey's neutral tone emphasises the problem rather than masking it. There is a problem even in his classical sources. In Ovid, Hercules is told:

> matris adulterio patrem petis: elige, fictum
> esse Iovem malis, an te per dedecus ortum.
> (Metamm. IX. 25-6)

Even the greatest of the gods cannot readily be absolved from crime, nor — still more relevant to our study of Arthur — can the son escape from shame. Where the most amoral of Roman poets condemns, will a Christian cleric absolve? As for the Alexander story, many medieval authors react violently against it, insisting that Alexander was the legitimate son of Philip.[16] A dubious demi-godhead is, to such authors, no substitute for legitimacy and the royal succession. No such choice is given to Arthur: either Uther is his father, or nobody. The blood royal carries the stigma with it, and so the moral question cannot be as easily shelved as it can with Alexander.

The fathers of Hercules and Alexander accomplish their own shape-shifts, but Uther cannot. In Geoffrey's story, the father-character is split between Uther and Merlin. Now Merlin, the accessory to, if not the instigator of, Uther's crime, is in many important works also Arthur's mentor. Therefore the problem of Merlin's morality, embryonic in HRB, later becomes very urgent, for Arthur may take the taint from him as well as Uther.

The moral knot which Geoffrey ties has two further strands: Ygerne, the innocent victim, and Gorlois, the wronged husband. Both have their part to play in later shapings of Arthur's destiny.

As for Arthur himself, he is indeed a child conceived and born in sin. His problem is potentially legal as well as moral and personal. The question of what made a bastard, whether a bastard could be legitimised, and of what he could inherit, was an important part of any medieval legal system. Geoffrey's data could be exploited to place Arthur in a very difficult position. Authors' reactions to this sort them into camps. Those hostile to Arthur will make capital of the bastardy charge; those favourable to him will try in various ingenious ways to refute it. In any case, the consequences of the birthtale may colour Arthur's whole life, and not merely add excitement to its beginning.

Let us consider the strands of the problem separately. The first question is whether Uther's guilt affects Arthur morally as well as through legal entanglements. Authors differ in their opinion of Uther, but most consider him to be no more a sinner than the rest of mankind. It is Robert de Boron who gives the closest consideration to Uther's guilt. He passes some of the stigma on to the unimportant Ulfin, but there is clearly evil in Uther himself. Boron does not himself suggest that this evil passed from Uther to Arthur, but his successors in the Vulgate, and especially in the post-Vulgate, make Arthur himself guilty of sins of lust. In these cycles, as in every account, Uther escapes all punishment for his lust. This means that he gets away with a sin which is really far worse than that of Arthur with his unintended incest. No doubt the reason is chiefly one of scope: there is no room for full treatment of two tragic, sinning kings in one cycle, and Arthur's destiny impresses most strongly if it is unique. But we may also consider that God withholds from Arthur a grace which he grants to Uther. Arthur does not slay his begetter, as Mordred does; Arthur is not evil, as Mordred is. Grace, we understand, is granted, not earned. Perhaps, indeed, Arthur expiates Uther's crime as well as his own. Both of them, and Mordred, are links in a chain of sin which ends only with the extermination of the family: they are a medieval House of Atreus.[17]

One author senses the presence of such a curse, and tries to remove it. This is Malory.[18] According to him, the war between Uther and the Duke is nothing to do with Uther's lust, but is of long standing, and the Duke is the aggressor, an over-mighty baron in rebellion against his lawful sovereign. Uther's sight of Ygerna is the consequence of a well-intentioned peace initiative on Uther's part. In the love intrigue, Uther is humbly obedient to Merlin. The Duke is already dead when Uther lies with Ygerna,[19] so that Uther is guilty of adultery only in intention, not in fact. Malory does everything to absolve Uther short of suppressing the conception story altogether, which he cannot do because it is essential to later developments. He does so because he wishes no taint to light on Arthur.

The morality of Uther can thus be used to doom Arthur, to release him from doom, or can be a separate question altogether. The same is true of Merlin's morality. In chronicle accounts, Merlin vanishes from the story after the conception, so his moral state has no effect on Arthur, there being no link of blood along which a stigma could be passed. In the great prose romances it is a different matter.

Robert de Boron clearly has great difficulty with Merlin. Boron's own antecedents story makes plain that Merlin is committed to God, in defiance of his semi-demonic ancestry. How is this new Merlin to be reconciled with the HRB character, who so enigmatically connives at a breach of God's holy law? Boron does something to mitigate Merlin's guilt by removing him from Uther's fatal feast, and by emphasising the positive good which results from the crime: Arthur's birth and reign. He cannot eliminate the guilt, however. Instead, by a brilliant volte-face, he makes Merlin's sense of guilt, and desire to expiate it, into the motivation for Merlin's actions subsequent to the conception. Ironically, that desire itself produces further crimes: the terrorising of Ygerna and the removal of her child. How far Merlin's machinations chime in with God's overall plan is unclear: Boron sounds the ultimate mystery of predestination, but leaves its depths unplumbed. What is clear is that the bringing of moral judgment to bear on Merlin had radical effects on Arthur's own story: the nature of his upbringing and accession depends on Merlin's guilt.

For Boron (if we may trust the evidence of the Didot *Perceval*[20]) Merlin's expiation is successfully completed by the accession; in any case, his subsequent fate does not affect Arthur. In two later works, however, his guilt continues to reverberate throughout Arthur's life. In the *Suite*, Merlin's anxiety for his own spiritual state dictates his refusal to help Arttur eliminate Mordred, and so seals Arthur's ultimate fate (I. 158-9). Boron's presentation of Merlin clearly determines that of the *Suite* at this vital point. In the Spanish *Baladro*, Merlin's sin over Ygerna is the direct cause of his death; and that death, according to Merlin himself, prevents him from saving Logres on the final Day of Destiny.[21] Merlin's guilt thus dooms Arthur from his very birth.

How alert and intelligent Boron, the *Suite* author and the *Baladro* author were in exploiting the possibilities of Merlin's guilt, can be estimated from comparison with other, independent prose works. LP and *Perlesvaus*, like Boron, judge Merlin on an ordinary human level for his sin over Ygerna, and find him guilty.[22] Since they do not make Merlin into Arthur's mentor, however, nor describe his machinations after the conception, they cannot make Merlin's guilt significant for Arthur's career. In LP, Merlin is destroyed through lust. This seems a fitting punishment for his original crime; but LP misses the connection, preferring the notion – dear to the medieval mind – of the sage who succumbs to a woman's wiles. In VM, which professes to continue Boron, Merlin is Arthur's mentor and perishes through lust (II. 451-2), but the significant connections between these facts are entirely missed. It is in such hit-and-miss ways that Arthurian development often proceeds: authors often do not realise the riches inherent in their material, invented or inherited. Geoffrey begins the interweaving of Merlin's and Arthur's destinies; Boron develops it; the *Baladro* completes it. The intervening periods produce countless works, both romance and chronicle, which are blind to the possibilities of the story. For every Arthurian author who has inspiration, there are ninety-nine who contribute only perspiration.

As for Ygerna, there is scarcely a hint in all the material that she is anything other than an innocent, faithful, loving and virtuous wife: Alcmena with – in Boron at least – overtones of Lucretia. Her complete innocence of connivance at the crime has one important consequence for Arthur. Legally speaking, it means that he is the child of rape, for while Ygerna consents to the intercourse, she does not consent to Uther.[23] No author specifically draws attention to this unpleasant fact: it is left for the consideration of the alert reader. We may hold that Ygerna's purity redeems Uther's crime, just as, according to Boron, the purity of Merlin's mother cancels out his father's demonic nature (Huth I. 19-20). In this case we may say that Ygerna's character affects Arthur's, helping to explain his general virtuousness – at least in the HRB tradition. In the Boron tradition, such an inheritance is less likely, for an interesting reason. In that tradition, Arthur is suckled not by Ygerna, but by Kay's mother. The Middle Ages held that character was communicated through the mother's milk, and this is certainly the case with Arthur, for Boron draws specific attention to it. In the Boron tradition, therefore, Arthur can inherit fate and character from Uther, but not from Ygerna. Nevertheless, in the *Suite* and Malory she does influence his career at a later stage. In the former, her contribution to the establishment of Arthur's identity is considered to be vital (Huth I. 164-74). In Malory, she is even accused of having affected Arthur already by her silence: '... and she wolde have uttirde hit in the lyff of Uther of the birth of you ... then had ye never had the mortall warrys that ye have had' (I. 45). This reproach is justified in Malory, where alone Ygerna learns the truth about her child's father before his birth.[24] But it is only in Malory that Ygerna has such opportunity to influence events, for good or for bad. Normally, in HRB and in the prose traditions, she is a victim, deceived, manipulated, terrorised by the ruthless forces of male lust and male political ambition. Perhaps her most significant contribution to Arthur's career — apart from his very life! — is the note of tragic pathos which she introduces. Arthur comes to birth and power through her suffering: thus, from the beginning, his story expresses the cruelty of a fallen world.

Ironically, the real key to the problem of Arthur's conception story is the least interesting of the four protagonists: Ygerna's husband. In the Hercules and Alexander stories, the mother's husband survives to become entangled in the intrigue, with consequences that may be comic or tragic. This means that the seducer cannot marry the wife. If the seducer is a god this is a convenience, not a problem, and the child enjoys a dual inheritance. A parallel situation obtains in relation to Christ himself — whose story is far from irrelevant to consideration of Arthur, as we shall remark again in discussing the accession.[25] It is expedient for Christ to have a putative earthly father as well as a heavenly one. But in Arthur's case, for Gorlois to live would be a disaster. The child would — by English law at least — be legitimately his, and its hereditary right to the throne impossible to prove, especially with such a crowd of witnesses to testify to 'Gorlois'' presence on the fatal night. Gorlois must, therefore, die before Ygerna's pregnancy becomes known. The time and manner — especially the time — of his death are potentially very important to Arthur's career. This brings us to the question of Arthur's bastardy.

The whole discussion of Arthur's bastardy hinges upon a precise point of law, views on which were different in England and in France. Under English law, a child born outside of wedlock was a bastard and could not be legitimised if its parents later married; a child born in wedlock was held to be the lawful issue of the husband, and the burden of proof was on those who claimed it was not. These rules were not changed until 1926.[26] The key word for our purposes is *born*. A child conceived outside wedlock, but born in it, was perfectly legitimate. In French law, by contrast, a child born to an unmarried woman could be retrospectively legitimised as an 'enfant de paile'; but a child *conceived* in adultery by a married woman could not be legitimised, and could not inherit, if his parents later married, even if they did so before his birth.[27] However, from the evidence of manuscripts of Beaumanoir, it appears that there was some dispute over the latter point. One manuscript holds that a child conceived in adultery, but born to his true parents after their marriage, could be considered legitimate.[28]

We now perceive that the question of Arthur's bastardy is complex. The rationale of Geoffrey's original story is plain. Since Uther and Ygerna marry after Gorlois' death, but before Arthur's birth, there is no reason at all to consider Arthur a bastard. Problems would arise only if Arthur were born before the marriage, or while Ygerna was still married to Gorlois. This is why Gorlois is so promptly dispatched. Whether or not he is still alive when the adultery takes place, however, is immaterial, and Geoffrey does not specify.

We may further perceive that Robert de Boron is either following English law,[29] or accepts the second Beaumanoir view. In Boron, there are two 'reasons' for smuggling Arthur away: the ostensible one, proposed by Uther to Ygerna, and the true one, held by Merlin and by the author. The former is merely a device to induce Ygerna to surrender the child. Nowhere is it suggested that Arthur really is a bastard. Uther affects to believe that the child is neither his nor the Duke's, and so threatens to prove Ygerna unchaste: it is this threat, not the risk to Arthur, that induces her to give him up. The true purpose, however, is precisely to remove from Arthur every obvious right to the throne, in order that his eventual accession may seem a mighty demonstration of God's omnipotence.[30] If Arthur were born to Ygerna in Uther's house, his right to the throne would be hard to dispute.

Other French texts differ on the bastardy question. The *Suite* shelves it: Merlin tells the story of Arthur's parentage in such a way that it seems that he was both engendered and born in wedlock (Huth I. 166-73). The birthtale is not politically important. Its facts are important in another way, however. It is because he is unaware of his origins that Arthur commits incest with his sister (Huth I. 147): thus Uther's crime, and Merlin's concealment of it, have direct practical, as well as ideological, links with the cause of Arthur's doom.

Perlesvaus and LP independently take a harsher view. *Perlesvaus* is clear that Arthur was conceived before the Duke's death 'en pechié'. This must be taken to mean that he is a bastard. The author drives the point home later by an implicit contrast with Gawain's birthtale. Gawain was born outside wedlock, but was conceived by an unmarried woman, and so was legitimised after his parents' marriage. Arthur can make no such claim. However, the revelation of Arthur's birth has no immediate political consequences. Clearly, he has been successfully passed off as Uther's heir; and since the secret is not made public, his throne is not threatened. It is told to Arthur himself at this point — at the beginning of his Grail pilgrimage — so that he may learn humility, realising that he holds his throne only by the grace of God. The timing of the revelation is also important in another way. Arthur's pilgrimage is the climax of his career, but it is also the beginning of the end — as the news of Loholt's death indicates at the outset. To the reader, therefore, the birthtale shakes Arthur's security: he depends on God's grace, and that grace is shortly to be withdrawn. In *Perlesvaus* as in Boron, the bastardy issue is not a legal point, but a vital link in the narrative *sen*.

LP is even more overt in its accusation of bastardy. The *preudom* who gives

Arthur a spiritual flaying during the Galehaut war tells him:

> . . . tu ses bien que tu ne fus engendrés ne nés par assamblement de loial maraige, mais en si grant pechié come est avoltire. Si dois savoir que nus hom mortex ne te baillast a garder la signorie que tu tiens, mais que Dieu seulement.
> (III. 216)

It will be noticed that LP defies HRB in saying that Arthur was not born in wedlock: this is an attempt on behalf of the hostile LP author to make the bastardy absolutely clear — as it is, in this passage, under either French or English law. The object is, once again, not to topple Arthur from his throne, but to teach him humility in the occupation of it. LP and *Perlesvaus* arrive by different routes at the same conclusion.

Spreadeagled between the Boron vindication and the LP accusation is VM, whose hapless author frequently encounters such contradictions. He makes good use of this one, however. Instead of trying to reconcile the two notions, he makes them the polarising agent in the wars between Arthur and the barons. Arthur's faction accept Merlin's assurances over Arthur's parentage; the barons — following Beaumanoir's first alternative — consider him a bastard (II. 91). The author could invalidate the barons' case by having Merlin state that Arthur was engendered after the Duke's death. However, either out of respect for Boron's silence on that point, or because he wishes to leave the question open, the author does not make this clarification. Instead he continues Boron's own policy of rooting all Arthur's claims in the will of God, which overrides the barons' political claims — however justified.

We see then, that the major French texts are not unanimous that Arthur is a bastard, while even those who consider him such have to bend Geoffrey's data to make the point clear — and even then they do not seriously suggest that Arthur's right to the throne is invalidated. Nor do they suggest that the revelation of his origins has a traumatic effect on Arthur; even in *Perlesvaus* he is only slightly embarrassed (I. 282). Bastardy, after all, was not such a terrible stigma in medieval times: many bastards climbed to honourable positions in real life, and they do so also in romance and epic. It is not the suspicion or the fact of bastardy which shapes our view of Arthur, but the way in which the authors colour the suspicion and the fact.

When we come to the Middle English authors, we find some rather surprising reactions to the bastardy charge. The author of *Arthur and Merlin*[31] follows his source in presenting the barons' contention without comment on its justification — although by English law they have no case at all. We should not, perhaps, expect this relatively unsophisticated author to have a detailed knowledge of the law; if he has any at all, he subordinates it to respect for his sources. It is slightly more surprising to find the fifteenth-century author of the short chronicle *Arthur*[32] declaring that Uther 'begat Arthour in avowtrye' (I. 28). This need not, however, involve an accusation of bastardy: it is Uther's crime, not Arthur's origins, which is being condemned. Most surprising of all is Malory. He is anxious to eliminate the doubt of Arthur's legitimacy which VM allows to persist. To this end he not only points out that Arthur was born in wedlock, which is sufficient proof under English law; he also says that Arthur was engendered before the Duke's death. Either Malory is confused over the state of English law — and VM itself is certainly enough to confuse anybody — or else he wishes to purge Arthur's origins of the faintest taint of irregularity and crime, whether they affect his political career or not. Probably both reasons obtain. Malory's treatment is a warning to us not to assume that all legal points are treated by romance authors as if they were writing a legal treatise. Ignorance and narrative intentions may often distort the mirror of real life.

It is sometimes claimed that chronicles like *Polychronicon*, *Flores Historiarum* and Portuguese *Nobiliario* suppress the details of Arthur's birthtale in order to make him appear legitimate.[33] In view of what we have already said, however, it seems more likely that such authors suppress the story because they find it incredible. Higden, at least, suppresses much else for the same reason. It is, in any case, possible to keep the accusation of bastardy while suppressing the more incredible elements, like the shape-shift. This is proved by the Scottish authors, to whom we now turn.

All the authors we have hitherto considered have accepted Arthur's right to the throne, bastard or not, because they have no other claimant to suggest. This is not so with the Scots. Pressing the claims of Loth and Mordred, they have an interest in making the bastardy as clear as possible. It would not occur to even the most hostile French authors to do likewise, because Loth and Mordred claim through the female line, a thing forbidden by Salic law. However, Boece and his successors 'prove' the bastardy by the same means as does the LP author (though certainly independently): they suppress the notion that Uther at any time married Ygerna. Uther does not even attempt to disguise the fact that Arthur is a bastard: he is openly acknowledged and reared as such. As for the shape-shifting story, Boece suppresses it, together with all romantic details which tend to gloss over the brutality of Uther's crime.[34] Buchanan even suggests that Merlin and Uther concocted the story as a cover-up.[35] By selection, suppression and invention, Boece and company suppress every relish of salvation in the birthtale, so that Arthur succeeds 'violato non modo Britannico, sed et gentium iure', defying elementary rules of human decency. It takes four hundred years for the danger with which Geoffrey unwittingly threatens Arthur to be realised; but when it is, it deprives Arthur of all moral, legal and political standing from the outset. As in the post-Vulgate, so — by a different process — in Boece: Arthur's birthtale settles his eventual doom in advance, and determines the very way in which Mordred is to destroy him.

The story of Arthur's conception is, then, a rich and complex one whose legal, political, moral and narrative implications are fully and intelligently exploited by a variety of authors with contrasting aims and viewpoints. By contrast, the story of his birth and early youth proves far less of a trigger to the medieval imagination: perhaps because there was no one precise point on which to dispute, dispute being very productive of narrative enrichment. One would expect the time of Arthur's birth to be marked by the authors with awe and reverence. Instead, all we find are endless colourless permutations on Geoffrey's brief comment over the conception 'Concepit . . . celeberrimum virum illum Arturum, qui postmodum ut celebris foret mira probitate promeruit'. Of all the innumerable romance and chronicle authors who follow Geoffrey, only three embroider on this pathetically bald statement. This is the more surprising – and disappointing – in that the birth of Alexander was marked by prodigies, and so was that of Christ, whose circumstances Arthur may echo from afar in his birth, as he certainly does in his accession. A few authors do embroider the story a little – most notably Layamon and the author of the Second Continuation of the *Perceval*[36] – and Boron does dramatise the account a little. However, for Boron the significance depends not on the birth of a wonder-child, but on the dramatic circumstances ensuing from Uther's decision to smuggle away the child. Even then there is nothing intrinsically mysterious about the child's disappearance, as there is (for example) about Pryderi's, or even Lancelot's in LP.[37]

There is one thing which, in modern eyes, does give Arthur's birth a romantic colouring: the belief that it took place in Tintagel. There is, however, no warrant for this belief in early medieval texts. Arthur is engendered in Tintagel in HRB, but this is not because Geoffrey considers Tintagel a suitably dramatic setting for the hero's appearance. It is simply because Tintagel is an eminently defensible place for Ygerna to be in. In Geoffrey as in later accounts, we must assume that Arthur was born in whatever palace Uther and Ygerna were living in at the time – and that is unlikely to be Tintagel. Once the Tristan story became popular – and even more when it was integrated with Arthur's – the association was even less likely to be made, for Tintagel was accepted as Mark's castle. As far as I know, it does not appear until the fifteenth century, in John of Glastonbury.[38] John makes an erroneous assumption from his sources, which is very often still made. This is our first example of Arthurian beliefs being held in the teeth of the evidence. More will follow.

Having come quietly to birth, Arthur has fifteen years to wait until he ascends the throne. There is little to learn from our authors about those years, but this should not tempt us to seek in their silence a profound, mythological significance – as Lord Raglan does.[39] Geoffrey is silent simply because he never wastes time over inessentials. Were he writing a romance instead of an avowedly sober chronicle, he might be tempted to describe Arthur's boyhood deeds and education. Hercules, after all, strangled serpents in his cradle, whilst Alexander's boyhood deeds were already a favourite theme with romancers. If Geoffrey had any interest in Celtic legend – which is unlikely – he might have been inspired by boyhood deeds such as Cuchulainn's, Finn's or Pryderi's.[40] Instead, he restrains himself; and his authority, acting this time as a dead weight, deters even the most romantic of his followers, however many Alexanders, Rolands, Tristans, Percevals or Gawains they had for inspiration.

There is, however, one important dispute over Arthur's boyhood. In the HRB tradition we must assume that he was brought up quite normally in his father's house: an assumption which is automatically made, for example, by the author of *De Ortu Walwanii* and by Jean d'Outremeuse, and which we also find – *mutatis mutandis* – in the Scottish chroniclers.[41] In the Boron tradition, however,

Arthur is reared in Antor's house, and is thus removed from the mainstream of the story: another deterrent to the would-be describer of his boyhood. Layamon's position is particularly intriguing on this point. He is firmly within the HRB tradition, yet he had Arthur spend his youth in Brittany (*Brut* 1.9898). Now, it was common for young noblemen in the twelfth century to be sent away for education. It is natural to send Arthur to Brittany, for his family is Breton and the Breton king sheltered his father. All the same, there is no need for Layamon to send Arthur away, and it seems to me possible that he was inspired here by the original Boron *Merlin*.[42] We shall find further warrant for this belief in the next chapter.

Can we learn anything of Arthur's upbringing? The Scots tell us that Uther thought highly — too highly — of him, while Jean d'Outremeuse assures us that he was a promising trainee knight (II. 182). Such individual gleanings amount to little. In one place only do we really meet the boy Arthur: in the conversation with Antor which reveals that Antor is not Arthur's father. Boron's own version of this is touching, but infinitely more so is Malory's, which is a masterpiece of selective adaptation. In Boron, Arthur is a rather feeble, tearful youth, while Antor is grasping, self-centred and intent on turning the situation to his best advantage. In Malory, Ector is humble, kindly and noble, while Arthur is affectionate, attractively naïve, grateful and desperately sincere, a beautifully brought-up child who will always strive to act generously and fairly: 'I shalle not faille yow. God forbede I shold faille yow.' One very significant cut is made by Malory. The explanation of Kay's unpleasantness in Boron undermines Arthur's own good character by implying that he owes it entirely to Kay's mother's milk: it is really Kay's character, which Arthur has stolen. Now Boron is not one of those French authors who are hostile to Arthur. Preoccupied with explaining Kay, he has not considered the repercussions on Arthur; but it seems that Malory has. Otherwise, both Malory and Boron present to us a convincingly 'young' Arthur, and this is the only locus in the literature where such a one appears. Boyish, he yet possesses in embryo the qualities which distinguish him as a man. The conversation immediately precedes Arthur's accession. With that, he abandons youth for ever: our first glimpse of the boy is also our farewell. It is a fitting point at which to end. Malory's noble version reminds us that human goodness always has value, even if evil eventually destroys its possessor; and that ill deeds — Uther's and Merlin's machinations — may eventually come to good — Arthur's obviously happy childhood. Evil will come of the evil, but at the moment of Arthur's accession it is in suspense.

Our survey of treatments of Arthur's conception and birth has shown us one opportunity magnificently taken, and one almost completely missed. The missing *enfances* may be lamented; but the conception tale makes up for the lack. It is superbly well adapted to the favourite medieval technique of many-layered presentation. It can be anything from an exciting tale of magic and intrigue to a part of a great tragedy making deeply significant statements on the condition of fallen Man. Its appeal is perennial: it cannot be dated except by disbelief in the shape-shifting, and rejection of that cannot alter the basic problem. It can only be altered by suppressing the whole story, as Higden does: and even such a suppression evidences a positive response, of scandal or disbelief, to the story. The basic moral of the tale is that no man is an island. A single thoughtless action may have repercussions on generations yet unborn. A good intention may turn fantastically awry; alternatively, divine intervention may distil good from human mismanagement. Neither magic nor prescience can control the consequences of Uther's desires: only the unfathomable designs of God, or of Fate, encompass all the possibilities. The corporate genius of the major medieval authors gives to these undying themes an urgency and a fascination which transcends the historical circumstances under which any or all of the writers lived.

III

ACCESSION

The discussion of Arthur's accession, like that of his birth, begins with HRB. In early Welsh literature he is not invariably called a king, and even where he receives that title — as in the saints' lives[1] — there is no interest in the circumstances of his accession. Here is further proof that the Welsh did not think of Arthur biographically, nor have any clear notion as to who and what he was. 'King' was in any case a little-used title in early medieval Wales, and there would be little point in attaching it to the Welsh Arthur. Even the post-Geoffrey, continental-influenced *Tair Rhamant* prefer to call Arthur 'amherawdr',[2] a title at once more honorific and less specific than 'brenhin'. Arthur is not a Welsh king, and there is nothing Celtic about his kingship, or about his accession, in any text.[3]

In non-Welsh literature, by contrast, Arthur compelled attention by the mere fact of his kingship.[4] It therefore becomes important to inquire into the circumstances of his accession, for it is the fulcrum of the significance of the medieval Arthur.

Arthur's accession is a creation of the high Middle Ages. We should, however, beware of assuming that its circumstances will automatically reflect the theory and practice of king-making as it obtained at the time and place of any one author. Arthur's accession will echo contemporary conditions, but will not give a mirror-image of them. His accession is always *his* accession: not a treatise on the coronation, or a blurred photograph of William the Conqueror's or Philip Augustus' or Edward IV's — let alone Brian Boru's.

Simply by accepting the notion that society has a natural and inevitable need to be headed by a king, the Arthurian material opens itself to a flood of complex notions. The assumption is not as automatic as it might appear. Political theorists — notably the enormously influential John of Salisbury[5] — held that in a perfect society, kings would not be necessary. The idea certainly percolated as far as the romancers, for we find it expressed in the early LP (III. 115).[6] It was also plainly stated in the Old Testament for all clerics to read (I Samuel 8-10). If Arthur is king, therefore, there is bound to be a certain realism in his presentation. Even folktale king-makings reflect reality to a considerable extent: the hero may become king by ritual combat (fighting the old king), by merit (killing the dragon), by inheritance through the female line (winning the princess's hand in marriage) or by designation (the king offers his kingdom to whoever will perform a certain deed). All are quite complex notions. Much more complex are those in Arthurian literature.

There were, indeed, several alternative means of becoming king in medieval western Europe: by conquest, by usurpation, by deposition, inheritance, co-opting, designation, acclamation, election, consecration or by a combination of any of these factors.[7] Despite attempts at evaluation and codification by churchmen and lawyers, no hard-and-fast rules were established even by the end of our period. Even such rules as there were were often hard to apply in particular cases: witness the disputes over the accession of such widely-separated monarchs as Pepin, William the Conqueror, Philip of Valois and Guy of Lusignan.[8]

Where reality was so complicated, the Arthurian authors could tap rich veins of inspiration. They could cull facts and theories from real life and recombine them as they chose; be realistic or imaginative, practical or theoretical, as they wished.

Geoffrey creates for his kings a system of succession which is broadly in accordance with contemporary reality.[9] That reality, however, was itself fluid, and overstepped the bounds of twelfth-century England. The system described in HRB has its roots in the Old Testament and still has echoes today in European coronations, for the conservative maintenance of ritual is of the essence of king-making. Geoffrey's scheme is loose enough to leave ample room for later authors to develop their own ideas without rejecting the 'facts' given in HRB. Geoffrey himself is not interested in the theoretical complexities of king-making:[10] in HRB, Arthur's coronation is hedged around and conditioned by a fascinating tangle of unique events. It illustrates the pragmatism of royal accession, the bending of rules to fit the needs of the moment.

There is an august precedent for Geoffrey's practicality. The circumstances of Saul's accession were determined by the urgent needs of war (I Samuel 7-8). So with Arthur: 'arguebat enim eos necessitas, quia . . . Saxones concives suos ex Germania invitaverunt . . .'. Now it is clear that Arthur, though Uther's only son, does not automatically accede at his father's death; nor has he been co-opted or designated by Uther in his lifetime. The first is not surprising, for in the twelfth century it was the unction, not the mere fact of inheritance by primogeniture, which made the king.[11] The second and third argue a failure in Uther which would strongly impress both French and English readers, for Normans, Angevins and Capetians all made colossal efforts to ensure a peaceful succession by designating or co-opting. The notion of kingship as an institution which was unaffected by an individual king's death was not yet fully developed; an interregnum meant almost certain chaos, as people believed that the law perished with the king.[12] It is this notion which Geoffrey's invading Saxons are playing on. Uther does have the excuse of sudden and unexpected death (HRB 431; cf. Wace, l. 8996, William of Rennes, l. 3006), but his failure still puts Britain in a dangerous position, and lays a heavy burden on the Britons, who are forced to seek alternative methods of selecting a king. Heredity guides their choice, and simplifies it, for Arthur is the one obvious claimant. It does not, however, suffice. Arthur has to be 'suggested' by the barons, and this implies an election, which is more than a formality even though Arthur has no rival. Geoffrey's opening praise of Arthur is clearly meant to show that he is *idoneus*[13] for election. However, the final word rests with the Church — as Geoffrey, a churchman, doubtless considered most fitting. The Church in real life held that a king should always deserve his throne and not merely assume it through inheritance:[14] thus Geoffrey's praise of Arthur also ratifies his being chosen as king in the Church's eyes, although the bishop, like the barons, defers to the pressure of military *necessitas*. The people's acclamation, even as a formality, is not mentioned. This is not because Geoffrey considers the people irrelevant to a king-making, for he includes their acclamation in the crowning of Uther (419) and of Ambrosius (399). It is merely that the urgency of Arthur's case precludes a full assembly. The role of the people in Arthur's accession is left for later, less urgent authors to develop.

The ideology and practice of Arthur's king-making in HRB is thus in perfect accordance with what one would expect, given a combination of twelfth-century notions and circumstances peculiar to HRB. The same could be said of the attendant ceremonies. Geoffrey has no time to describe them in detail; besides, that would rob the later, leisured crown-*wearing*[15] of its thunder. But his brief allusions: '. . . diademate regni insignivit . . . insignibus itaque regiis iniciatus . . .' are sufficient to convince the reader that all is done decently and in order. A fuller description must await a more leisured context. In HRB, the rich symbolism of kingship as expressed in oath, sword and unction must give way to the practical demonstration of kingship in council, legislation and, above all, battle.

What of Arthur himself? He expresses no will in the matter, being neither a Constans nor a Vortigern. His pliancy is, however, a virtue, which demonstrates his perfect adaptability to be a vessel of the will of God expressed through the Church, which is the theoretical ideal of early medieval kingship.[16] His consecration will act on him like a burning-glass, focussing and directing the *innata bonitas* which makes him morally suited to kingship. He already has *gratia*: not only grace of mind or body, but God's grace, set on him as an individual and ratified by the unction. Geoffrey does not mystify the account of Arthur's coronation, but the perfect suitability of the man for the moment has something almost mystical about it. It is the unction which makes the king, setting him apart from all other men; but he will be a good king only if his own character pre-disposes him to it. This is Arthur's case.

Brief as is Geoffrey's account of Arthur's coronation, it is the most detailed one in HRB. His other descriptions of coronations mention factors which do not appear in Arthur's, such as the consent of the people, or the *regia ornamenta* (361), but none has quite the same denseness of meaning. Geoffrey has clearly taken great care over these few brief sentences, and it would not be surprising if later authors were stimulated by them. But were they?

Wace, Geoffrey's most influential adaptor as far as later developments are concerned, fails his master sadly over the coronation. Normally given to expansion and to comment on the text, he rejects all such opportunities as are afforded by the coronation, reducing it instead to a mere three lines. He concentrates more on Arthur's virtues, but generalises them, not relating them in any way to the coronation. As far as the ideologies, the ceremonies, even the particular significance, of Arthur's coronation are concerned, Wace furnishes his followers with a *tabula rasa*.

That it was possible to adapt and reinterpret Geoffrey's data within small compass is proved by Wace's fellow-chronicler, William of Rennes. He throws Arthur's coronation into prominence by placing it at the beginning of his seventh book, where it is preceded by a tremendous encomium of the hero. This approach isolates the coronation from the peculiar historical circumstances, giving it a special significance. William compares Arthur to the heroes of the Antiquity which he loves, showing that he judges him not by contemporary or even HRB standards, but by those of the eternal warrior-paragon. In the king-making itself, William introduces delicate shifts into Geoffrey's data in order to emphasise the Christian importance of the ceremony: Arthur, though comparable to the classical heroes, is nonetheless a most Christian king. The grace which commends him to the electors is now overtly *Christi gratia*. His other virtues are those of a sage as well as of a warrior. William's Arthur is Achilles christianised, or perhaps Charlemagne with classical overtones. William's whole portrait of Arthur expresses, in a different medium, the same twelfth-century rediscovery of antique heroes as is expressed in the vernacular *romans d'antiquité*. They contain classical heroes medievalised; William's Arthur is a medieval hero classicised. The coronation paragraph fitly introduces such a hero.

William, then, is distinctly more original at this point than Wace.[17] But William had no successors; doubtless his work smacked too much of the schools to win favour over the lively vernacular of his rival. William is to Arthur what Gautier de Châtillon is to Alexander, though the former never attained the success which both deserve. Wace is more like the original *roman d'Alexandre*, well-placed to begin a ramifying vernacular tradition. It is from Wace that spring the two most interesting adaptations of Arthur's coronation story: Layamon's and — most important of all — Boron's. Layamon, of course, remains within the HRB story, but his version still has considerable originality. That it spawned no such new tradition as Boron's did is probably due to the undeveloped state of the English language at the time, rather than to inferior quality.

The two accounts also exhibit some striking similarities, which may even indicate direct borrowing on Layamon's part. In the first place, the two agree that Arthur is not on the spot when Uther dies. The reason for this is different in each case, being tied to two wholly different sequences of events, but in both cases the effect is to prolong the king-making and leave room for extra detail. Arthur must be sought, and this involves deeper consideration of his right to the throne. Both authors make play with concepts of succession not introduced by Geoffrey. Most notable is designation, which is hinted at by Boron, clearly stated by Layamon. This new emphasis does not reflect a change in contemporary circumstances, for designation was as much and more a live issue in Geoffrey's time than in the later authors'. It indicates a more leisured consideration of legal forms — remembering that both Layamon and Boron start not from *HRB*, but practically from scratch, from Wace. Layamon does not consider designation sufficient: he emphasises the hereditary aspect even more than does Geoffrey.

By contrast he tones down the elective principle, though the 'husting' is still important in that it ensures the correct following of precedent. Clearly Layamon wishes Arthur's accession to have every possible stamp of legality. To this end he is even prepared to distort the fabric of the story, for whereas Arthur is told that Uther designated him, there is no hint of this in Uther's death-scene. It is possible that Layamon himself conceived the idea of designation: but it is also possible that he distilled it from Uther's death-scene in Boron, which we shall consider shortly. The combining of two versions would explain the distortion of the *Brut* context.

Layamon and Boron also share an emphasis on Arthur's self-dedication to the ideals of kingship, under the guidance of leading ecclesiastical dignitaries. In Boron, this dedication takes the form of a ritual coronation oath. In Layamon there is no formal coronation ceremony at all; but in the new scene between the deputation and Arthur, the aims and ideas of kingship, which the coronation ceremonies symbolically express, are expounded in words by the deputation. This deputation, being led by bishops, can claim the same authority as that held by Dubricius in HRB, Wace and Boron. Moreover, its recommendations amount to an informal coronation oath. They are three in number, like the *tria promissa* of the oath in the contemporary English *ordo*.[18] They do not correspond exactly to the *promissa*, but the similarity is close. Arthur is not told to keep the peace, but the injunction to drive out the enemy amounts to the same thing.

Is Layamon actually copying an English *ordo*? It is unlikely that, in his Worcestershire backwater, he would have had access to one.[19] But the Boron *Merlin* contains an oath whose provisions agree more closely, though still not exactly, with Layamon's: to maintain the Church, peace, and justice.[20] It cannot be proved that Layamon used the *Merlin* oath; but the accumulation of slight similarities is beginning to acquire some weight.

The relative informality of the 'oath' in Layamon has the effect of emphasising the element of free will in Arthur's espousal of its provisions. It is not a prepared formula which he could pronounce without any intention of fulfilment: it is a challenge, to which Arthur responds quickly and resolutely, but with full under-standing of its implications. A determined, dedicated man, of quick decision, and no one's puppet: here indeed is Layamon's Arthur, fitly introduced. And yet he does have something of the humility – if not exactly of the passivity – which we have seen to be desirable in a new king, for his first words in the scene express a submission of his will to God's. Layamon does not describe the sacral transformation of man to king through the unction, but he clearly shows Arthur to be the servant of Christ.

Layamon's version represents the most extensive reworking of the scene within the HRB framework; but his alterations still amount to modification, not transformation. If he borrows from Boron,[21] he integrates the borrowings very thoroughly into his own context. He still accepts the basic propositions that Arthur's right to the throne is undisputed, and that the context for the succession is the urgent *necessitas* created by the Saxon wars. Boron, by rejecting these propositions, transforms the story completely.

Boron has the same 'real-life' data available to him as do his predecessors, but he works it into a new *sen*. The change hinges on a shift of emphasis from human to divine agency, and from action to theory. Instead of infusing new ideas into an old story, Boron creates the story afresh round his new ideas.

HRB-based accounts of the succession do not neglect the ideas of divine grace and choice, but they concentrate on the human agencies which raise Arthur to the throne. Boron acknowledges the working of human agencies, but shows their powerlessness in the face of the divine will. To this end, as we have seen, Boron removes from Arthur all trace of an obvious right to the throne. This involves great effort and some distortion of Boron's own story: not only the introduction of the complex Antor intrigue, but a deliberate abdication by Merlin of that omnipotence which, during the previous reigns, he strove so hard to establish. On Uther's death, the barons automatically consult Merlin over the succession; Merlin replies: 'se je disoie que vous fesissies de l'un de vous roi, je feroie bien a croire, et drois seroit. Mais a vous est biele aventure venue . . .' — the 'biele aventure' being a total suspension of human activity in favour of the direct intervention of God, who here by-passes Merlin, His usual agent.

Arthur's removal to Antor's house obscures the claim of inheritance. Merlin's refusal to guide the council impedes the workings of the elective procedure, as it is intended to do: 'pour cele election (i.e. Christ's) sera rois sans election d'autrui'. Nor does Uther designate Arthur — though it is easy, from a hasty reading of Uther's death-scene, to assume that he does. In fact he merely accepts Merlin's assurance that Arthur will succeed: an assurance which is given only because Uther is dying and unable any longer to influence events.

This elimination of Arthur's rights is disconcerting to politically-minded readers. Hence the efforts of Boron's followers to replace the wordly proofs which Boron has so carefully removed.[22] Such imitators either misunderstand or reject Boron's *sen*. For Boron, the king of the Grail country must come unheralded and unacknowledged, like Christ himself, until events reveal his importance in the sight of God. Merlin, who is aware of Arthur's advent but does not bring it about, is a sort of John the Baptist. The Christological bent of Boron's account becomes increasingly obvious as it proceeds. He is not, of course, the first to introduce Christological thinking into the concept of king-making; it is inherent in the whole medieval concept of kingship.[23] But Boron adapts it to his personal concept of the environment of the Grail quest.

Boron's Arthur, like Christ, comes to an ignorant and hostile world. The council, which would unhesitatingly have accepted Merlin's recommendation or the normal political proofs, are highly dubious about the predicted sign from God: 'moult estoient fol qui cuidoient que nostre sires mesist entencion de roi eslire'. The parallel with Christ becomes quite explicit when the Archbishop chooses Christmas day as the expected time for the miracle: 'prions a Jhesucrist que il nous fache hui demoustrance d'avoir roi . . . si voirement que il nasqui au jour d'ui'. Now, the gospel for Christmas day, which must be read at the Archbishop's mass, is the opening of St John: 'In propria venit, et sui eum non receperunt' (John I.9). The lesson is a warning to the congregation — and to the reader — that the rejection of the forthcoming miracle, and the king designated by it, will amount to rejection of Christ.

The Jews awaited a Messiah, but did not recognise him when he came. Just so the Britons, under the guidance of the Archbishop (who now assumes Merlin's role as John the Baptist), dispose their minds to receive the expected sign. Their reward is the appearance of the sword in the stone.[24] Both sword and stone are obviously loaded with significance, some of which Boron expounds, while some is left to the reader's deduction. (The anvil has no obvious significance, being merely a formidably solid lodging for the stone, and most of Boron's imitators wisely eliminate it as superfluous.)[25] The stone probably represents Christ, the corner-stone, or his Church, following the text 'tu es Petrus . . .'. It tells us that the new king's power will be drawn from God and sanctioned by Holy Church. The sword symbolises Justice. It will do so again at the coronation, as it does in all real-life *ordines*, for to the medieval mind the maintenance of Justice was the primary function of kingship.[26] But this particular sword of justice comes directly from God, as if it were the concrete manifestation of the Sword in the Apocalypse (Revelation 19.15). Stone and sword thus put the new king into a uniquely close relationship with Christ. *Christus domini* by virtue of the unction, he will be by their virtue almost an *alter Christus*.[27]

The inscription on the sword puts this special relationship into words: 'Cil qui osteroit cele espee, il seroit rois de la terre par l'election Jhesucrist'. Symbolically, he will receive his synechdochic function of Justice from Christ and the Church. The choice of the sword-test as king-making motif may even have been suggested — though not uniquely inspired — by the same passage from Revelation: 'et de ore eius procedit gladius ex utraque parte acutus' (Rev. 19.6). Arthur's advent does indeed have some overtones of a Second Coming.

Since Boron has eliminated all Arthur's earthly claims, it is clear from the sword's message that the actual drawing of it will make him king. It is at that moment that Christ's 'election' singles him out. The withdrawal does not demonstrate a pre-existent right, as do the many best-knight tests of the romances. It realises Arthur's potential, just as the unction does in one medieval line of thought, the father's death in another. Many of Boron's imitators fail to grasp this notion. Thus AoM labels the sword with a vague: 'Icham yhote Escalibore/unto a king fair tresoure', which removes the king-making function of the sword altogether. Malory, anxious to re-assert Arthur's worldly claims, reverses the significance of the withdrawal: 'whoso pulleth oute this swerd of this stone *is* rightwys king *borne* . . .' According to Salazar — who supplies defects of memory with an imagination which gives rise to a wholly different *sen* — it is Merlin who engineers the sword. It neither makes the king nor demonstrates his right: it is merely a magically-contrived reference for the job. Merlin is restored by Salazar to that omnipotence which Boron firmly removed from him at this point. These alterations through misunderstanding are significant for the overall development of Arthur's legend. Misunderstanding of a Celtic magical motif is supposed to be a very common occurrence in Arthurian romance.[28] Sometimes the misunderstanding produces a new and acceptable interpretation. The fate of Boron's sword-inscription shows that, for this process to work, the original does not have to be Celtic or folkloric. It also shows how difficult it may be to decide whether the author has misunderstood his original or altered it deliberately. The legend did not, after all, grow steadily according to a universal grand design. The sword-inscription exemplifies the haphazard and contradictory way in which it did grow, with mistakes being sometimes as productive as intelligent adaptation.

Returning to Boron's own story, we find a slowing-down of the action after the sword's appearance. There are several reasons for this delay before the coming of the Chosen. Firstly, it gives time for the methodical testing of the whole social hierarchy, which underlines the uselessness of obvious worldly merit. Secondly, it introduces dramatic suspense, as the characters wonder who will be king, while the reader wonders when Arthur will appear. The story thus becomes more compelling, which makes the reader more receptive to its *sen*. Thirdly, the delay introduces a well-tried folktale motif, that of the despised Younger Son (Arthur's actual status *viv-à-vis* Antor) who succeeds in a test after everyone else has failed.[29] This popular motif increases the story's attractiveness. Fourthly, there is the Christological parallel, for the delay corresponds to the period between Christ's birth and his baptism, the beginning of his actual ministry. When Arthur arrives, the carelessness of the sword's guards in going off to the tournament provides yet another Christological parallel, this time reflecting the Second Coming. 'Vos estote parati, quia qua nescitis hora Filius hominis venturus est' (Matthew 24.44). As with Christ's coming, so with Arthur's: vigilance is lacking.

The actual withdrawal is rich in many-layered significance. Arthur's total unawareness of what he is really doing exhibits to perfection that passivity which we have seen to be desirable in a new king. He is purely a vessel for the grace which steals upon him at the moment of withdrawing the sword. In strict logic it is scarcely credible that Arthur should be ignorant of the sword's meaning, which is well-known to Kay. This, however, accords with the Younger Son motif, in which the hero performs the essential deed without thought of any advantage to himself. It also emphasises the disarming *niceté* of young Arthur, already demonstrated by his tears at missing Kay's own sword. Pathetic innocence, contrasting with a later rise to fame and glory, characterises several popular medieval heroes,[30] including the 'yongë child' of may a Christmas carol. Boron's illogicality does, however, present a problem to his imitators. AoM and Salazar circumvent it, without altering the *sen*, by insisting that Arthur has never seen the sword. Malory increases the awkwardness by having Arthur aware of the sword, but not of its significance. Malory's first tale has several hiatuses of this sort: they may be the slips of a youthful writer, imperfections which would have been eliminated in a final version, or trifles which an impressionistic writer expects his readers to ignore in pursuit of the overall conjointure.[31] Generally, however, all Boron's imitators, however clumsy, appreciate his contrast between the innocent, ignorant child and the *novus homo* which he is soon to become.

Arthur's first withdrawal of the sword makes him king irrevocably, by Christ's election. But one cannot be king *in vacuo*. Here, therefore, Boron abandons Christology and begins to reintegrate Arthur into the human world. In Boron's own work this is a comparatively simple business; Arthur faces only some natural reservations about his suitability for kingly office. This suitability he demonstrates in the testing-time before the coronation, which latter consummates the reintegration. This testing demonstrates only worldly qualities, not worldly *qualifications*, for Arthur's kingship must continue to depend only on God's will. But Boron, who is not totally unrealistic, realises that Arthur must rule in a world of things, not merely of ideas.

Boron makes little of the coronation, having transferred most of the king-making ideology to the withdrawal. Even the unction, normally the climax of the *sacre*, is scarcely mentioned. Christ has already 'sanctified' Arthur, and human symbols are unnecessary. The sword replaces the unction, which in French coronations was believed to have come straight from Heaven.[32] The sword links heavenly election with earthly coronation. All other coronation symbols are mere trappings, and Boron (like Geoffrey) lingers over them only long enough to convince us that all is done decently and in order.

The coronation maybe does, however, contain one more biblical (not Christological) parallel. It happens at Pentecost. Pentecost was already established as a common date for Arthurian events, as we see in HRB, Wace and Chrétien. It was similarly important in real life, if only for reasons of convenience in assembly.[33] Boron, however, is surely thinking of the first Pentecost, at which God's holy spirit descended on His Chosen, equipping them to go forth and labour effectively in the world (Acts 2.1-12). Thus Arthur's coronation launches him on his earthly career. The connection between Pentecost and coronation was not widespread in medieval theory or practice: the idea seems to be Boron's alone.

Arthur is equipped not only by coronation, but also by knighthood and by accepting the coronation oath. The knighting does not mean as much to Boron as it does to most Arthurians, whose passion for *chevalerie* is proclaimed in every romance. More typical of that attitude is AoM, which completely subordinates the coronation to the knighting.[34] To what extent Arthur can be both knight and king is a subject of perennial interest to authors, as we shall see in a later chapter.[35] Boron himself attaches much more weight to the kingship; but the knighthood is necessary if Arthur is to govern a world of knightly endeavour. As for the oath, it defines Arthur's field of secular activity, and by accepting it he launches himself into that activity. The subsequent disappearance of the stone shows not only that God's will has been wholly accomplished, but also that Arthur has fully entered into his earthly kingship. The coronation, which sets an ordinary king apart from other men, brings Arthur closer to them again; but there is still a very real difference. Boron emphasises not what resembles contemporary life and thought in Arthur's accession, but what makes it different and unique.

There is little doubt that, in Boron's original schema, Arthur's right to be king was never challenged after his coronation. He 'tint la terre . . . de Logres lonc tans a pais'. This concluding sentence — immediately negatived by the Vulgate and post-Vulgate continuators — is very important to Boron's overall *sen*. It marks a shift of parallelism. Before, Arthur is a type of Christ. Afterwards, interest is focussed on the Grail knight, who takes over the role of Messiah, while Arthur becomes Augustus, the Prince of Peace.[36] Boron never forgets that his true subject is the Grail. His constant playing with biblical symbolism is designed to remind the reader of that fact: it determines the nature of his *sen* and thence of his *matiere*. Both are so rich that they offer ample opportunity for re-orchestration by imitators, some of whom we have already glimpsed at work. But Boron's account is the fullest, the most original and complete, dwarfing all other efforts both previous and posterior. It is arguably the masterpiece of Boron's work, as far as this can be reconstituted. Narrative, political and theological elements combine to create one of the most fascinating episodes in the whole Arthurian literature.

Successful as Boron's version is, it is of course not accepted by other Arthurian writers as definitive. There is no such thing as a definitive version of any Arthurian story — or, indeed, of any medieval story. The authors, wary of claiming originality for themselves,[37] were no more ready to respect it in others. Boron's *Merlin* did acquire a certain prestige, being incorporated unchanged into both the Vulgate and the post-Vulgate.[38] But the *sen* of the accession episode is so complex that it cannot survive even retrospective allusion, such as it receives in VM and the *Suite*. Translation and adaptation risk altering it completely.

Most of Boron's followers are, in a way, throwbacks, though not intentionally. They tend to re-create the two conditions which Boron eliminates: that Arthur needs, and must have, worldly claims to kingship, and that his accession takes place against a background of *necessitas* created by war. This need not be Saxon war; VM furnishes the alternative of the barons' rebellion. Inevitably, these worldly preoccupations shatter Boron's allusive and mystical atmosphere and return us to harsh realities, which each author interprets according to his interests and abilities.

The simplest adaptation is that of the Welsh translation. It purports only to explain, more fully than the *Bruts*, the circumstances of Arthur's birth and accession. The account is not influenced, save on a superficial level, by any Welsh traditions of Arthur, but it does introduce shifts of emphasis. The Saxon *necessitas* is restored, under *Brut* influence: hence a return to warlike realism and urgency. Politicisation is apparent in the increased emphasis on the barons' disputes and their disastrous consequences: instead of justifiable doubt, there is ferocious rivalry. Malory takes the same line. The two texts are certainly independent, but both may be reacting to similar contemporary conditions. Certainly both are acutely aware of the dangers of baronial power, and sharpen the dichotomy between the insurgent barons and the common people, who support Arthur. This sharpening may be influenced by knowledge of VM, but it could also be an independent intensification of Boron's Christology: Christ abrogated his high station to make common cause with the poor and lowly. Certainly the Welsh author is aware of biblical parallelism, for he twice quotes openly from the gospels, and echoes them when Kynyr beseeches his fosterling: 'koffau i pan ddelych ith deyrnas dy hun'.[39] Further, his version of the sword-inscription, couched in solemn Latin, emphasises its status as a symbol of God's power. The terse Welsh prose does not communicate Boron's mysticism, but the translator appreciates it, despite his political bent. His Arthur is a secular king, as the brief and pragmatic account of the actual coronation shows, but the account still induces some contemplation of the essential nature of kingship as a God-given institution, and of the problems of applying it in the 'real' world. That 'real' world is the world of HRB: hence the throwback nature of this apparently close translation. It attempts to reconcile 'chronicle' and 'romance' traditions.

Thomas Gray sets out, quite independently, to make a similar amalgamation. He considers HRB to be more authoritative than the post-Vulgate, his chief romance source; but he is seduced by the Boron accession – not by its ideology, but by its picturesqueness. He does, however, make some attempt to reconcile the two ideologies; his struggles (unlike the Welsh author's) are in fact painfully obvious. He cannot accept the Boron idea that Arthur has no obvious claim to the throne; in any case, HRB gives him the idea that Arthur was on hand all the time, his identity widely known. On his own authority – perhaps misunderstanding Boron – he adds that Uther designated Arthur (*I fatti* p.50). The sword is thus politically superfluous, but Gray cannot resist the story. He therefore has to create a new difficulty for Arthur; in defiance of both his sources, and in desperation, he falls back on the bastardy charge: '. . . les grants du realme en avoient doute pour ceo que le temps de son (sic) naisence estoit trop pres la solempnité du matremoin le roy et por ceo que l'aventure n'estoit pas discouvert, pur l'oneur la royne, vivaunt le roy' (cf. *I fatti* p.50) – that is, Uther might not be the father. Gray also uses the notion, hinted at by Boron, that the barons have rival candidates – which gives them a motive for opposing Arthur, however impressive his claim. Gray takes these doubts to be sufficient warrant for the appearance of the sword, which is to give magical ratification to Arthur's claim. The origin of the sword is not explained; Gray massacres Boron's complex religious parallelism. The protests of the unbelievers therefore appear eminently reasonable, instead of sacrilegious as in Boron or even Malory; the overall result is confusion, a sacrifice of *sen* – or simply of sense – to *matiere*.

Gray, having dispensed with the divine sanction of Arthur's claim, is now obliged to calm the suspicion of bastardy which he has himself raised. He does so by having Ulfin disclose the full story of Arthur's birth: a measure which is considered unnecessary by Boron (though it is taken as an extra precaution in the Didot *Perceval*, perhaps in defiance of Boron's own intention), tried in vain in VM and delayed for narrative reasons in the *Suite*. Here, it is so immediately effective that Gray's contrivance creaks at the seams. He ends on the same note as the Welsh: Arthur's acclamation as a suitable leader against the Saxons (*I fatti* p.51). But whereas the Welsh smoothes over the initial and final allusions to the HRB tradition, Gray unintentionally focusses attention on the transition. He does succeed in communicating his own enjoyment of Boron's bizarre story, but cannot convince us that he has devoted any intelligent thought to it. His account is a warning to any reader, medieval or modern, who seeks to read such a story on only one level, that of narrative incident. To ignore the deeper meanings introduced by a skilled author is to imperil the coherence of the narrative itself, and rob it of the power which ensures its perpetuation.

Both French continuations of Boron imply retrospectively that the manifestation of God's power did not silence the doubts of all Arthur's subjects. The two major English adaptations, AoM and Malory, both read this attitude back into the coronation scenes, though in different ways. In both we find a refusal to discount the importance of worldly proofs. This is not a consequence of their Englishness or of their respective dates, for the same attitude obtains in French, Spanish and Anglo-French (Gray's) adaptations. Boron is altogether exceptional in his unworldliness.

Both English authors stress that Uther designated Arthur: probably because they misunderstand Boron, although the idea (which is shared by Layamon and Gray) could have been conceived independently. It is not, however, a contemporary reference, for designation grew steadily less, not more, important between the twelfth and fifteenth centuries.[40] Be that as it may, open designation and primogeniture give Arthur an exceedingly strong claim. The sword-test is not wholly superfluous, however,[41] because of Arthur's concealment. It does not make the king: it singles him out in an ordinary 'best-knight' way. But it still demonstrates God's approval — as it does not in Gray or Salazar, where its origin is uncertain. This reduction of the sword-test, however, potentially throws more weight on the coronation itself, which must now be a true king-making. This is the more so, as in both versions the caution of the barons between test and coronation becomes downright malevolence. Here, the attitudes of the two works (which are quite independent of each other) diverge. AoM prepares us for the wars of VM by identifying the hostile barons with the rebellious subkings. Their contumely is emphasised by having Arthur's identity — the worldly proofs — revealed *before* the coronation, at which the subkings are indeniably present (ll.3055-3172). It is further underlined by their brutal refusal of homage, a refusal which gives Arthur a legal right to make war on them.[42] In no other text is the rationale of Arthur's war with the subkings so clearly explained: in VM and the *Livre d'Artus* it is unclear whether they were at the coronation or not, while Malory — as we shall shortly see — utterly confuses the whole issue.

Unfortunately, the somewhat earthy-minded author of AoM misses the opportunity of emphasising the sacrilegious and damnable nature of the rebellion by bringing out the mystical and symbolic elements of the coronation itself. It is plain, nonetheless, that the barons are defying Arthur's just rights at the very moment when they are most solemnly demonstrated. Such defiance, even if it does not shock Heaven, threatens to set at naught all human organisation and cause political chaos — which does, indeed, ensue. Thus the circumstances of Arthur's accession are dictated, as in HRB, by the *necessitas* of the realm, though here the threat is internal. Once again, Boron's prince of peace is turned into a war-lord, though for a different war. AoM does not mirror contemporary conditions: if anything, it mirrors the troubles of Philip Augustus, fossilised in the source.[43] But the problems of rebellious barons, and of an uncertain succession, are relevant to any medieval century or country. That is why adaptations of Boron tend to revert to an HRB-type attitude, even if their authors have never seen HRB or even Wace.

The author of AoM, though unsubtle, has a stout grasp of the basic issues of the accession and rebellion, as he recounts them. Malory, though in every other way a far better writer, does not. Throughout the accession scenes he seems uncertain whether to prepare us for the wars of VM, or give us pure Boron. Thus at one moment it is only 'some of the grete lordes' who oppose Arthur, while others form a faction which guards him day and night. At another moment, all the lords are against Arthur, all the commons for him — as in Boron, but with more contumely. The coronation itself is no mystical consummation, but a time of violent action in which the people's formal *acclamatio* becomes a forcible elevation of the new king in the teeth of the barons. At this point, if the war is to be explained, some at least of the barons ought to refuse homage to Arthur, as in AoM. Instead, Malory, like Boron, shows 'both ryche and poure', the 'lordes and comyns', accepting the new king, while Arthur successfully exacts homage from '*alle* lordes that helde of the croune'. The subsequent wars, which Malory then briefly mentions, seem to be not rebellions but suppressions of the disorder consequent on the interregnum, and perhaps pacification of that perennial trouble-spot, the Scottish border. Up to here, then, we have a complete, if slightly confusing, story which does, this time, mirror contemporary conditions. Young Arthur could stand for Henry VI, manipulated by one faction, rejected by the other. The intervention of the commons mirrors the growing power of Parliament in the fifteenth century, with, perhaps, a general popular reverence for the true king against usurpers. Now it seems to me that Malory did not originally intend to recount the subkings' rebellion at all, but to end with 'thurgh the noble prowess of hymself and . . . the Round Table'. Later, he took up the story again, but without altering his original conclusion. The accession story would then represent Malory's own substitution of harsh political realism for Boron's Christology. Arthur must have not only the right, but the power, to impose his rule. Defensive caution and a display of force do more to reconcile the suspicious barons than religious fervour and a display of virtue; but they are convinced eventually, and Arthur is able to impose the peace with which Boron's own account concludes.

Suspicion, force and intrigue destroy any sense of mysticism in Malory's account of the coronation ceremonies; but again it is clear that they are properly performed. Naturally, the greatest emphasis falls on the political settlement: Arthur swears a deeply secularised oath, which is a compact between him and the people rather than between him and God.[44] He also swears to right the wrongs done during the interregnum,[45] indicating an awareness of the theory — well established in the fifteenth century, though not always respected in practice — that the heir became king at the moment of his predecessor's death, and is responsible for the maintenance of peace and justice from then on.[46]

Malory's alterations amount neither to a comprehensive reworking of his source, nor to a mirror-image of contemporary events. Rather does he select from his source elements which can construct a picture relevant to his own times, but not tied to them. His methods are a little confused, but the central ideas emerge clearly enough.

One group of writers stands out from the rest in its attitude to Arthur's accession. They are, of course, the Scots. While all others accept Arthur's right to the throne, however demonstrated, and implicitly or explicitly condemn all opposition to it, the Scots turn the story to an exactly opposite purpose. They, too, retain an atmosphere of *necessitas*, and play on the idea of a disputed succession, which is much more acute than it is elsewhere because the rival claimants have a distinct justification which no action of Arthur's will induce them wholly to renounce. Arthur still has claims acceptable in other circumstances: he is designated, elected and acclaimed. But his bastardy is held to invalidate them. This accords with late medieval trends, but the reason for the Scottish insistence is not modernity but their ubiquitous nationalistic prejudice. This same prejudice doubtless explains why no coronation is described in the Scots. Even an usurper derives from that ceremony a certain sanctity, and the Scots do not wish Loth's opposition to appear sacrilegious. Its very absence in the Scots underlines its importance elsewhere, save in the unique Boron. However briefly described, the *sacre* clinches all the other claims with which Arthur is variously endowed.

In all the works which we have considered, Arthur's accession story remains uniquely personal to himself. Real-life elements of king-making, which change little from century to century and from country to country, despite shifts in their relative importance, do feature in the story; but each author selects from them only what he considers to be most relevant to Arthur's particular career. This fact is underlined when we realise that, despite the vast amount of material — descriptive, ritualistic, formulaic and symbolic — available on coronations, Arthur is never shown to undergo the full ceremonial. This is the more striking in that most authors conceive of Arthur's life as being largely regulated by elaborate ceremonial. So fascinating and individual were the contexts created by Geoffrey and Boron, so rich their *sen* and its potential, that no imitator chose to linger on mere description, or to give a bland reproduction of real life. The HRB combination of irregular birth, *necessitas* and theory is the key to the story's success, making it virtually impossible (*pace* Wace) to dismiss Arthur's accession as a natural, inevitable and uninteresting occurrence. Malory's phrase 'made king by adventure and by grace' perfectly sums up the nexus of inventions surrounding the accession.

IV

ARTHUR AT WAR

With this chapter we must alter our strictly 'biographical' method of investigation. Birth and accession are, obviously, fixed points in Arthur's career. The same cannot be said of his later activities, to the time of his death. Accounts vary so widely, and so many of them dispense with a biographical approach, that it is impossible to discuss Arthur's warlike (and other) deeds chronologically. I shall, therefore, treat Arthur's wars according to type, not in order of occurrence.

There is, however, one preliminary 'biographical' question of universal applicability. What proportion of Arthur's life is spent in war? To the medieval mind, war is endemic.[1] According to Erich Köhler, this is not so in the Arthurian world, which is the literary realisation of a hoped-for *future* peace: the peace preceding the Last Things. Arthur's realm, being timeless and unsituated, realises these hopes in a temporal suspension which is neither real nor unreal.[2] For reasons which will, I hope, become apparent, I do not agree with Köhler's generalisation, even as applied to Chrétien, almost his sole source. No medieval author of my acquaintance implies, much less states, that Arthur's reign was a period of uninterrupted peace. Some, indeed, state the exact opposite: that Arthur, like any real-life medieval king, was perpetually troubled by war. For a society largely geared to war, such a situation held a greater fascination than some vaguely-imagined future of unbroken peace. The moral, technical and political problems of warfare are mirrored in romance no less than in epic.[3] Outstanding among these problems is the king's role in war, and its exposition in the Arthurian material unites all its various branches.

There are few works in which Arthur is wholly unconcerned with war. The Welsh material and the verse romances cannot, by their very nature, compute how much of Arthur's life is spent in war. The Welsh Arthur is basically an uneasy blend of two personalities, anti-Saxon hero and legendary adventurer. The former, represented in the Nennian paragraph and one triad,[4] exists for no other purpose than war; but, as he has no biography, we cannot tell whether this purpose occupied a lifetime. The latter often fights — sometimes against non-human enemies — but does not engage in systematic campaigns except in *Culhwch*,[5] which from this viewpoint resembles the verse romances more than the Welsh fragments. The verse romances show awareness that Arthur has been involved in many wars, by listing or evoking his conquests.[6] Some show him at peace in the present, but many do not: he may not be perpetually engaged in the same war, but must be constantly on the alert for spasmodic outbreaks. His very gathering of renowned knights around himself means that he is always on a potential war footing.

Chronicles and prose romances permit of a more accurate estimate. Geoffrey and (even more emphatically) Wace lay far more emphasis on Arthur's wars than on his peacetime activities, although it is possible to calculate that their Arthur must have spent at least half of his reign in peace. All Geoffrey's imitators see Arthur as a warrior-king first and foremost. As for the great romances, all, in their various ways, bring out the importance of war in Arthurian society. Not all are as emphatic as the *Livre d'Artus*, but a remark in that work may stand as a fair summary of a widespread Arthurian belief: '[Arthur] onques n'ot pais a nul jor de son vivant des que la vie li encommença dusqu'a sa mort'.

If Arthur is widely seen as devoting most of his time to war, this creates the possibility of developing several differing approaches to his role as warrior-king. In medieval theory and practice, it is upon the king that the multiple problems of war and peace, and their relative desirability, ultimately devolve. While the clergy — with exceptions — are assumed to favour peace, while the knights desire war and the people's opinion is ignored, the king must decide between the two. According to medieval law, he alone can formally declare war.[7] He is responsible if his subjects wage war without his consent, or if they force him to declare it against his better judgement — as when Ebrauc in Layamon's *Brut* is forced by his council to wage a war which he knows to be unpleasing to God. This puts the king in an acute conceptual dilemma. He contains in himself elements both of priest and of knight. Churchmen, theorists and his coronation oath continually exhort him to keep the peace. On the other hand, one of the most ancient and universal concepts of monarchy is that the king should be an eager, invincible conqueror.[8] Theorists try to reconcile these notions by defining areas of justifiable conflict: defence of the people, restoration of the peace which has been disturbed by foreign invaders or rebellious subjects.[9] But it is hard to regulate real life according to theoretical ideals — even if one wants to. Thus, medieval accounts, 'historical' or 'fictional', of a king at war are interesting from many viewpoints: psychological, moral, legal and practical. Arthur's case is one among many; but, once again, his wars, whatever they may reflect of literary and historical models, remain an integral part of his own story as the various authors conceive it.

The many wars of Arthur's long literary career fall into distinct types, which bear some relation to categories laid down in medieval treatises,[10] but do not follow them exactly; Arthur's wars do not constitute a theoretical textbook. I categorise them as follows:

(i)   Saxon wars
(ii)   Defensive wars, including wars against rebels
(iii) 'Altruistic' wars, on behalf of vassal or ally
(iv) Wars of conquest
(v)   The Roman war: a category in itself

Arthur's last wars against Lancelot and Mordred are, like the Roman war, a category in themselves. Unlike the Roman war, however, they have a fixed place in Arthur's biography, and my discussion of them will be found in the last chapter.[11]

It will be noticed that I have not employed the favourite medieval division into 'just' and 'unjust' war. This division is hard to fix even in theory, and in practice – including Arthurian practice – it is far harder. This is strikingly demonstrated by Arthur's wars in the alliterative *Morte*, for critics have been unable, despite long debate, to agree on how far they are 'just' or 'unjust'. Probably the author was not sure himself;[12] and such contradictions abound in the Arthurian material. A war praised by one author may scandalise another. The distinction is therefore useless for purposes of classification, though it may sometimes serve as a guide to authors' attitudes.

Another point may be noted. In many medieval manuals, it is assumed that the combatants in a 'perpetual' war are always the same, so that any 'peace' is really a truce. The model for this is doubtless the long Franco-English conflict.[13] Arthur has such long-term struggles, with Saxons, Romans and with Claudas, which even overlap his own reign. Most often, however, Arthur faces, simul-taneously or successively, a variety of enemies. This is a different kind of perpetuity, and it can bear contrasting interpretations: either that the invincible Arthur can overcome innumerable foes, or that he is continually harassed and on the brink of disaster. With this as with every variation on the war theme, the author's manipulation of the reader's beliefs and prejudices can throw light on the author's general conception of Arthur, as we shall attempt to show while we examine the categories in turn.

(i) Saxon Wars

Saxon war is perhaps the most unvarying constant of Arthur's career. Two basic ideas, that Arthur fought the Saxons, and that he was justified in doing so by Saxon wickedness, spring from Dark Age British history, and link themselves so firmly to Arthur that succeeding Arthurian writers make great efforts to adapt them so as to retain their impact. These efforts continually affect the development of Arthur's legend.

Whether there was a real Arthur who fought the Saxons, or whether British hatred of Saxons transformed a purely legendary Arthur into an anti-Saxon champion, will never be known for certain.[14] It is certain, however, that the earliest writers on Arthur[15] shared in that bitter, unrelenting, determinedly ignorant race-hatred of dispossessed Briton for usurping Saxon which permeates early Welsh literature. The 'Nennian' Arthur is the quintessence of this hatred. He exists only to kill Saxons, and the much-disputed title 'dux bellorum' serves above all to dissociate him from all peacetime interests.

But he is also, by virtue of Guinnion and Badon, a Christian champion,[16] fighting pagans. Such a figure could appeal to a wider audience than the Welsh – but the appeal would have to be enhanced by a progressive updating of the enemy so as to stimulate the prejudices of the hearer. We can see Geoffrey doing this by developing such incidents as the Treachery of the Long Knives, which demonstrates the Saxons' betrayal of universal human values. And he goes further still when he introduces into Dubricius' famous pre-Badon speech unmistakable echoes of Turpin's speech at Rencesvals. Arthur's Saxons thus take on the colour of Charlemagne's Saracens, and Arthur is implied to be an opponent of the most feared and hated enemy of high medieval Europe, Islam. This concept was to win enormous favour among Geoffrey's successors. It emerges most clearly in VM, which belongs to the great days of the Third Crusade, and which treats Arthur with a whole-hearted enthusiasm unusual among the French authors of its time. It draws heavily on the French crusading epic,[17] so that in VM and in its imitator, the *Livre d'Artus*, we see Arthur's Saxons transformed into very palpable Saracens. By the time we come to AoM (ll.75-6) and Malory (II. 633), there is no distinction at all between 'Saisnes' and 'Saracens'. Moreover, as the Saxon/Saracen equation develops, all Arthur's traditional enemies tend to take on exotic pagan connotations — Rion in VM, for example (II. 92 et passim), Ariohan in *Palamède* (Lathuillière 229).

Thus, by adapting itself to a major literary and historical interest of the Middle Ages, this most ancient Arthurian theme keeps its primacy throughout the tradition. Always an ultimately hopeless struggle, the Saxon war exhibits the same tragic fascination and urgency as the real-life defence of the Latin Kingdom of Jerusalem. Arthur is, indeed, a crusader in his own land. Few authors bother to send him to Outremer,[18] for the Saxon/Saracen theme turns Arthur's Britain into a focal point for Christian unity. The old Welsh nationalism is reapplied, in the French prose, to express supranational and religious preoccupations. The presence of the Grail in Arthur's Britain is, indeed, as potent a religious symbol as the Cross itself: thus the defence against the Saxons may be linked in many authors' minds with the most central, spiritual theme of the great Arthurian cycles.

Though the Saxons maintain their importance as a theme, the magnitude of Arthur's achievement against them is not everywhere emphasised, even in the chroniclers. In Higden Arthur makes little impression on the Saxon hordes; in the Scots his very success carries the seeds of his own moral corruption; Gray, trying to reconcile Higden with Geoffrey, states — firmly if not quite logically — that Arthur's success was partial and temporary. Even in Geoffrey, Arthur's Saxon victories are but the springboard for higher endeavour, and even so prove impermanent at the last. In VM, the Saxons are only one element in the young Arthur's tangled situation, and they even favour him in as much as they eventually force the rebels into repentance. Here indeed Arthur is the archetypal medieval king, struggling to put the lid on a cauldron of conflicting interests; yet simultaneously — such is the adaptability of the Saxon motif — he is a glorious crusading leader. His glory is personal as well as regal and ideological. This brings us to a consideration of the Saxon wars as a theatre for Arthur's personal achievements. In HRB, he grows through them from a gracious stripling into an invincible hero who is equipped to challenge all of Europe. His active participation in the fighting is taken for granted and given an almost mystical importance. Both the *Livre d'Artus* and VM enthusiastically echo Geoffrey's opinion. By risking death, the king approximates to the model of Christ,[19] inspiring his men to fight with religious enthusiasm. VM very neatly evades the charge of unnecessarily exposing the king to danger. In VM, Arthur is no longer a strategist as in HRB, this role being vested in Merlin. Arthur thus escapes the full weight of kingly responsibility and human fallibility, while retaining his personal valour and the mystical aura of kingship. His self-exposure in battle cannot seem irresponsible under Merlin's guidance, and the two opposing views are reconciled. Arthur and Merlin combined make the perfection of warrior-kingship, and the war-leading Arthur of Wace is harmonised with the omnipotent Merlin of Boron.

Thus far, the works which we have considered have taken for granted the favourable presentation of Arthur as an anti-Saxon hero. This is not everywhere the case, although the Saxons themselves are never vindicated.

Two examples will suffice. The first part of LP startles a Wace-fed reader with its unsympathetic picture of Arthur's Saxon war in the Camille episode. The war itself is, as usual, approved of, but Arthur himself participates for the wrong reason: not to defend his country or Christendom, but to impress a hoped-for mistress. The author makes the general point that one should not fight for unsound reasons, and the particular point that Arthur is morally inferior to Lancelot.[20] He also contributes to the undermining of accepted Arthurian values which can be detected in many of the French prose romances.

Palamède also uses the Saxon wars to determine an attitude. Like VM, it interweaves them with a civil war, and shows how the Saxon threat eventually reunites king and rebels (Lathuillière pp. 229-34). The moral *sen*, however, is reversed. In the VM, it is the rebels who repent. In *Palamède*, it is Arthur who is compelled to reverse his attitude to the rebel Meliadus. Thus two near-contemporary French works, both using the same sources and the same basic situation, come to opposite conclusions about Arthur's position. For one, Arthur is the type of king endeavouring to restore order and Christianity, and deserves praise and obedience. For the other, Arthur is tyrannically endeavouring to suppress the independent spirit of his worthy barons. Individual prejudice transforms an identical story, under identical real-life conditions.

The development of the Saxon motif remains always within fairly narrow parameters. Not even Layamon, in whom religious prejudice overcomes any possible racial sympathy, will speak for the Saxons. They never feature save as enemies on the battlefield. It is a measure of the ingenuity of Geoffrey, the VM author, and others to a lesser degree, that they can so enrich a limited motif. Were it not for their injection of new *sen*, it would wither and die in the new world of Lancelot and the Grail.

(ii) Defensive Wars

In a well-known article, A. E. van Hamel argues that both Arthur and Finn were originally mythological Defenders, protecting the sacred Land against all manner of threats.[21] His theory has not won general acceptance, but it is still worthy of consideration. Neither Arthur nor Finn is a king in his earliest literary appearances. But in almost every society, it is precisely the king who is thought of as defender of the Land. Now, in early Irish society, the king was taboo-ridden, and defended his land in subtle, magical ways rather than in battle.[22]

Such a concept might give rise to the imagining of a secular figure to fulfil the fighting role assigned elsewhere to the king. Finn might stand in this relation to Cormac, and Arthur to the 'reges Britannorum'. Then, in a changed society which accepted the notion of an active warrior-king, both Finn and Arthur might be thought of as kings *because* they were known as defending warriors. But – in Arthur's case at least – there is no solid evidence that such was his 'original' role. His activities in the early literature are multifarious, and by no means all concerned with defence; nor are they so at any point in his development. He may, however, engage at any time in defence, because both heroes and kings are universally expected to do so in time of need. Defensive war is perennially relevant to Arthur's legend, but neither monopolises it nor explains its ultimate origin.

At this stage we shall concern ourselves only with defensive *wars*: not challenges by individuals such as the Green Knight, nor invasions by non-humans such as Twrch Trwyth. These are similar in a way, but demand a different kind of response to that required by an invasion by a human army. Such an attack demands the mustering of all Arthur's forces, and an assumption of responsibility by himself. 'Defence of the *patria* required a just war waged on the authority of its legitimate protector.'[23] Let us see how the authors apply such maxims to Arthur.

Defensive wars are even harder than Saxon wars to fit into a generalised schema of Arthur's life. The former, unlike the latter, can occur just as easily in a timeless verse romance as in a chronicle or prose cycle. They can be on a small or large scale, span days or years, form a tiny incident in a work or decide its whole structure.

In the HRB tradition, Arthur does not fight defensive wars in the sense that he waits to be attacked before taking up arms. Such passivity is alien to Geoffrey's concept. The Saxon, Roman and Mordred wars can all be construed as defensive, if only for the purposes of moral arguments, but the overall impression is of a victorious aggressor. The HRB structure must be abandoned before Arthur can truly go on the defensive. The verse romances, which reck nothing of that structure, might therefore seem to have an infinity of scope. These, however, impose a different limitation. If the equilibrium is to endure, defensive wars must not impose too great a disruption.

This does not mean that the threat must not seem serious at the time, for, of course, it must if the reader's interest is to be held. Angres' rebellion in *Cligès* is an excellent example of combined seriousness and stability, and succeeds in preserving much of the excitement of its source – Mordred's rebellion in Wace[24] – without reproducing that source's destruction of the Arthurian *status quo*. Everything is carefully scaled down from the beginning, when Arthur leaves Britain not for a mighty invasion, but on a peaceable routine 'eyre'. Concentration on the lovers further reduces the feeling of danger to Arthur, as does the relatively small scale of the rebellion, which does not re-activate the Saxon threat as Mordred's does. Conversely, there is tension and excitement, issuing in the first place from Arthur's own desperate concern and huge preparations for a counter-attack. Nor can he be accused of over-reacting, because the rebellion as first announced to him sounds much more serious than it actually turns out to be, especially as Angres is said to be in control of London, which in this entirely non-Celtic romance — as in real life — must mean domination of the entire country.

Within the equilibrium thus constructed, the siege of Windsor takes place. Chrétien, concerned with his love-story, deliberately neglects the graver political implications; but Arthur's reactions are important throughout as a secondary and interacting theme. He emerges as a strict but just king, whose personal hatred is translated into royal *mautalent* and thus acquires the impersonal force of law; his sternness actually complements the mildness of Guinevere and Alexandre. Behind the sentimental main story lies a firm demonstration of the king's God-given authority over that most loathsome of criminals in medieval eyes, the traitor.

'Actif et énergique'[25] in his first reaction, Arthur does not figure in the actual fighting. He is not to be condemned for this, however. All medieval sieges were essentially stalemates; they left room for individual exploits — which in this case means Alexandre's. We must admit, nonetheless, that Arthur's inactivity in *Cligès* is typical of all his sieges, and in this he contrasts with the impetuous Alexander of both history and romance. This should not, however, trigger accusations of *fainéantise*. Arthur is always less impetuous than his partial analogue, Alexander, and less thirsty for personal glory; and Alexander's *fougue* in sieges endangered his whole expedition more than once.[26] Arthur is wiser. A siege requires long-term strategy and wide direction, and we may assume that Arthur provides them.

We have lingered over *Cligès* because, despite his lightness of touch, Chrétien here manages to incorporate a range of questions concerning the king's role in defensive war. Other verse romances are less detailed, but introduce fresh aspects. Such is Chrétien's *Perceval*, which contains his only other allusion to defensive war (ll. 834-1119).

It is an odd episode. Arthur's court, when Perceval enters it, is already on a war footing, having successfully dealt with the aggressor, Ris. Why then does Arthur fail to defy the new aggressor, the Red Knight? His peculiar inactivity certainly puzzled Chrétien's imitators. *Peredur* and the Second Continuation keep the challenge firmly on an individual basis, thus mitigating Arthur's failure. *Percyvelle* accepts the war theme, but alters and backdates it.[27] What these works evade, but Chrétien boldly advances, is the idea that Arthur has somehow lost the ability to stimulate his own will, and that of his realm, into the huge effort necessary to meet an aggressor. It is our first sight of him in *Perceval*, and it prepares us for the progressive loss of faith in all aspects of the worldly Arthurian ideal which is so central to that romance.

Despite Chrétien's attitude here, the later verse romances continue evidence of Arthur's vigorous reaction to aggression. In *Durmart* and *Li Chevaliers as deus espées*,[28] Arthur himself reacts vigorously to a threat to his territory, and the hero's efforts are complementary to Arthur's own instead of replacing them as in *Perceval*. In each case it is clear — as it often is not in individual peacetime adventures — that the hero acts for Arthur and in his name. It is no shame for

Arthur, in war, to rely on his knights, for they are as helpless without his directing authority as he is without their prowess. The war is won by individual effort — but then, all wars are won by the sum of individual efforts, a fact which the medieval habit of describing battles through a series of single combats repeatedly makes clear. The verse-romance hero's settlement of a defensive war expresses that symbiosis of knight and king which, in other contexts, is often strained, challenged or completely eliminated.

Defensive war does not bulk large in the whole verse-romance corpus, for it threatens too much disturbance. As we move away from the verse-romance world, the problems of defensive war become more insistent, and Arthur's reactions more complex. This is exemplified in the Second Continuation, which moves slightly but discernibly away from the verse-romance equilibrium. Its defensive war, against Carras, touches on many problems. To begin with, it is long-standing:

> ... trop grand posnee
> a faite, voir, li rois Carras
> et ses freres li rois Claudas ...   (ll. 31304-6)

says Gawain, looking back over a long, intermittent struggle. The relative chronology makes it impossible that this idea should have been borrowed from LP: rather, LP borrowed both notion and nomenclature from the Continuation.[29] In the Continuation, the background details are unimportant, but the basic notion of perpetual war is significant, because it affects the normal Arthurian peacetime occupation of errantry. Gawain reluctantly, but instantly, abandons his Grail-quest to join in the war. This mirrors the feudal duty of real life. It also looks forward to LP and the prose cycles, in which the same duty is codified in the Arthurian law:[30] the ever-present menace of war is thus officially acknowledged, as it never is in the verse romances. The Continuation also demonstrates the importance of justification, even in a basically defensive war, in the value which Arthur attaches to Gawain's ratification. Here, we encounter a piece of legal theory. Is a prince whose territory is threatened justified in eliminating the threat definitively by carrying the war into the aggressor's territory? At least one Romanist lawyer opined: 'when the rightful lord of a property violently expelled the present possessor without judicial authority, he lost the ownership of his own property through his illegal violence'.[31] Gawain's advice takes a similar line, and gives the sanction of the acknowledged paragon of Arthurian romance to Arthur's decision. Evidently the author is sensitive to contemporary notions of the morality of warfare. However, unlike a verse romancer, he makes quite clear that war is woven into the very fabric of Arthurian life, and that Arthur's kingdom is perpetually menaced.

Defensive war bulks very large in the great prose cycles. One of their distinguishing attitudes is that Arthur is never wholly secure. Progressively, the awareness of Arthur's approaching end permeates and shapes the whole account of his life,[32] so that every threat echoes the menace of final doom. The defensive wars are no longer brief interruptions, easily and creditably settled. They are protracted, often indecisive, struggles for survival. The enemies are great lords:

Claudas, Madaglan, Rion, Galehaut, Mark, the Five Kings, Lot and his confederation. Their continuous menace undermines Arthur's status as conqueror. Some of them also undermine his moral status: Galehaut and the Lot of the *Suite* are good and noble men whose excellence challenges the justice of Arthur's defence.

Perlesvaus, though maintaining its uniqueness, partakes of these attitudes. In it, Arthur fights defensive wars against Brien and Madaglan, and is threatened with a third from Claudas. All three are interrelated, and variously linked to the narrative and ideology of the whole work. Occurring in quick succession towards the end of the work, they threaten the destruction of Arthur's kingdom, not simply by military conquest, but by a combination of external and internal disturbance, and overall the apparent withdrawal of God's grace from Arthur, hitherto His principal champion. Over and over again, Arthur acts in accordance with the laws and customs of Arthurian society – and the outcome is disastrous, because that society is in decay and its laws no longer obtain. The effect is almost apocalyptic. Cause and effect join in a many-layered *sen*: the three wars constitute a superbly dramatic story, a political lesson, probably a historical allegory,[33] certainly a demonstration of how men's best intentions go awry when unsanctioned by God. They also augur a forthcoming account of Arthur's final end by a combination of treachery – by Brien instead of Mordred – and unwilling betrayal by Lancelot, as compelling as, though utterly different from, that of the Vulgate *Mort*. Truly this is a 'moult bele conjointure'.

In *Perlesvaus*, Arthur's kingdom suffers no military conquest, but the threat of one creates the conditions for internal collapse. Within this framework, the author creates his own frames of reference and justification. The same can be said of the early LP's treatment of Arthur's defensive war against Galehaut, which brings Arthur to the lowest political and moral position he reaches in the whole LP. The earliest pages of LP show us an Arthur beset by wars, but acquitting himself well on the whole and achieving a glory which impresses even Claudas.[34] Now, however, a new star arises in the LP firmament: Galehaut, who possesses all the noble, kingly attributes earlier attributed to Arthur. Neither virtuous indignation nor rash courage (so often successful in medieval war stories), nor all the power of Arthur's knights, nor even Arthur's own moral regeneration, can prevail against the newcomer. The whole Arthurian structure, political and literary, is on point of collapse when Lancelot persuades Galehaut to spare Arthur. Lancelot thus becomes the pivot of equilibrium between the two warrior-kings, both of whom henceforward (though for rather different reasons) depend on him utterly. As the romance proceeds, Galehaut is eliminated and Arthur restored to his former place, but the reader is never allowed to forget that he retains in on loan, once from God and once from the hero. Through Arthur and Galehaut, all kings are given the lesson of humility and moderation. And like the *Perlesvaus* author, that of LP constantly reminds us of the all-importance of God's grace and immanent judgment.

Later prose romances show no clear, progressive line of development in the treatment of defensive war; each adapts it to a different *sen*. In *Perlesvaus* and LP the defensive-war motif is used destructively. VM, in contrast, uses it constructively: Arthur becomes the archetype of the defending, and ultimately peacemaking, monarch. Moreover, it is the Saxon menace, combined with reaction against their fathers' rebellion and the allure of Arthur's victories over both, which attract to him the young knights who are to constitute his court. The traditional Arthurian organisation is forged in the heat of defensive war.

VM's conclusion is optimistic. It is that wars fought in the right spirit can have a happy and constructive issue. Misguided Christian opponents can be persuaded, instead of exterminated, and Arthur, in accordance with the best contemporary theory, fights to restore peace. That peace creates the conditions for Arthurian adventure — a fact which increases the interest of the whole process.

The *Suite* offers a profoundly original treatment of the defensive-war theme. It involves deep and disturbing questions of justice — not just legal problems, but the basics of human conduct. Through the defensive wars, the author probes the relative importance of individuals and the realm, of the king's private and public personae. Spanning all is the basically theological question of Arthur's sins: the actual sin of incest, the intended one of murdering the babies. Theological theory apart, these sins relate very directly to the wars. They cause rebellions both intended and actual, and the rebellions in turn complicate what began as a straightforward defensive war against Rion. Rion's chances obviously increase enormously when the realm is rent with internal dissension. God's immanent justice hovers very close over Arthur in both wars; more clearly than in LP, his moral state determines the outcome. His uncommitted sin is not punished, wherefore Lot's rebellion fails. But unbeknown to Lot, Arthur's real sin, his incest with Lot's wife, actually justifies Lot's rebellion. Therefore — as Arthur is well aware — Arthur's victory comes through God's grace, not his own merit. This is only a prorogation of sentence; in the end Arthur, and Logres, will pay in full for his sin. But Lot is not the predestined instrument of vengeance, and the cause for which he consciously fights is unjust. It is thus not true to say that Lot is an innocent man sacrificed to preserve a guilty one, especially as he condemns himself by his refusal to accept Merlin's explanations. But certainly he is sacrificed for the good of the state, for the preservation of the king's public persona, not for Arthur the sinful man: 'que il li prenge pitié de la couronne, que li honours del roiame ne dechie par le defaute de lui' (I. 247). Individuality is abrogated on both sides. Natural law yields to politics, though both ideas are complicated by the ultimately insoluble problem of God's justice and of Fate. Much of the post-Vulgate is concerned with the conflict between the 'natural' law of blood-feud and the man-made rules of civilised behaviour. Lot's dilemma therefore adumbrates much: and, of course, there is a direct link between Lot's death and his sons' long-drawn-out feud with the Pellinors.[35]

The *Suite*'s use of defensive war is complex and subtle. There is still plenty of excitement, but the author moves beyond the problems of war and national safety to probe universal questions of eternal relevance. Questions of patriotism and Arthurian organisation seem petty by contrast: even *Perlesvaus* can scarcely rival the *Suite*'s achievement.

It is, as we have seen, largely in French works that Arthur's defensive wars are treated. They exhibit a general reluctance to treat him as a mighty conqueror, an attitude which must surely have some nationalistic preoccupation behind it.[36]

In the post-Vulgate *Queste* Arthur cannot even fight off the despicable Mark (*Demanda*, 249-50). This French reserve over Arthur's military standing did not pass unnoticed abroad. Malory, for instance, avoids the whole of the post-Vulgate *Queste*, and reduces Galehaut to an obedient satellite of Arthur, in what is surely a deliberate refutation of attacks on Arthur's prestige. It is surely no coincidence that there are no full English translations of LP and TP, though manuscripts of both abounded in England; whereas the less reserved VM was Englished at least three times.[37] The Scots *Lancelot of the Laik*, by contrast, finds the LP Galehaut episode very easy to adapt in order to express the contemporary Scottish nationalistic and anti-Arthurian prejudice.[38] Thus do authors' varying interests stimulate controversy over Arthur, and keep interest in him alive.

(iii) Altruistic Wars

In a fully feudal society, everyone save pope and emperor was someone else's vassal. Under such conditions we may expect that Arthur, whose lands are often thought of as roughly coterminous with the Roman Empire, should frequently engage in wars on behalf of vassals — as well as allies. Naturally, under the later idea of 'rex est imperator in terra sua'[39] Arthur is seen as the ultimate appeal. Never does Arthur himself obey a summons to assist a feudal overlord. He acknowledges none — least of all the Roman emperor.

'Altruistic' interventions could be seen as a normal part of a suzerain's duties, not calling for particular comment. However, we shall discover that this theme, too, can express a variety of authorial attitudes. Again, the contributors are mainly French: because altruism negates conquest, and also simply because the French authors bring the greatest originality to bear on this theme, as on many others.

Cligès, which presents the first Arthurian defensive war, also launches the 'altruistic' theme with Arthur's protracted attack on Alis. The project, though aborted by a *deus ex machina*, has great conceptual importance. It is entirely altruistic, for Arthur is bound only by a very tenuous family obligation. The identity of the enemy, however, raises intriguing questions. Arthur challenges the formidable Byzantine Empire; and, although Arthur's dominions seem to be no greater than those of the contemporary Angevin kings, Chrétien plainly sees him as an emperor equal to Alis. Arthur is poised to achieve the perennial dream of reuniting Eastern and Western Empires. But Chrétien shrinks from allowing Arthur to achieve the colossal conquest. Hence Alis' convenient death, which makes possible the kind of harmonious east-west relations which were sadly lacking in twelfth-century reality. Such harmony would create ideal conditions for a crusade: a point which Chrétien does not mention, but which might well resonate, to Arthur's credit, in contemporary readers' minds.

Certainly at least one medieval author was excited by the prospect of an actual war between Arthur and Byzantium; for in *Floriant* — written a hundred years after *Cligès*, its obvious source — such a war occurs. The author, however, still shrinks from allowing Arthur to conquer Byzantium: HRB 'history' and the verse-romance equilibrium both forbid such a colossal change in his fortunes. Therefore, the conflict — which is again purely altruistic, Floriant being neither vassal nor relative of Arthur — is localised in Sicily. Moreover, Arthur's final victory is rather moral than military. However, Arthur and the Byzantine Emperor are treated as equals throughout: once again, he has the status of Western Emperor. The kindly father-figure, who resolves his knight-children's problems, is also an awesomely successful monarch.

Elsewhere, too, the altruistic war theme works favourably for Arthur: in the Latin *Meriadoc*, the French-derived *Lanzelet*,[40] the English *Percyvelle*. In each case, the alliance between king and current hero redounds to the credit of both. This optimistic use of the theme is unconfined by genre or nationality, appealing to authors individually. But the pessimistic view is a powerful counterforce.

Pessimism features even in the verse romances, for in both *Deus espees* and *Yder* Arthur is criticised for neglecting his clear feudal duty of aiding vassals in their need. The criticism is harsher in *Yder*, where Arthur neglects an altruistic war to pursue an unjust one, than in *Deus espees*, where there is merely a lack of communication between lord and vassal. This difference fits the overall *sen* of the works, for, whereas *Yder* is everywhere harsh to Arthur, *Deus espees* views him, on the whole, favourably. Indeed, *Deus espees*' attitude implies not criticism of Arthur but simply a touch of realism, countering the Arthurian grapevine which in many romances spreads news with uncanny rapidity. In *Yder*, the criticism contributes to the portrayal of a man whose personality often militates against the abstract demands of his kingship. Thus we have not only variations on the altruistic theme, but also variations on the variations. We notice, however, that the equilibrium requires that Arthur's prestige be eventually restored; this is done by both the verse authors.

The dynamism of the prose romances, by contrast, permits any number of failures in altruism. Not that Arthur is deliberately neglectful, as in *Yder*; most often he is too far away, or too busy, or simply has not heard of the trouble.[41] Such failures were doubtless common in the difficult careers of real-life monarchs. Yet such realism contrasts sharply with the confidence of the verse-romance or chronicle Arthur, who, in Layamon, can even impose peace on pain of death. The allusions are not frequent in the entire prose corpus, and they sometimes jostle with praise of Arthur and his great and peaceful courts; nevertheless they do indicate criticism, for they are conceptually linked to a vast failure of protection which spans the whole of the LP, and must therefore influence the entire corpus. This is the ever-postponed war with Claudas. It is introduced in the first pages of LP; it oppresses Arthur's conscience; it dominates the preudome's reproaches and thus purports to explain Arthur's defeat by Galehaut. Thereafter, the postponement lasts some twenty-three years, during which it is kept in our minds by repeated allusions. This failure, unlike the others, is inexcusable. As Arthur's debt to Lancelot mounts, the failure becomes more damnable: the obligation is both feudal and moral.

The obligation is, however, finally discharged, as is vital to the entire structure of LP. Moreover, the ending of the obligation is allowed to reflect considerable credit on the king. To this end, the HRB war against Frollo is incorporated into the Claudas war. Naturally, Arthur does not actually wrest France from a French king, for such a notion is naturally distasteful to a French author.[42]

(Of course, Frollo in HRB is a Roman tribune.) In fact, Arthur already owns France by right of inheritance from Uther, and his victory simply reasserts that right, nearly forfeited through inaction: 'Sire, si m'ait Dieus, bien devés avoir le royaume, quar bien l'avés deservi!', as Lancelot himself admits. Arthur's action is simultaneously self-interested and altruistic, and it restores his moral and political viability. Despite this, however, we carry away from LP an impression of tottering prestige. We also absorb a limited justification of belligerence: peaceableness in a king is not laudable if it inflicts suffering on his own subjects. LP projects both a general and an intensely 'Arthurian' lesson.

On the whole, however, Arthur's altruistic wars do not stimulate theoretical discussion, because their rights and wrongs are too clear. They serve to express the author's opinion of Arthur himself; their connection with plain kingly duty provides a useful measuring rod for his success. There remains one class of supremely altruistic wars which demand a higher level of duty: crusades to Outremer. We have seen that the Saxons and the Grail can turn Britain itself into an Outremer, obviating the need for an expedition abroad.[43] In any case, we should perhaps not expect French authors to send Arthur gloriously to Outremer; and the verse-romance and HRB structures leave little room for such an invention. We might look to Middle English authors to fill the gap. As a national hero, and above all as one of the three Christian worthies, Arthur would profit from crusader status such as Charlemagne and Godefroi de Bouillon enjoy. But he scarcely gets it. Four strangely-assorted texts involve Arthur with Jerusalem: the chronicle of Jean d'Outremeuse; the *Prophécies de Merlin*; the thirteenth-century Vatican MS of Nennius; and *Golagros and Gawain*.[44] Of these, d'Outremeuse's version is most like a true crusade, but it is too chaotic and phantasmagorical to give Arthur a solid reputation. It may, however, propose him as a prefiguration of Charlemagne – who later in the Chronicle shows great interest in Arthur. The *Prophécies* take a different line. It is not Arthur's active intervention in a crusade which is solicited, but his financial aid; moreover he is excommunicate at the time.[45] His generous response to the appeal fits his current circumstances marking his redemption from the False Guinevere's clutches.[46] Moreover, the author's mercenary attitude towards the crusades and their funding is not sarcastic, but realistic. However, it does detract from the original exalted crusading ideal; and since Arthur has recently been flagrantly neglecting his own anti-Saxon 'crusade', an active Outremer expedition would be just the thing to restore his prestige. By denying it him, the author asserts his low opinion of Arthur as altruistic warrior.

The Vatican story can be dismissed as a mere local legend,[47] though it may hint that there are – as we have suggested – makings of a true crusader in Arthur the anti-Saxon warrior. In *Golagros*, Arthur's visit to Jerusalem is only a frame to the main story. The idea is developed from a suggestion in the alliterative *Morte* (ll.3216-7),[48] but whereas the *Morte* clearly envisages a crusade, *Golagros* thinks rather in terms of a pilgrimage. Doubtless the crusading ideal retained little force in fifteenth-century Scotland, whereas the mystique of a visit to Jerusalem remained. Arthur's piety in *Golagros* is not meant to clash with his aggression: both combine to construct a character whose religion is sincere, but never allowed to interfere with his worldly preoccupations – realistic enough for a late medieval monarch.

These isolated instances only emphasise the silence of most authors. If Arthur 'crusades', he does so at home. When he wields arms abroad, it is often in aggression against fellow-Christians. To the fraught subject of aggression we must now turn.

(iv) Aggressive Wars

Aggressive wars are both dangerous and necessary to Arthur's prestige. The doubts of jurists, of course, have little hold on the popular mind, which thrills to a tale of conquest so long as the 'right' side wins. The conqueror himself may use law and theology for *post hoc* justification, but is far less likely to be deterred by them beforehand.

The earliest text to mention Arthurian conquest, *Culhwch*, avoids controversy in the simplest possible way, by putting all the conquests in the past so that any suffering is comfortably forgotten. The places conquered are so fantastical that nobody's sensibilities can be injured, and Arthur gains his conqueror's glory without cost to anyone. But such conquests cannot establish a hold such as Arthur has on the high medieval imagination. To become an international hero, he must conquer real places: otherwise he will remain a purely local hero, as Finn does. But if he conquers real places, he will become controversial, and, with some, unpopular. A pre-Christian hero, such as Alexander, may partially escape controversy by remoteness and the removal of the religious dimension. Alexander is at worst a pagan conquering pagans, at best an agent of God. Criticism of his conquests – which bulks small in the sum of medieval criticism of Alexander[49] – concentrates on the deterioration of the conqueror's character, and on the ultimate vanity of his successes. But Arthur, as a Christian and British figure, who at Geoffrey's behest takes Europe as his field of conquest, cannot escape calumny.

The message of HRB is that the British race in its prime was destined, by its very nature, to conquest. Moral doubts are practically crushed by this natural impulse. Such moral discussion as occurs is based – though not always overtly – on national prejudice.[50] Nevertheless, Geoffrey attaches considerable importance to such discussion, particularly in the Arthurian section. Its main argument is precedent: an act which is repeated often enough becomes rightful. Arthur claims no lands not hitherto conquered by his ancestors. Later medieval lawyers and historians imitated the argument when they based territorial claims on Arthur's HRB conquests.[51] Medieval monks forging land-grants used the same principle; it governs large areas of law-making to this day. But, of course, Geoffrey's arguments will satisfy only the pre-converted!

Later authors' reactions are mixed, and largely personal. French prose authors tend not to insist on Arthur's conquests, and the Scots play them down for political reasons. Chroniclers such as William of Newburgh do the same, but for different reasons, rooted in disbelief, not in nationalism. In Boece the two motives are combined.[52] All such authors consider the conquests creditable, and none suppresses them in order to clear Arthur of blame.

The French verse romances exemplify this admiration. They steer a middle course between *Culhwch*'s fantasy and HRB's brutal realism. For them, Arthur is 'cil qui les terres conqueroit':[53] real countries, but conquered in a comfortably far-off and unreal past. Present-day aggression is always levelled at imaginary countries, often vaguely thought of as being within Britain, and therefore does not arouse violent political feeling. There is some theoretical discussion, however. *Hunbaut* directs a mild irony at the Arthur who, like Charlemagne and Alexander in other mildly ironic French works,[54] constantly seeks new worlds to conquer:

> Est-il donc nus n'a val ne mont
> qui ne tienge de moi sa terre?   (ll. 92-3)

The irony passes swiftly, being only a means to launch the story. Vaunting ambition appears again in *Rigomer*:

> ne perderai plain pie de terre,
> ains vaudrai sor autrui conquerre.   (16205-6)

Here the tone is admiring of the warrior-king's 'primitive' thirst for personal victory and glory. Criticism becomes slightly more insistent in *Durmart*, in which the hope of territorial gain induces Arthur to intervene in a war without first determining its justice — and to join the 'wrong' side. The point is not laboured, and Arthur eventually rallies to the just cause; nevertheless the condemnation of wrongful conquest is adumbrated. Harsher still is *Yder*, in which Arthur's aggression is wrong both in conception and execution. Here, the point is laboured — but in general, not exclusively Arthurian, terms. Alexander would have served his purpose just as well.

These doubts are countered by a blast of enthusiasm from the First Continuation:

> ou fust par force ou par amour,
> tuit li font lijance le jor   (TVD 2043-44)[55]

Conquest is in no way intrinsically wrongful: 'force' is as valid a reason for proffering homage as 'amor'. The text goes on to describe Arthur's struggle against the single recalcitrant. The issue is potentially a lively one, as *Golagros*' development of it shows;[56] but the Continuation author acknowledges no moral dimension. Arthur's resolve to conquer is as laudable as Brun's to resist. War is a game: it is pleasant to win, but not very terrible to lose. All the verse-romances partake more or less of this light-heartedness, showing little consciousness of suffering and pain,[57] and because of the romance equilibrium, no person of importance is ever killed — certainly not on Arthur's side, a fact which obviates any need for Arthur to show vengeful cruelty to his enemies. The worst which can befall a defeated opponent is to gain the honour of a seat at the Table. Being fundamentally a good man — and he is so even in *Yder* — Arthur makes a good conqueror. Only in the Short Version of the First Continuation is there a harsher note of realism, where Arthur's enemies are said to resent his domination (ASP 3407-8). Certainly this criticism was not intended by the original author. On the whole, the verse romancers approve of Arthur the conqueror, any criticism being abstract and unimpassioned.

If not all French writers disapprove of Arthur the conqueror, it is equally true that not all English ones approve of him. Many of them are moralisers to whom Arthur is *exemplum malum*, a point which has been amply demonstrated by previous critics.[58] We must notice, however, that Arthur is never dismissed as wicked beyond redemption. Even the alliterative *Morte*, the *Auntyrs*[59] and *Golagros*, which are most overt in their criticism, acknowledge both Arthur's good qualities and his success. *Golagros* persists in doing so despite its role as a piece of Scots propaganda.[60] The arrogant self-reliance of its Arthur would be anathema to Boece or Stewart. Moreover, this Arthur is not only a successful conqueror, but capable of enough self-restraint actually to curb his conquering ambition: 'I mak releasing of thin allegiance . . . fre as I the first fand' (1356, 1361). This renouncing of victory and homage is unique in Arthurian literature, and it pays Arthur the conqueror a compliment which only Malory, in his 'Tale of Arthur and Lucius' (II. 246), ever equals.

Most English criticism of the 'conqueror kene' (a favourite English title for Arthur) is, as in the French, theoretical, making Arthur the text for reflections on the favourite late medieval theme of Mutability. Condemnation is not absolute, and the final English verdict on Arthur would probably echo LP's on Galehaut: 'nuls homs qui tant ait conquis comme vos avés no porroit estre sans trop grant charge de pechiés'.[61]

We should expect the Welsh to welcome Arthur the conqueror even more enthusiastically than the English. And indeed, although the Welsh contributed little to the elevation of 'their' hero to European status, they adored him in that guise, as the number of 'Brut' translations shows.[62] Ironically enough, Welsh literature also contains perhaps the strongest condemnation of Arthur as conqueror. This is in the pre-HRB Welsh-Latin *Vita Gildae*, where Arthur's attack on Huail is reproved by the full majesty of the Church and with full awareness of the human suffering involved.[63] The attack, however, remains isolated. The Huail story long remained popular in Wales, but on the level of anecdote rather than saga.[64] For unexplained reasons it never took root on the Continent, and so a *locus classicus* of condemnation remains entombed in the narrow grave of a Celtic saint's life. Arthur's disinterment of Bran's head in an early triad hints at conqueror's hubris, but this too is an isolated instance. Post-HRB Welsh continues its hymns of praise to all-conquering Arthur long after the end of the Middle Ages. Indeed, no nationalistic resentment, nor moral or metaphysical doubts, no awareness of Arthur's tragic destiny, can crush this popular conception. Arthur dominates medieval story by right of conquest.

(v) The Roman War

In our first chapter, we recalled how the 'new' nations of medieval Europe delighted to discover for themselves a common origin with Rome.[65] However, ex-barbarian nations who liked to feel a link with the old Empire might well feel differently about submitting themselves to the authority of a present-day emperor − or pope. We have no time to survey the complex progress of theory and practice which led eventually to the emergence of sovereign states owing no allegiance outside their borders.[66] Suffice it to say that the issue was a live one throughout the high Middle Ages — that is, throughout the period of vigorous Arthurian development. Therefore, to involve Arthur with Rome, in peace or war, was to give a boost to his literary success rivalling that given by his mysterious end, or his surrounding by paladins. The latter two contributions pre-date HRB: it could therefore be argued that the Roman war is Geoffrey's principal contribution to Arthur's success. Of course, he did not create it unaided. Gildas and Nennius had described the Romano-British interaction, but Geoffrey was the first to link it with Arthur, and so assure him European notoriety.

So complex are the treatments of the Roman theme in Geoffrey and his successors that it is possible here only to analyse briefly the most important elements and lines of development. I shall focus on three vital components: the context for the war, its morality, and its outcome — as they relate to Arthur's story. Let us first survey Geoffrey's handling of them.

For Geoffrey, Arthur's Roman war is the culmination of a Romano-British rivalry which stems from the nations' common origin in Troy. Simultaneously, it is the clash of Arthur's virile 'new' nation with Rome's outworn monarchy:[67] a theme of contemporary interest for Geoffrey's readers, though it also has a literary source in the Alexander/Darius clash.[68]

Geoffrey himself favours neither side in the complex moral contest which precedes the physical one: rather does he allow both rulers to express their own, obviously twisted and biased, attempt to settle on the other the stigma of aggresssion. This examination of war-mongering sophistry is of perennial relevance. However, the force of prophecy which backs Arthur, together with the slight 'crusading' dimension given by Lucius' unexpected summoning of oriental forces, does something to tip the moral balance in Arthur's favour — even if Arthur himself, in council and at Siesia, cynically extols and exercises brute force. All in all, Geoffrey presents the war as a problem for moral discussion, proposing some lines of argument, but offering no solution. Is there a moral judgement in his halting of Arthur on the brink of conquest? Certainly one is entitled to believe so; but historical verisimilitude may (for once) determine Geoffrey's decision, as may his overall *sen*, which is hastening towards the inexorable collapse of Britain. Note Geoffrey's distinction between Lucius, the consul/general, and Leo, the shadowy emperor. The former may perish to Arthur's glory, but the latter preserves Eternal Rome. Failure to grasp this distinction causes confusion in many later accounts.

Geoffrey's Roman war episode is so tightly constructed that it is impossible to make even minor modifications without introducing new *sen* — as we can see, for instance, even in Henry of Huntingdon's so-called 'excerpt' in the *Letter to Warinus*,[69] or in William of Rennes' epically sonorous re-telling. But many authors dare to make a far bolder re-use of the morality theme. The author of the alliterative *Morte*, for example, gives it an entirely new *sen* by an almost brutal re-shaping of the HRB antecedents which produces the impression that Arthur's ancestors have been in almost continuous possession of Rome. Thus it is Arthur, rather than the emperor, who desires to castigate a rebellious subject; the emperor's demand for tribute becomes a mere piece of insolence.

Thus the alliterative author, cutting through Geoffrey's web of moral complexities, disposes his audience to approve Arthur's claim not only on the evidence presented in the romance itself, but also because it panders to their own nationalistic prejudices.

While the alliterative *Morte* re-uses Geoffrey's arguments, the Didot *Perceval* goes further, combining those arguments with new motifs so as to introduce a technique which is to become the hallmark of the great prose cycles: multiple causation.[70] In this early work, the multiplicity is not well handled. Arthur's HRB appeals to history, and Geoffrey's evocation of prophecy, become inextricably entangled, with Didot's own notions of the fatal cessation of the 'enchantments' and of the sacred destiny of the Three Tables. The ultimate confusion occurs when it is categorically stated that God wishes Arthur to become emperor; yet – as the source demands – in the outcome he never does. What then is God's real opinion of, and purpose for, Arthur? Certainly Arthur himself is not in control of his own destiny: in Didot he is manipulated by God, by circumstance, and by his own underlings, and so loses the imperial impressiveness which he had in HRB – which in turn diminishes the power of the war episode. We must judge the Didot account to ba a valiant, but unsuccessful attempt to make a new 'conjointure'.

The great French prose cycles tend to diminish the importance of the Roman war very radically, perhaps because it tends to elevate Arthur to a status very near that of the French Charlemagne. LP certainly shows knowledge of the HRB material, both in Part I and in the Claudas war, which draws heavily on HRB. But the Romans themselves remain largely in the background, and there is no suggestion that Arthur could ever conquer the Eternal City. In view of this attitude in LP, it is rather surprising that the Vulgate *Mort* should trouble with the Roman war at all, especially as Arthur's tragedy can be satisfactorily encompassed by developing the Lancelot theme to its logical outcome. A lingering respect for historical 'truth' here leads the *Mort* author into a lapse from his usual narrative excellence.

Despite this cursoriness in the *Lancelot-Graal*, the HRB war does find its way into the complete Vulgate cycle, in VM. The VM account is certainly an interpolation,[71] ill-suited to its context in both style and content – for VM proper assumes a continental situation extrapolated from LP, just as we should expect. Whatever its contradictions and absurdities, however, the interpolation makes, by its very positioning, an interesting adaptation of *sen*: the expedition becomes an expression of Arthur's youthful fougue instead of the culmination of his career. This idea appealed to Malory, as we shall see.

The post-Vulgate cycle, though it leaves Geoffrey almost out of sight, does momentarily yield to the fascination of the Roman war. Lucius' challenge is presented, in an oddly isolated episode, and is so handled as to become an expression of the contemporary *rex est imperator* doctrine – a doctrine which would appeal particularly strongly to Capetian France.[72] This is the theme's last coherent appearance in the Arthurian romance. It is never altogether lost, and it can still be forced to accept new *sen*; but Geoffrey's structure was never improved upon. It bears a sort of internal copyright, and is the hardest to use of all Geoffrey's bequests. However, later authors continue to be fascinated by its bearing on Arthur and his story, and it is as a part of that story — rather than as an illustration of any abstract theories of warfare — that it usually survives.

Hitherto we have examined the use made by Geoffrey's followers of the context and background of the war. Let us now look at their notions of its outcome — for on this the whole *sen* of their treatment of Arthur may depend. Geoffrey's own story bears an inherent tension. The *sen* demands failure to take Rome; yet there is also a strong feeling — induced, for instance, by the Sibylline prophecies — that Arthur ought to become emperor. Both ideas are stimulating to new interpretation. By far the profoundest moral examination of Geoffrey's conclusion is that of the alliterative *Morte* (which has already received ample critical attention).[73] But Didot, too, gives an interesting new slant. By emphasising Lucius' pagan connections, it makes Rome into a sort of equivalent Jerusalem, centre of Christianity but occupied by its enemies.

The alliterative *Morte* and Didot give the best tragic analysis of Arthur's failure to conquer Rome (in the former, Arthur is offered the crown, but never assumes it). By contrast, the patriotic chronicler, Hardyng,[74] explores the equally tragic implications of temporary success. It might seem absurd to have Arthur crowned emperor, only to fall immediately. Hardyng, however, exploits this absurdity to make Arthur exemplify not Nemesis, but the blind cruelty of Fate. The increased measure of his triumph raises to a pinnacle the glory of the blameless English worthy; but it also gives him further to fall, and his fall provokes the reader to cry out against the perennial injustice of life.

It is Malory who finally makes Arthur the emperor. Malory adapts from VM the positioning of the Roman war early in Arthur's career, and from Hardyng (perhaps)[75] his elevation to the imperial throne. Of course, the question then arises of what Arthur is to do with Rome for the rest of his long reign. Malory answers it by having him administer it as a province, thus implying a *translatio imperii* from Rome to Britain; and in his later books he is careful to include no Vulgate material which would contradict this notion. In Malory, for the first time, the pseudo-historical Roman war is satisfactorily fitted into a 'romance' biography of Arthur, and so attains a new artistic truth which is evidence for that late-medieval literary phenomenon, the separation of history from romance.

The Roman war, then, can exhibit Arthur as a moral, political and national exemplum, and can be used to determine the nature of his tragedy. Just as important, however, is his personal status through the war. As far as the military virtues are concerned, this is invariably high: Geoffrey creates a paragon warrior-king who never loses his appeal. His is leader, supreme commander, strategist and tactician. In pitched battles he over-matches any knight, but holds himself in reserve until the battle has taken shape, and does not risk himself uselessly.[76] In between battles he will not adventure, but remains as directing intelligence and rallying point. He is generous to his subjects, implacable to his foes, honourable to all. No author accuses him of cowardice or inefficiency. He dominates the war, despite the attention paid to individual exploits; and his participation in the fighting, in which all authors and readers delight, raises him to a lofty pedestal in every mind. Geoffrey, in his care for military verisimilitude, does not allow him to kill Lucius in single combat as he had killed Frollo, and most certainly does not allow him to kill the Roman emperor. Other authors, however, in their enthusiasm for Arthur — and their ignorance of the difference between Lucius and Leo — do allow Arthur this ultimate military triumph. Among them, surprisingly, is Didot, whose Arthur is markedly less strong-minded than HRB's; but Didot interestingly turns the combat into a sort of judicial duel, in which Arthur as the challenged party is legally compelled to respond. Another approach to the combat is exhibited in the Vulgate *Mort*, in which the aged Arthur's victory over the knightly young emperor is seen as a tragedy rather than a triumph: a defiance of the natural order which accords well with the *sen* of the whole work. The most emphatically favourable view of the combat is given by Malory, for whom it makes Arthur 'emperor himself thorow dygnité of his hondys'. Malory's version is the final working out of Geoffrey's suggested clash between imperial opposites, but Malory's *sen* is opposite to that of HRB. The evolution of the Roman war takes Arthur through nemesis and denigration to glory.

For indeed, despite all the moral complexities which authors introduce, the Roman war must always show Arthur as an almost titanically impressive figure. He compels admiration for his vigorous espousal of this supreme challenge. Overproud or greedy for land he may seem, but he must be the very antithesis of the *roi fainéant*. Above all, the Roman war is a tale of action: all ideological and theoretical discussion must yield to the overmastering excitement. It is one of the principal arteries of the living legend of Arthur.

69

V

PEACETIME

Despite the importance of war in the Arthurian universe, romance works (unlike chronicles) require periods of peace in which individual knights may depart on adventure. In such periods attention is, inevitably, less often focussed on King Arthur. But Arthur himself began as an adventurer in the early Welsh sources; and later authors show considerable interest in the question of how active and adventurous the peacetime Arthur can be.

Throughout the material, Arthur's peacetime activities may be broadly divided into four categories: hunting, giant-killing, adventuring, and the maintaining of justice. This may seem a strange classification, but it is dictated by the development of the medieval conception of Arthur. Hunting expresses his 'primeval' role as active defender of the land from destructive forces. Understandably, it features at the very beginning of the development; but it never loses its importance. Giant-killing stands for Arthur's status as an individual hero, characterised – like many popular heroes – by a particular kind of exploit. Adventuring introduces the 'romance' Arthur, who participates fully in the knight-errant world of which, at the height of the Arthurian development, he is the symbol and the head. Finally, justice evokes the 'realistic' consideration of Arthur's fulfilment of his kingly duties. It may be well to state that the persistence of these four themes does not at all derive from the persistence of 'Celtic' beliefs about Arthur. Arthur in the early Welsh is a hunter and adventurer; but these activities have a universal and timeless appeal, being proper to the 'Hero with a Thousand Faces'.[1] They may have a Celtic flavour in the Welsh, but no more. Later continental authors draw on basically the same stock of universal themes as the Welsh do, with the same purpose of keeping the current hero alive and interesting. Sometimes, on the continent as in Wales, these themes are used to degrade and mock Arthur instead of glorifying him. The urge to mock what is normally revered is deep-rooted in the human mind. Such degradation is part of the hero's role as intermediary between mankind and the supernatural: the latter is brought under closer control if the hero is proved to be of common stuff after all.

(i) Hunting

The mythological and social importance of hunting in 'primitive' societies is, of course, colossal. The hero's hunting expresses victory over the forces of darkness, chaos and evil. Deeper significances apart, hunting was, to the medieval mind, the sport of kings *par excellence*. It was the peacetime channel for warlike energies, and, like war, demanded of the king both individual prowess and the ability to organise the efforts of subordinates. It united him with his nobles in a common passion. Arthur is never expected to hold aloof from hunts as he may from tourneys and adventures. This acceptance of hunting as a proper activity has an important corollary. Hunting takes one into the unknown, the forest which, to medieval Europeans, represented both imagined and very real dangers. The hunt is one of the ways to Adventure. In contrast to the custom of not eating until an adventure materialises, which seeks to entice Adventure to court, hunting challenges Adventure on its own ground. Hunting is the best way to isolate Arthur in the face of the unknown. This can happen to any character, of course; but with Arthur it is more important, since it is ordinarily so difficult to isolate a king. Thus Arthur's hunting may acquire an importance which transcends that of chase and quarry in themselves.

There is, however, one universal hunting theme in which the quarry is supremely important: that of the pursuit of one exceptional beast by a particular man or men.[2] The beast may possess exceptional size or cunning, or be under enchantment, or totemic, or symbolic, or altogether unique and bizarre. Arthur's quarries variously possess all those qualities. Kings and heroes are often called in by lesser men to deal with a particularly destructive animal, even if they are not 'professional' hunters. Hercules, Perseus, St George and often Arthur himself are examples of all-round heroes who turn their hands to monster-killing. Sometimes heroes band together in such an enterprise, an attitude which also features in Arthur's legend.

Arthur as a hunter of exceptional beasts need not, then, be an exclusively Celtic figure. But these is one Arthurian hunt which certainly begins in early Welsh and persists, albeit obscurely, through centuries of Arthurian development: that for Cath Palug.[3] Cats are significant in many mythologies, but not usually as hunting quarries: this applies as much to Celtic mythology as to the rest.[4] The cat's importance to Arthur was never codified. Only in VM, where it counter-balances Arthur's giant-fight, does it have a definable narrative role. Here, the cat-fight approximates to the familiar international theme of the itinerant hero who delivers the locals from a destructive monster. This common theme is used to give *sen* to an obscure and exceptional story. Elsewhere, this Celtic survival has little meaning, and does little to shape either Arthur's biography or the concept of him as a hunter. It probably survives through the attraction of its bizarreness, which can outweigh the impossibility of integrating it into Arthur's mainstream biography.

The cat apart, the hunting theme never coalesces round particular hunts — as the war-theme tends to coalesce, thanks to Geoffrey, round the Saxon and Roman conflicts. The Twrch Trwyth hunt may have had some persistent currency in Welsh legend, but it does not survive on to the continent — or at least, if the name travels it travels without the story,[5] while the theme (unlike that of Huail, for example) falls from use even in Wales. But there is one unifying element which connects all the stories of destructive beasts. This is the notion that the beast is demonic, an enemy of God. Now Christianisation of pagan monster-legends is common enough: a famous example is Grendel. But it is particularly interesting in relation to Arthur because it approximates his hunting activities to his Christian wars. Indeed, Twrch Trwyth and the Boar of Inglewood,[6] with their malign intelligence, are little more monstrous than many of Arthur's 'human' enemies, and Arthur's expeditions against the two dragons and Twrch Trwyth are very like wars. Here, from another direction, we again approach the idea that hunting is the peacetime equivalent of battle. The Christianisation is not necessary to maintain interest, as in the case of the Saxon wars, but legitimises responses in the audience which really spring from universal, primordial feelings. Arthur was probably not originally a mythological hunter, but his hunting can express a Christian myth of the saving of souls from the Evil One. As intermediary between Christ and the people, the king-hero prevents the two being separated by eliminating evil threats, protecting his subjects' souls as well as their bodies. The people need not necessarily be Arthur's subjects, for there is nothing political about this myth. He need not even be a king. Hence the variation in characterisation of Arthur in the various stories, from the rather reluctant hero of the early Welsh *Life of Carannog*[7] to the piously resolute champion of the *Avowyng*, does not affect the fundamental myth. It allows a favourable presentation of Arthur which no local, national or temporal evolution can invalidate.

Not all exceptional quarries are destructive. Ysgithrwyn in *Culhwch* and the White Stag of *Erec* are prime examples of non-destructive quarries. The hunt of Ysgithrwyn is not a mere couplet of that of Twrch Trwyth, but different in kind. Ysgithrwyn is important not for himself, but for what he can provide; the hunt for him does not resemble a war, but rather a quest for one specific object. It is not Arthur's individual quest, and he is compelled to participate by the *geis* which Culhwch has laid on him, even at the expense of contradicting earlier data. The prowess and enthusiasm which Arthur demonstrates here exemplify his role as mainspring of the action. Throughout the tale, he initiates the quests. Infinitely energetic and versatile, he is a hunter not by nature, but when, and because, the occasion demands it. Here, in fact, his hunting has a fresh, lighter, more personal meaning.

The first Arthurian adventure ever recounted by Chrétien is, most interestingly, a hunting exploit of Arthur's: the chase of the White Stag in *Erec*. Thus we have a link, in theme if not in actual imitation,[8] between the Celtic Arthur and the new, French one. We also notice that, while *Erec* (sometimes described as 'the first Arthurian romance')[9] already has a totally sophisticated courtly background for the 'still-centre' Arthur, it also introduces him as a vigorous, impulsive, adventure-minded prince in whom glorious majesty co-exists with an almost boyish exuberance. Chrétien is to modify this picture in his later works, in which he becomes progressively more critical of Arthur and the Arthurian ideal; but in *Erec* adventure is certainly a part of Arthur's kingly make-up. It is true that the tale of the stag itself presents many contradictions and ironies; Chrétien may have misunderstood an originally coherent source-story. But he was equally certainly aware of the inherent absurdity of the whole 'fier baiser' episode — which is scarcely modified by its ingenious resolution via the Erec-Enide story. It seems that, even here at the beginning of his Arthurian career, Chrétien is inclined to satirise the notion of Arthur as maintainer of 'custom', anticipating by a hundred years the sarcasms of Dinadan.[10] It can truly be said that Chrétien, the very formulator of the high medieval Arthurian world, also furnishes the means of its destruction.

The verse writers are quick to follow Chrétien. *Fergus*, indeed, borrows the White Stag episode, but purges it of its ironic and disconcerting elements — as does the Welsh *Geraint* (col. 194) — and makes it into an orthodox and exciting chase (*Fergus* ll.50ff). In *Fergus* and *Geraint*, Arthur is restored as a lover of hunting for its own sake, keen and courageous, respecting his noble quarry as an enemy worthy of his steel. This is, indeed, the trend of Arthur's hunting in continental literature generally. His quarries do not tend to be magical, though they may be monstrous or demonic. This does not reflect a paucity of magical beasts in European or even Arthurian tradition. But it is not Arthur's part to hunt such beasts, though he may be afforded brief glimpses of them and their meaning.[11] This is because such hunts tend either to be long-drawn-out, or to work a profound transformation in the hunter who discovers their true meaning, and are thus generally alien to king Arthur, who cannot be wholly severed from his kingship or from his own fundamentally secular nature. Arthur's hunts are generally more realistic, part of the evocation of his day-to-day life and personality. They are not realistic in the sense that they involve exposure of the techniques of venery — though in late Middle English Arthur does demonstrate his competence in this, as in most other kingly crafts.[12] Nor are they executed because the court needs meat: Arthur's court always has a romantically unexplained superabundance of provision. They are simply a pleasure, an enrichment of life.

There is never a hint that Arthur's passion for hunting is frivolous or excessive, save in a post-medieval French folkloric explanation of his ghostly leadership of the Wild Hunt.[13] Contemporary laments over the destruction caused by the King's hunting, or the cruelty of the forest laws, do not percolate into the aristocratic and autonomous Arthurian universe. But Arthur's hunting *is* taken seriously. He ennobles the sport by his devotion to it, and *vice versa*; and readers who share his enthusiasm feel themselves linked to him in an exalted fraternity. It is somewhat curious that he was never credited with the invention of hunting techniques — as he was with that of tourneying, mourning in black, giving the accolade and so on.[14] It is Tristan who receives that distinction, not because he was originally a Celtic hunting god (there is no evidence for such a supposition),[15] but because the continental versions of his legend pay much attention to his youthful hunting accomplishments and his self-sufficient sojourn in the forest. He is the master of a highly civilised art. It is doubtless because his story was first codified in romance form, rather than in chronicle like Arthur's, that he snatched from Arthur the palm of hunting innovator. This, we must note, shows that, while chronicle and romance often share the same material, the overall concept of a character may be greatly influenced by the medium in which he first, or most commonly, appears. Arthur is unique in this legend in his domination of both genres, and this must be one of the keys to his success. Even in the present case, Arthur does not entirely lose out to Tristan, because if Tristan belongs to the Arthurian period, his credit will reflect on the king who presides over the flowering of all the noblest pleasures.

Enthusiast as Arthur is, his hunting is not always an end in itself. The notion of hunting as a way to adventure appears, fully developed, in *Pwyll*,[16] but it is needless to suggest that continental authors drew on that or any other Celtic source. It was doubtless always easy for a hunter to lose his way, even in a carefully maintained game-forest.[17] The king would naturally be better mounted than most, and it would be easy for a particularly keen huntsman, such as Arthur, to become separated from his companions.

The 'adventures' which Arthur encounters in his 'hunting isolation' are not normally of an orthodox knightly type. Rather is he brought sharply up against the fact of his kingship and its relation to his private persona. The ordinary knight courts isolation because, by the inner law of the Arthurian universe, isolation is a catalyst for adventure. Arthur cannot do so because he is not, like the knight-errant, a unit entire of itself. If he is lost, universal chaos will ensue. This viewpoint is strongly put three times in the prose cycles. In two instances, Arthur's isolation, and the ensuing adventure, are contrived by an enemy. In the False Guinevere episode of LP, Bertholai plays on Arthur's hunting enthusiasm and his duty of protection to isolate and ambush him, with the precise intention of causing chaos in the realm. The adventure, which normally happens 'naturally', is here realistically motivated and contrived. Therefore, the 'natural' romance law, which normally safeguards the knight throughout his adventures, does not operate for Arthur, and he is overwhelmed.

The second example of contrived danger is less realistic. In the Accolon adventure of the *Suite* (II. 174-7), the hunt, the isolation and the magic ship appear 'natural' at first, and only gradually do we realise that Morgain is solely responsible. Now, 'adventures' designed by enemies to entrap Arthur and/or his knights are fairly common in the French,[18] but are normally precisely located, waiting for the victim instead of engulfing him. Morgain's contrivance here is more alarming because it indicates that she can govern a complex concatenation of circumstances, including the falling of night. The author may not fully have realised the complications of his invention. Be that as it may, the end result is once again to cause chaos by the removal of the king. As in LP, Arthur is unable to escape solely by his own efforts, as an ordinary knight can, because the 'rules' work differently for him.

Our third example is Samaliel's planned vengeance in the post-Vulgate. As in the case of Morgain, the danger is from a personal enemy of Arthur; but the whole realm, and also the international institution of knighthood, are explicitly threatened. The isolation is not, this time, contrived by the enemy: the author uses the 'natural' motif, somewhat clumsily, to make Arthur helpless. Ironically, it is his helplessness which saves him, by giving Samaliel time to reason himself out of his vengeance. His kingship is also instrumental: it is this, not Arthur's person, which the politically dutiful Samaliel resolves to spare. Knightly prowess has nothing to do with Arthur's survival.

In these examples, Arthur's isolation emphasises the importance of his kingship, but this is brought home to the reader more than to Arthur himself. In other occurrences of hunting isolation, Arthur – this time like many an adventuring knight – has the opportunity to learn the truth about himself. One possible example occurs in early Welsh. The Peniarth 96 version of *Englynion Arthur a'r Eryr*[19] is prefaced: 'Yr englynion a fu rhwng Arthur a Liwlod i nai . . . pan oedd Arthur yn i fforest gwedi colli helynt.'[20] This title may be little earlier than the fifteenth-century MS; the poem itself does not tell how Arthur met the eagle. But the examples of Pwyll, and of Math, who follows an animal in order to meet the eagle Lleu even if he does not actually hunt it,[21] shows that the hunting-isolation motif was known in early Welsh, and certainly the Eliwlod poem looks like a classic case of it. In it, the Eagle forces Arthur to acknowledge the inadequacy of his *Weltanschauung*, and to accept a new one based on better understanding of Christianity. The Eagle is neither symbolic nor angelic, but, being an avatar of a dead man, it evidently has access to certainties beyond the reach of ordinary humanity. Arthur, isolated from society with its flatteries and opportunities for self-deception, is compelled to accept those certainties. Isolation in the wilderness can bring temptation, but also purges and strengthens the soul. Christ, Buddha, Mohammed and countless other great teachers sought enlightenment in the wilderness. On a correspondingly lesser scale, Arthur here participates in the universal motif.

In the long and β versions of LP[22] (Micha I. 157-9; II. 95-9) a similar hunting 'isolation', followed by a spiritual flaying, is used to mark the end of Arthur's enslavement to the False Guinevere. Amustans, like the Eagle, is an informed messenger of God who ameliorates Arthur's Christian understanding. Arthur's sojourn with him cures both his soul and society itself. In these LP versions, the False Guinevere episode thus begins and ends with a hunting isolation: the first endangers Arthur and the realm, the second liberates them. Whatever we think of the relative merits of the three versions of this tale, it is undeniable that the repetition of the motif in the Long and β versions makes a more satisfactory pattern than the abrupt ending of a.

Even more important to Arthur, and to a whole narrative, is Arthur's isolation in the *Suite* which leads to the seminally significant conversation with Merlin. Here Arthur learns the most basic truths about himself, his identity, his present spiritual state and his ultimate destiny. Again he learns from a heavenly messenger, for this is Merlin's role here. Again Arthur is measured against Christian standards, and forced to recognise the real nature of his actions, his responsibility for them, and the inevitable outcome. Nor is it forgotten that the fate of Arthur the man is inseparable from that of king and kingdom. The *sen* concerns the universal human condition, but it is also political. On several levels it expresses the truth that no man is an island. Arthur in the wilderness may reach an understanding of his fate, but in this case understanding will not help him escape the consequences of his actions. He must return to society and play out his part there. Clairvoyance is no protection against inexorable fate.

These are the most sophisticated uses of the isolation motif. They introduce a pure discovery of truth, with only the thinnest covering of adventurous action. From an end in itself the hunt has become the means to an end, and so has the adventure which the hunt introduces. We see how the theme of hunting, like others we have considered, can work on many levels, from pure enjoyment of the chase to mythological expression to vehicle for philosophy. Like the war theme, it induces on the whole a favourable attitude towards Arthur. It demonstrates his prowess, reveals new layers of interest in his character, and prevents his peacetime persona from atrophying.

(ii) Giant-Fights

We have indicated that the only thing which Arthur the hunter lacks is a particular beast, like Palomides', Theseus' or Captain Ahab's. The multiple demands of his career forbid the development of such an obsession: he is no King Pellinor, lightly abandoning his realm to pursue the Questing Beast.[23] But there is another monster, no animal but hardly a man, whose destruction is pronounced on HRB authority to be Arthur's special province. This is the Giant of St Michael's Mount.

Why should Arthur's particular monster be a giant? The Mount giant himself is probably a local legend which Geoffrey adopted for his hero's glorification. Giants are universally popular in folklore, being more truly 'international' than most motifs,[24] so Geoffrey could be confident that a giant-story would appeal, even outside its own area. The biblical David — whom Geoffrey probably had in mind at least when beginning his account of Arthur[25] — was famed as a giant-killer. We know that Arthur's exploit reminded at least one alert reader (William of Newburgh) of David's.[26] Arthur and David are both saviours of their people by virtue of this supreme exploit. But what is puzzling is that HRB suggests that Arthur was an habitual giant-killer. Now, all the British giants were exterminated by Corineus, and although Arthur's twelve-year peace might furnish an opportunity to go giant-killing abroad, this is hardly consonant with his overall presentation in HRB. It is often suggested that Geoffrey is here drawing on traditional Welsh material. The mere fact that Arthur, in pretendedly sober chronicle, kills a giant need not argue such borrowing. We must look for evidence of giant-killing propensities in early Welsh Arthuriana. The Welsh Bruts add nothing to Geoffrey's account of the Mount giant or of Ritho; and there are no giants in the Arthurian saints' lives or triads. Involvement of Arthur with giants in recent folklore is certainly inspired by the HRB tradition, by a familiar process of popular borrowing from a literary text.[27] (Indeed, Sion Rhys' seventeenth-century collection of giant-stories uses the very words of Ritho's challenge in HRB.[28] The only notable evidence of a Welsh connection is in certain resemblances between the killing of the two HRB giants and the killing of Dillus in Culhwch. It has been sweepingly claimed that the HRB Ritho tale is 'based' on that of Dillus.[29] Actually, the only common point is the importance of the beard, and the reasons for this are utterly different in the two stories. Now, the importance of the beard as a symbol of manhood was not confined to Wales; indeed, the medieval Welsh were reportedly *not* bearded.[30] Any medieval European could appreciate the enormity of the insult offered by Ritho in

Geoffrey's story — as its later popularity proves. There may indeed be a folkloric (not necessarily Welsh) source behind it, but there is no reason why Geoffrey should not have invented it. As for the resemblances between the Mount giant's story and that of Dillus, they amount to the eating of pigs' flesh, and the presence of Kay and Beduer. They are noteworthy, but do not constitute positive proof of a connection. It is most unlikely that Geoffrey read *Culhwch* as we know it, whereas it is at least possible that the *Culhwch* episode at some time underwent *Brut* influence.[31] Even if Geoffrey did use something resembling the *Culhwch* story, it would not convince him that Arthur was an habitual giant-killer: he is not even present at the killing of Dillus. Altogether it is highly probable that Arthur's giant-killing reputation stems entirely from HRB. HRB establishes that Arthur fought many giants; that he killed the Mount giant; and that he fought the giant Ritho over a beard-mantle, presumably at a fairly early stage in his career. Let us investigate these notions in later literature.

Geoffrey himself plainly enjoyed Arthur's giant-fight more than any other incident in HRB. He tells it in his most elegant and graphic style, and so loads it with *sen* that it risks distracting attention from the smooth progress of the Roman war. The giant-fight is not, and never later becomes, organically related to the war. HRB deliberately emphasises its separateness by the division of opinion over the significance of Arthur's dream.) It increases Arthur's prestige, of course, as the climax of his career approaches. It recalls the exploits of earlier kings: Corineus, Morpidus and — for sheer intrepid unusualness — Bladud with his attempt to fly. Arthur is linked to his predecessors, but has a greater sum of qualities than any of them.

The varied *sen* of the HRB fight may be summarised as follows. The giant, coming 'ex partibus Hispaniae' is a foreign invader who must be repelled. Spain being a Saracen land, he may be vaguely thought of as a pagan threat. He has animal characteristics; he does not, probably cannot, speak, and thus has less claim to rationality than Twrch Trwyth or any such enchanted animal. Therefore, like Arthur's other monster opponents, he represents a demonic and chaotic threat to civilisation and Christianity. His lust and anthropophagousness excite repulsion, especially as he has approximately human form — as if Man the divine reduced himself to the level of beasts through utter moral and physical degradation. By slaying him Arthur purges the realm of corruption. Arthur is also out for family vengeance, the giant having killed a relation of his: a powerful motive to the medieval mind, and strongly emphasised by Geoffrey.

Despite this abundance of teleological and symbolical overtones, Geoffrey concentrates most on the excitement of the fight. Arthur here does not represent terrified humanity desperately struggling against the forces of evil, but is the superhuman hero, offering his help with arrogant and laughing readiness[32] to lesser mortals, Hercules rather than Beowulf.

Geoffrey's story is a very fine literary accomplishment, and not, like much else in HRB, a mere outline to be filled in by others.[33] Imitators can change it or shift the emphases, but hardly improve on it. Thus Wace emphasises the social consequences of the giant's advent, rather than the savagery and horror of his behaviour. The giant is made less inhuman by the elimination of the cannibalism and the gaining of a name, while Arthur becomes correspondingly less superhuman.[34] The fight even acquires some elements of comedy, and Arthur emerges as a strong and bold, but basically ordinary human being who surmounts terror by courage and common sense. It is as if he awoke the country round about from a nightmare, whereas the Arthur of HRB and, later, of the alliterative *Morte*[35] must become part of the nightmare, destroying its denizen but not cancelling its terror. Wace's Arthur is the other kind of hero, the hero that dwells in Everyman.

The version of William of Rennes is of great interest as representing the reaction of one highly-educated, talented high medieval Latinist to the work of another. It is, indeed, the *literary* quality of this story, in some ways a folktale, which William appreciates. His elegant hexameters seem to be inspired by both the Ovidian and the Virgilian accounts of Polyphemus.[36] Geoffrey himself may, indeed, have drawn on this classical story of an anthropophagous 'monstrum horrendum, informe, ingens' (*Aen*. III. 658), even to the detail of the giant's blinding in the fight. If so, William has recognised and extended the borrowing. William's giant in some ways resembles the medieval wild man of the woods[37] – particularly in the hair which covers him instead of clothes – but he also has the 'barbam concretam sanguine foedo' (1.3656) of Ovid's Polyphemus (*Metamm*. XIV. 201). Like Virgil's Polyphemus, he is horrifying to all human senses and unamenable to speech. Like all the Cyclopes, he is 'terrigena' (ll.3654, 3678, 3681). But if William's style is determined by classical models, the overall *sen* is entirely his own. To him, Arthur and the giant are indubitably established by Arthur's dream as fated opponents. The social implications, even the vendetta, are toned down. Arthur stands as the defender – or avenger – of virginity and purity against hellish lust and evil. Hellish the giant certainly is, with his maw 'Acherontis ad instar' (1.3658). As 'terrigena', he is close to primeval chaos – by both classical and biblical standards.[38] Arthur is Perseus, Ulysses and Hercules in one; he is the rational principle, the original king-hero who represses Chaos – and he is the saviour of souls. Classical and Christian myths combine. To William, this episode is the quintessence of all heroic monster-killings.

Layamon's giant, though quite unconnected with William's, has something of the same significance. Like Grendel[39] he is an evil spirit, the enemy of Christian civilisation. Like Grendel again, but unlike William's giant or Wace's, he is malignly intelligent, a conscious hater of the values defended by the hero. Arthur accords him the respect due to a human foe when he declines to slay him sleeping, and afterwards converses with him. The giant is cunning in his well-planned depredations, cunning again in the fight; but Arthur is more so. This is why the fight is no longer won by brute strength, but through intelligence. The humanisation of the giant makes the episode in Layamon seem much less isolated from surrounding events. Arthur's character and attitude are also the same throughout – fearless, ruthless, clever[40] – and altogether the fight makes a powerful and effective contribution to Layamon's portrayal of Arthur.

These are just three of the variations on Geoffrey's multiple theme. Any number of others are possible, from the complex excellence of the alliterative *Morte* – in which Arthur appears as a new St Michael, vanquishing the demonic monster in the high places — to the pathetic botch in VM, in which Merlin's directing intelligence eliminates all doubt and all excitement from the tale, and the fact that Arthur has already fought many 'giants'[41] removes even the charm of novelty. Not all developments in Arthur's legends are improvements: the VM giant-fight is a forcible reminder of that fact! Even the poorest version, however, cannot entirely kill the appeal of the story. Some writers do resist that appeal: Higden and Boece reject the story, along with the complete Roman war; the Didot *Perceval* rejects it because it is undeniably a distraction to the war narrative. But to the end of our period the story was always widely available. This is important not only because of the opportunities thus supplied for inventive adaptation, but because the story keeps alive the notion of an active, independent, heroic Arthur. It is a standing encouragement to believe that adventurousness is not forbidden to the great king of legend, however socialised or politicised that legend may become.

We must now consider Arthur's more general reputation as a giant-killer. Actually this notion, despite its fostering by HRB, does not gain great currency in either chronicle or romance. Its most positive expression comes in an early and (undeservedly) little-known French adaptation of HRB:

> si fait monstre *solt* il sol agraventer
> e par sa grant vertu abatre e sormonter.[42]

Such a pronouncement, however, needed no encouragement from outside HRB itself. Nor are chroniclers likely to depart from the HRB framework so as to include new giant-stories. It must be in romance, if at all, that such a process occurs. This does not happen in any of the verse romances. Apparently it is too dangerous to bring Arthur, the cohesive centre of rationality, into too close contact with the phantasmagorical ambience in which the average verse-romance giant dwells. The sole exception to the rule is *Yder*, in which Arthur challenges three giants. But Arthur here is no expert giant-killer: he shows cowardly fear of the monsters, and Yder is the real hero of the adventure. The analogue in *De Antiquitate Glastoniensis Ecclesiae*[43] demonstrates that Arthur originally had nothing to do with the episode. *Yder* brings him in only to exemplify the enmity between Arthur and Yder, and the latter's superiority. Far from proving Arthur's giant-killing expertise, *Yder* negates it.

In the prose romances, as in the verse, giants abound; but again Arthur's involvement with them is limited. Moreover, most of them — unlike the Mount giant — are simply large people (we recall that Galehaut himself is a giantess's son), and so an encounter with them has no great mythological overtones. The nearest approach to a true giant-killing Arthur is in the *Livre d'Artus*, where his largest Saxon opponent greatly resembles the giants of folklore, and even the Mount giant. This, however, is an isolated incident, as is the giant-killing reported in *Palamède*. Such incidents creditably maintain Arthur's heroic character, but do not denote a professional giant-killer.

It is in folklore that that notion receives the most credit. Sion Rhys' list fully accepts it, though Arthur here shares his expertise with Gawain and others. Recent Welsh lore proffers three stories of Arthur as giant-killer. Of these, one is onomastic, while others are versions of international tales, 'No-man' and the 'Three Truths'.[44] The idea of attaching them to Arthur was, however, probably suggested by an HRB-derived popular conception of him as giant-killer. This general conception may have been nourished by the belief that Arthur himself was gigantic: an idea which may even, if the Canons of Laon story be admitted as evidence, be pre-Geoffrey.[45] It is applied to many folk-heroes, some (like Francis Drake or Roland) indubitably historical. If Arthur were gigantic there would be nothing surprising in his fighting giants: thus, finally, is fertile ground found for the seed of Geoffrey's suggestion.

Arthur, then, is not generally seen as a full-time giant-killer. But what of Ritho? Actually Ritho enjoys a wider literary success than the Mount giant, but it is at the cost of losing his giant attributes. Many romance giants are, as we have said, simply large people, and HRB's Ritho is one such, having none of the animal characteristics of the Mount giant. As a result, French romance rapidly and easily transforms him into a rival king of Arthur's. The process was doubtless encouraged by a conflation of HRB's Ritho with the ordinary king, Rion des Illes, who fights Arthur in Chrétien's *Perceval*. The result — an ordinary king who collects beards — features in *Deus espees*, the *Suite* and Malory. In VM, Rion is still gigantic, but he approximates to humanity in another way, by turning into a Saxon.[46] There is, however, another obvious way of dealing with Ritho, whose appearance in HRB is so uncomfortably parenthetical. This is to conflate him with the Mount giant. It would be a delicate task, as the natures of the two giants differ, but it would greatly neaten and intensify the story. Only the author of the alliterative *Morte*, however, has the courage to attempt it. Even he does not do a very good job: the 'imperialist monster'[47] consorts ill with the dehumanised cannibal. The uneasiness of the conflation is all the worse because the author retains Arthur's allusion to a previous giant-fight, raising an uneasy ghost of the original Ritho. The conflation is attempted not to turn the episode into a condemnation of imperialism, as Matthews suggests, but to make Arthur's foe as formidable as possible, and to combine maximum interest with the minimum interruption of *ordo naturalis*. It is a laudable attempt which gives Arthur full credit in his supreme and unique giant-killing adventure.

Whether Arthur kills one giant or many, his acceptance of such a task automatically frees him from the rigid confines of kingship. Like hunting, however, Arthur's giant-killing has not quite the nature of pure adventure, and Arthur's kingship is still very much in play. We must now turn our attention to true Adventure.

(iii) Adventure

There is a 'hen wrthryfel'[48] in Arthur which never quite allows him to relinquish adventure even where he is most thoroughly a king. The ill-defined, fantastic world inhabited by the Arthur of early Welsh knows no 'normality', no detailed organisation. In it there is no point in mentioning Arthur *unless* he is adventuring. *Culhwch*'s world is a little more coherent, but comports the child's glorious expectation of exciting things happening at any moment. Arthur's court is not the still centre of this adventurous storm, but part of the storm itself.

The verse romances inherit from Celtic and folkloric models this expectation of adventure. But the more they organise Arthur's kingdom, with an eye to HRB and to contemporary institutions, the less automatic adventure becomes as part of the Arthurian universe. It is considered not so much natural and inevitable, as desirable.[49] The custom of not eating until an adventure appears, which at first is a recognition of the inevitability of adventure and an attempt to regularise its tumultuous spontaneity, is later used as a ritual compelling adventure to appear. Later still it is satirised, the adventure refusing to appear.[50]

The prose romances consider from a different viewpoint this problem of Adventure versus Organisation. From the Didot *Perceval* onwards, adventure is neither part of the natural scheme of things, nor yet a desirable excitement to be sought 'in the bounds of the world and its wilderness'.[51] It is the unique, distinguishing mark of Britain during Arthur's reign. It is at once troublesome and intensely desirable, its final ending a thing to be both desired and feared. Adventure, rather than Arthur's virtue and glory, is the reason why knights flock to his court. This concept, endowed with an ever-diversifying and intensifying *sen*, dominates all the prose cycles.[52]

Whatever the motivating force of Adventure, however, it is always accepted as particularly characteristic of Arthur's ambience. Naturally this suits the knights, to whom inaction is anathema. But a realm teeming with adventure cannot be peaceful and orderly; and peace and order are — in theory at least — the ultimate aim of every king. Therefore Arthur, in fostering adventure, betrays the highest ideals of kingship. Many authors evade this uncomfortable truth by doublethinking, pretending that the knights really disseminate peace and order. Many readers — then as now — have swallowed the deception. Gawain's smug dictum in Chrétien:

> ... bien savoies tu
> qu'en la terre le roi Artu
> sont puceles asseürees   (*Perceval* 7121-3)

sounds magnificent until one remembers that the speaker is a Don Juan from whom no maidenhead is safe. The *Livre d'Artus'* highflown assurance of the common people's love for the knights of the Round Table who rid the realm of evil things is equally impressive until one realises that the aforesaid knights never care twopence for the common people. Even Dinadan, that refreshing mocker, does not stigmatise the essential absurdity of Adventure, but only the absurdities of some of its devotees. It seems that Arthur himself must either accept the same doublethink, or must secretly resent the endless placating of knights to which the laws of the romance universe compel him.[53] Althoughshe is aware of the compulsion, he invariably espouses the former attitude. He himself is unendingly enthusiastic about adventure. This being accepted, it is natural that he should wish to participate. How else can he command the respect of his knights? how else truly appreciate their needs? But we can never forget the need of a king as focal point, sanctioning and rewarding his knights' efforts. Some knights are seldom at court — in LP and TP they even boast of the rarity of their visits[54] — but they still need to orient themselves upon it. Moreover, if Arthur abandons the court, the author must renounce the slightest pretence that he is fulfilling his kingly duties. Clearly there are contradictions here; authors' consideration of them produces some interesting results.

Although the court is normally the point of departure for adventure, some adventures are initiated, and even accomplished, in the court itself. In these Arthur must be involved, if only as an interested spectator. They include some of the most popular recurrent themes: the beheading game, the magic ship, the coming of the Grail, the horn/mantle test, the challenge of the Aged Knight, the Siege Perilous. In them Arthur neither appears idle and indifferent, nor has to abandon his proper place.

These motifs present a variety of adventurous concepts. The Siege Perilous, for example, is one of the chronic, static adventures set up on purpose — by God or Merlin in this case — to test, identify or entrap knights. Arthur is its keeper, and knights come to his court to attempt it, so that the court becomes not the point of departure, but the goal. Under these exceptional circumstances, Arthur is not debarred by his kingship from attempting the adventure; and Hardyng, for one, asserts that he accomplishes it.[55] Normally, however, he desists for a different reason — because he knows that only the Grail knight can succeed — and this abstention applies also to the vast majority of knights, those (Perceval and Galahad apart) who do attempt it being considered fools.[56]

The Siege Perilous is a unique case. Normally, adventures must come in from outside. Many, however, like the Siege, are tests which single out one outstanding individual. Unlike the Siege, most work by simple elimination, the adventure being attempted by all. In most cases, Arthur attempts it with the rest, a significant indication. In the horn/mantle test, the most widespread and possibly the oldest form of the motif,[57] Arthur is morally compelled to participate, for refusal would be more damning than failure. The *sen* of this test is general, satirical, moral and anti-feminist. A peasant would have an equal chance of success if — inconceivably — one should be present. Nevertheless it is important that, in attempting and failing[58] the test, Arthur is equated with the bulk of his knights. In singling out one individual who is not the king, the test temporarily eliminates the distinction between king and knights.

Arthur cannot hold aloof from this test. However, his participation may influence the function of the motif in other stories, for if Arthur takes one test, why should he not take others? Hence in the prose material, Arthur takes tests not from compulsion, but from a conviction of solidarity with his knights: a solidarity which is demonstrated, not created, by the test. The tests may reveal the excellence of the chosen knight, as in Balin's sword or the healing of Urry.[59] Or they may, on the contrary, expose unique criminality, as with Loholt's head in *Perlesvaus*, Lamorat's head — clearly connected with the former[60] — and the bloody sword in the post-Vulgate *Queste*. With one exception, Arthur 'fails' all these tests. His failure is, in every case, reassuring; obviously so in the criminal cases, but so also in the excellence cases because it gives the knights a feeling of basic equality with him. Arthur emerges as *primus inter pares*, which means that he is basically a knight. This idea may, in its turn, extend beyond the court-adventure context and influence a general 'adventurous' view of Arthur.

The exception to the 'failure' rule is Lamorat's head, which represents a different and more subtle use of the motif than most. To begin with, it is twofold, designating both the head's destined avenger and the *lineage* responsible for the murder. Lamorat's death is part of a long and complex vendetta, and the head involves Arthur in it in a complex way. As a member of the guilty *lineage* he is, by tribal law still ideologically operative in the thirteenth century, as guilty of the murder as if he himself had struck the blow.[61] But as king, he is also the destined avenger, who ought to avenge not through vendetta but through due process of law, employed implacably even against his own family. Personal allegiance is opposed to kingship, old laws to new. Hence this use of the motif passes beyond simple notions of solidarity and adventurousness.

There are two further exceptions to the failure rule. The first is the sword in the stone, which makes Arthur king and so *must* set him apart. The second is the floating-sword test of the Vulgate and post-Vulgate *Quests*. Arthur ought, by virtue of his previous success, to be particularly well-qualified for this one, but in fact neither author even allows him to try it, although the post-Vulgate, at least, makes him attempt the bloody-sword test immediately afterwards. The reason is that the Vulgate author does not wish to involve Arthur actively in the Quest. He is essential to the background, his kingdom being simultaneously the home of the Grail and the evil place from which the Grail must depart. Arthur's active participation would distort this *sen*. This is another personal and particular use of the motif.

On the whole, tests within the court assimilate Arthur to his knights. Rather different is the function of another popular motif, the general challenge. This appears at court in the beheading game and the Ancient Knight's visit. There are two versions of the former, in *Carados* and in GGK.[62] Arthur's reaction is radically different in the two versions. In the first, he does not consider himself included in the challenge. He thinks himself different in kind from his knights: if he is shamed, it is through them, not with them. In GGK he does consider himself included, and is therefore one with his knights. His kingship is not forgotten, for it is the chief reason for Gawain's adoption of the challenge. But it is an addition to knighthood, not a thing apart. There are further differences between the two Arthurs. *Carados*' Arthur in this scene is one of the feeblest on record, GGK's one of the strongest-minded and most vigorous.[63] But these differences are largely a matter of literary skill. Arthur can be aloof without feebleness, vigorous without kingliness. What matters is the fundamental contrast of attitudes, which is not easy to explain. Elsewhere in *Carados*, and in the whole First Continuation, Arthur is exceedingly active. His willingness in GGK, and his determent by a subordinate, are paralleled in *Culhwch*, in LP and in *Durmart*. Again we see how wide-ranging is the debate.

The debate continues in the Ancient Knight episode. Invented by Rusticiano, it is popular in French, Spanish and Italian.[64] The contrast of two treatments, in Rusticiano and the Spanish *Tristan*, will serve as illustration. In both, the basic *sen* is to prove Arthur's generation inferior to Uther's.[65] In both, Arthur himself wishes to take up the Knight's challenge, despite energetic protests from his court. In the French, Arthur persists, fights, and is defeated, in another demonstration of solidarity with his knights. In the Spanish, he and the Knight conclude an agreement whereby the latter is never to fight Arthur or any other crowned king. Clearly, in both texts, the characters themselves are divided over the nature of kingship. Arthur does not think it disqualifies him from adventure; the courtiers do, unless they simply doubt his prowess. The French author – not averse, like many another such, to humiliating Arthur – decides for the king, the Spaniard for the court. The Spanish thus partially spare Arthur the shame put on his knights. Its respect for royalty is paralleled in the Spanish *Baladro*; both seem to bespeak a general respect for kingship in fifteenth-century Spain, rather than a particular respect for Arthur. In both versions, Arthur's adventurous spirit and his restricting kingship are in conflict; there is also a suggestion that Arthur's chivalric abilities do not match his spirit. Here are new twists to the debate.

Some adventures involve more than one knight, though only one knight can complete them; they can occur at least partially in court and so involve Arthur. One such is the Magic Ship, which occurs in *Raguidel* (ll. 105-301), the First Continuation (ll. 14119-14432), *Perlesvaus* (pp. 183-5), and the Vulgate *Mort* (p. 57-90).[66] In each case, Arthur, alone or almost alone, discovers and enters the ship, and this is an adventure in itself, as Arthur claims in *Raguidel*:

> Lores avoit dit entre ses dens;
> 'Dius *m*'a aventure envoié
> dont ma cors ert joians et lié.'   (ll. 136-8)

Moreover, although the ship comes to Arthur's doorstep, he has to leave throne and court in order to board it, which introduces the vital 'departure' element. Each time, the motif reveals Arthur's desire for adventure. If he is restrained from it, this is not because of his kingship, but because he is not the Chosen.

The Grail experience in some ways resembles that of the ship. In *Perlesvaus* and the two *Quests*, Arthur experiences along with his knights the first appearance of the Grail. In the *Quests* he is debarred from the action, in *Perlesvaus* he is commanded to participate; but in both, the vision assimilates him to his knights in a spiritual 'adventure' of wonder and discovery. In that moment, Arthur's kingship is not important; as we learn from the heavenly voice in the Vulgate *Quest*: '*Rois* Artus, . . . en cest jor d'ui t'avendra la graindre honors qui onques avenist a *chevalier* de Bretaigne.' (p. 13). Kings and knights merge. Soon they will be sharply differentiated again, though it is worth remembering that the differentiation process does not stop with Arthur, but continues throughout the Quest. The vision resolves on a mystical level the king/knight dichotomy which in earthly terms sometimes appears irreconcilable.

We must now turn to the more difficult theme of Arthur's adventures outside the court. In the Welsh, Arthur's activities range from monster-killing to the composition of frivolous poems, from kidnapping maidens to kidnapping pigs. The outcome ranges from glorious success to farcical failure. Arthur may exhibit heroic exaltation on one page, 'heroic' degeneration on the next – without either being part of a discernible literary development. In general, if the Welsh Arthur receives censure, it is for precipitate action rather than *fainéantise*. If he can be characterised at all, it is as a man who will attempt any adventure which offers, even at the risk of humiliation. Now it is noticeable that the continental Arthur often exhibits the same traits, despite all kingly complications. Perhaps travelling tale-tellers did indeed bring this Arthur from Wales and help to keep him alive on the continent.

Arthur's adventurousness is, however, undeniably damped by Chrétien and his immediate successors. In them, Arthur never undertakes solitary adventure. If he is virtually confined at court, however, we may note that this appears to be true also of the vast majority of knights, only the current hero being given free range. Yet even in these works, Arthur engages in the corporate activities of hunting and war, and is not stigmatised as *fainéant*. What is more, the very concentration on the hero produces a new type of adventure which at first is Arthur's sole prerogative, but in the prose becomes the very stuff of routine knights' adventure. This is the search for the missing hero. In the early verse, Arthur always embarks on such searches with a vast retinue, bringing the mountain to Mahomet. Nevertheless his departure into the wilderness retains something of the essential adventurous impulse. In Chrétien's *Perceval* Arthur even makes the classic adventurous declaration:

> Jamais en chambre ne en sales
> deus nuis pres a pres ne jerrai
> jusques atant que je saurai
> s'il est vis en mer ou en terre.   (ll.4136-9)

And he uses the first person. Actually the whole court accompanies him automatically, and Chrétien makes merry over the upheaval thus caused. Nevertheless it is notable that Arthur is not content to sit idle whilst others search.

The *Perceval* search appears as an unprecedented upheaval, as if Arthur rebelled against the deadweight of his kingship, and it ends rather ridiculously soon. Later versions take the motif more seriously. Even in the Welsh *Peredur*, where no adventures are described en route, the search lasts longer and is treated without irony. This certainly need not be a reminiscence of the active Welsh Arthur, for far better developments are found in the French. In the First Continuation Arthur undertakes three searches. None of these involves Arthur in solitary adventures, but all show a willingness in him to endure travels and dangers, and − a significant change − to remain away from court for a considerable time; he is already beginning to shake off the deadweight. This tendency intensifies in the searches in *Hunbaut* and *Deus espees*. Indeed, the independence in *Deus espees* is so pronounced that it convicts Arthur of excessive adventurousness, when enemies profit from his prolonged absence to invade his kingdom. Somewhere between the rooted Arthur of Chrétien and the over-active one of *Deus espees* there ought to be a happy medium. We shall see the prose romancers in search of this; but they also demonstrate the difficulty of striking it.

In the searches, Arthur's court always accompanies him, and individual knights often abandon the cavalcade for private adventure, thus turning Arthur back into the point of departure. To be a true adventurer, Arthur must set out alone;

and in fact, not even the verse romances wholly deny him this. Even in *Yvain*[67] the germ of the impulse can be detected when Arthur resolves to visit Barenton (ll.661-672). This adventure, which involves single combat, is essentially an individual affair. Now in Chrétien, Arthur views the expedition as a picnic and scientific experiment combined, and (in set contrast to the fiercely individualistic Yvain) he does not dream of setting out alone. Nevertheless the experience brings him in contact with all the elements of private adventure. In the Welsh, he even wishes to take up the individual challenge (*Owein* p.19), and this is not wholly opposed to Chrétien's treatment. Chrétien's immediate successors curb, but do not deny, Arthur's adventurous spirit. Even *L'Atre périlleux*, which says little of Arthur in any capacity, ranks him with Gawain as the non-pareil of active chivalry, while slightly later romances, such as *Fergus* and *Yder*, loosen the reins even more. *Fergus*, which does not actually send Arthur on adventures, still implies that he ought to have them: both Arthur and his enemy express that conviction. The author concludes, albeit cautiously, that the maintenance of Arthur's reputation may depend on personal adventure.

The vigorous Arthur of *Yder* goes adventuring as soon as his wars are concluded. Although he has a motive ulterior to the pure desire for adventure — the encompassing of Yder's destruction — this does not negate his adventurous spirit, for he could have destroyed Yder without stirring from court, simply by imitating the wicked king of folklore who sends his daughter's (or wife's in this case) suitor on some fatal mission. The Arthur of *Yder* is an enfranchised character who never allows his kingship to interfere with his natural impulses, be they those of *gelosie* or of adventurousness. However, in *Yder*, as elsewhere, Arthur's credit as knight-errant is not high. 'Adventure' is no respecter of persons, and Arthur, his ceremonies laid by, must find his own level.

In *Yder* Arthur, being a king, still cannot set out entirely alone. *Rigomer* and *Papegau*,[68] both late works but firmly in the verse-romance tradition, shake off this conviction. For *Rigomer*, Arthur's knighthood is subsumed in his kingship: 'Si est tels chevaliers le roi . . .' (l.9). Thoughts of his prowess spur even Lancelot to emulation (l.5555). A knight excepts Arthur from a general challenge not because he is king, but because he '. . . a tant le cuer entir/ qu'a lui ne m'en ose ahatir.' (ll.15471-2). These increasingly favourable references culminate in a true adventurous departure:

> Dont soie je honis et cous,
> dist li rois, 'se ja y envoi
> nul autre *chevalier* que moi.'   (ll.16040-2)

The resolution causes consternation in court, with a division of opinion similar to that of the Ancient Knight episode. *Rigomer* being incomplete, we never discover whether the verse-romance equilibrium is shattered when the king is no longer at the fulcrum. The author seems to be on Arthur's side, and narrates his adventures with every sign of complacency. It seems that the tradition of the stationary verse-romance king is putting up a last struggle against a more adventurous concept, which has never been entirely dormant.

Papegau purports to recount 'les premiers aventures au bon roy Artus quant il porta corone premierement' (p.1). That Arthur should depart on adventure with the chrism scarcely dry on him is incredible from a normal Arthurian, or realistic, viewpoint, but *Papegau* has none such. Despite its starting-point at the coronation, it assumes throughout the verse-romance tradition of eternal stability. Once Arthur is launched, the author – or *remanieur* – completely forgets that Arthur is king. The setting-out, however, implies that the standard for Arthur's adventurous reign must be set by Arthur himself. Not only is he capable of being both knight and king: it is essential that he should be so. There is again consternation at his resolution, but it is directed at his youth, not his kingship.

The verse romances, then, move from rigid control of Arthur's adventurousness to enthusiastic indulgence of it. This is not a change from *roi fainéant* to more active king, but a relaxation of restrictions on an intrinsically adventurous character. The contemporary Latin romances, which employ a basically verse-romance structure, also indulge the adventurous Arthur. In *De Ortu* Arthur lives in considerable formality, but is accustomed to challenge all comers (in a reversal of the familiar motif of an incoming knight who challenges the whole court), in a perpetual proving of his knighthood. In *Gorlagon*[69] he sets forth impulsively, on a personal, self-imposed quest. This quest is only the frame for the main story, but the fact that Arthur is used and not a knight shows that the author has no objection to his departure on adventure.

In the ensemble of English works (excluding Malory and prose-romance derivatives), we gain little impression of a *roi fainéant*, though he has few personal adventures. *Lybeaus Desconus*[70] sums up the common opinion:

> . . . man of most myghtis . . .
> and ffloure of chevalrye
> to fellen his fone in fyghtis.   (ll.1587-1592)

Basically, verse-romance works, in whatever language, do not argue at length over the knight-king distinction, but demonstrate their opinion implicitly. 'Realism' has little to do with the question: in this, as in many matters, Arthur's court makes its own rules. The verse romancers sense these rules; the prose romancers often express and codify them. Let us see how they attempt this with regard to Arthur's adventurousness.

Perlesvaus, as often, is transitional between verse and prose attitudes. It discusses the king-knight problem seriously, but through action rather than authorial comment. The first branch forcibly demonstrates the universal truth that Arthur's existence at court is not *fainéantise*, but an unremitting exertion of the will which maintains the coherence of Arthurian society – perhaps of all Christendom. But Arthur is also an excellent knight in his own right, and this actually shows most clearly when he has been effectively unkinged by his 'volontez deslaianz'.[71] We conclude that knightly excellence is intrinsic to Arthur, whereas kingly excellence comes to him as a gift from God for the realm's sake. Arthur is most a king when he is least a knight, and *vice versa*; but he does not cease to be knight on becoming king, any more than Christ ceased to be God when becoming man. But an equilibrium must be found between the two natures, and normally this must favour kingship. This is, perhaps, *Perlesvaus'* solution to the problem; but it is full of tensions, and is expressed so intimately through the *matière* of *Perlesvaus* that it is hard to apply universally.

LP, the chief law-giver of the prose-romance universe, has equal difficulty in finding a solution. The most definite pronouncement is Bohort's speech after the Claudas war (Micha VI. 170).[72] Bohort opines that kingship and knighthood are totally incompatible, knighthood being the more creditable (and infinitely the preferable) state. For him and his relatives, Arthur — compelled into kingship by literary tradition — is a convenient scapegoat on whom to unload their own kingly responsibilities. In this speech, we must make allowances for Bohort's own character. The LP author(s) did not despise kingship or consider it inessential: the whole work negates that idea. Nor is Arthur rigidly excluded from knightly endeavour throughout, even if he never sets out alone. Galehaut, the non-pareil of kings, is also a paragon of knightly excellence. Bohort's speech is an attempt to lay down the law, but it is questionable by its very nature.

Bohort's opinions have echoes in later prose works, but are frequently contradicted. We have seen that, in the Boron *Merlin* and all its derivatives, knighting is an indispensable preliminary to Arthur's coronation.[73] The high medieval ceremony of dubbing actually resembled the coronation, especially in the dedication of the sword.[74] This fact, and the narrative juxtaposition of the two ceremonies, must suggest to many readers that knighthood and kingship are essentially compatible, and indeed, all medieval kings received the accolade, though normally some time before their accession.[75] The three sequels to Boron all follow up the suggestion. The Didot *Perceval* hails Arthur as 'li mieldres chevaliers que on seust' (p.139). In VM Arthur is a pure knight in war, but does rather take root in the later peace. We are left with the impression that he has knightly potential, but will use it sparingly.

The *Suite* is much more liberal. In it, the young Arthur is prepared to subordinate kingship to knighthood, and the author, while acknowledging the danger which this poses to the state, nevertheless sanctions Arthur's *fougue*. Merlin himself approves, appointing Arthur to the Round Table fellowship 'pour la bonté de chevalerie qu'd sentoit en lui'. There exists at least a hope of harmonisation; and in the rest of the *Suite*, harmony seems to be achieved. This is partly due to the author's new, negative attitude towards adventure, which becomes a discipline to be endured rather than a pleasure to be enjoyed.[76] In keeping with this, Arthur's adventures are forced on him by Morgain, and he tackles them with grim determination rather than cheerful *élan*. He defends the state through adventure instead of neglecting it to pursue adventure.

In later post-Vulgate fragments, the harmony breaks down, and Bohort's attitude reappears. Thus Arthur himself at one point: 'Ja dieu ne m'ait, se je fusse comme autre chevalier errant, se je james fusse granment a l'aise devant que je sceusse comment il (a challenger) scet ferir de lance et d'espee.'[77] Arthur himself confines his adventurous spirit by conscious adherence to a clearly codified rule. Obviously there is a change of attitude between the *Suite* and the later fragments. This may indicate a change of author, but it may also mark the influence, not of the Bohort speech directly, but of its interpretation by TP.[78] The speech itself hints that Arthur's *chevalerie* is no loss to the world, and that it is very agreeable that his renunciation should spare his betters the same sacrifice. For TP it is very regrettable that Arthur should have to make the sacrifice. He did not lose the qualities of knighthood when he became king, only the right to exercise them.[79] This is a loss both to Arthur and to the supreme good, *chevalerie*, and Arthur's duty to maintain knights does not compensate for his enforced inactivity. Moreover, through Dinadan the author expresses the fear that this inactivity may look like idleness and cowardice, and for this reason, TP breaks its own rule at least once, when it involves a very knightly Arthur in the adventures of Darnantes. Interestingly, this episode was popular with adaptors of TP.[80] In fact TP, far from seeking harmonisation, deliberately exploits the problem so as to stimulate fresh interest both in Arthur and in the institution of knighthood itself. It is often very hard to judge which, of TP or the post-Vulgate, is the innovator in any new departure, but so insistent is TP's discussion that I consider it to be the innovator here. It is interesting to discover, in a work which at various times casts doubt on the greatness of Arthur's achievement,[81] so favourable an estimate of his personal qualities. The TP author's passion for knightliness − which transcends all political and temporal boundaries − allows him to take a magnanimous view of Arthur's personal excellence.

Palamède inherits both Bohort's dictum and the TP/*Suite*'s tendency to rebel against it. The various versions complacently narrate innumerable knightly adventures of Arthur, and never dilate on threats to the kingdom. There is, however, a lingering unease, which one of the best versions (MS B.N. fr. 350) resolves by relegating all the adventures to Arthur's careless youth, after which 'pour toute la haute dignité n'eüst il laissié a faire d'armes com un chavalier errant, se ne fust le rois Uriens et li autre roi ... qui l'en commenchierent a blasmer et a reprendre'. Now it would be perfectly natural if Arthur went adventuring before his coronation. Even Bohort allows this, and we see it in Erec and Yder, whose stories end with their crowning. The secrecy in which Boron enshrouds Arthur's youth prevents such a development in his career. Instead, *Palamède* envisages a probationary period; possibly the complete post-Vulgate did likewise. Not all versions of *Palamède* make this clear, however: often Arthur rubs shoulders with kings of all ages, all happily adventuring. One version justifies this by asserting that the high reputation of Britain in Uther's and Arthur's days was due to the very fact that the kings went adventuring. This is certainly in accordance with the rationale of a totally adventure-geared universe. In a way, however, it means that the wheel has come full circle. The Welsh Arthur adventured freely in a disorganised world of fantasy. *Palamède*'s world also lacks realistic organisation. This liberates Arthur from the restraints imposed by a Chrétien or a LP. *Palamède* was not in its time accused of frivolity: it was as popular as LP itself, and at the same time. Moreover, it was stories of the *Palamède* type which provoked the most imitation in 'real life'.[82] Perhaps we should see *Palamède* as giving a different view of the LP world, rather than a new and degenerate concept, while neither romance gives the 'last word' on Arthur's knightliness.

Yet another viewpoint occurs in *Palamède*'s approximate contemporary, the

Livre d'Artus. Here again there is acceptance of an adventurous Arthur, but the problem of the king's responsibilities is not shirked. The author assumes a dualistic attitude similar to *Rigomer*'s, though in the prose the dichotomy is sharper. Arthur's departure on adventure rouses a sea of troubles for his subordinates: 'quar bien savoient ja en maintes contrees que li rois Artus estoit perdus . . . si cuidoient bien avior li pais a bandon sanz grant desfense'. Arthur's mere presence guarantees the security of the state, and his knights' efforts are useless unless channelled through him. But interlacing with these scenes are Arthur's adventures, related with great enjoyment, and without the least sense of urgency. Arthur is nowhere overtly criticised, and it is unclear how much criticism is expected from the reader, who is left to decide whether Arthur can reconcile the two roles.

By the late thirteenth century in France, then, it was possible to present Arthur as full knight-errant; but it is almost impossible to accept this without suspecting a dereliction of duty. Arthur is pulled two ways by the very nature of his king-centred, adventure-oriented universe. However, Malory, writing in fifteenth-century England, heir to all the prose-romance tendencies and with ideas of his own, achieves the harmonisation without sacrifice of narrative logic or political awareness. For Malory, knightliness is an absolute standard of goodness against which all things can be measured.[83] Therefore, if Arthur is to command favourable attention, he must be a knight first and foremost. This must not conflict with his kingship, lest it be suspected that there is something bad in knightliness. This is why Malory changes the people's consternation at Arthur's disappearance for his duel with Pellinor into whole-hearted approval. Subsequently, whatever source he is using, Malory deletes all suggestions that Arthur is no knight, or that there is a conflict between kingship and knighthood, while intensifying everything which shows Arthur to be intrinsically and actively knightly. Knightliness, far from unfitting one for kingship, is the major — perhaps the sole — criterion of it. Thus Arthur reigns 'as a noble knyght', while Mark is 'the shamfullest knyght of a kyng that is now lyvyng' (II. 580). Malory's approval of Arthur's knighthood is moving and convincing because it springs from the very foundations of his work. It finds echoes in many Middle English works, seeming to accord well with general English enthusiasm for Arthur. At last he is wholly at ease in his world: it is neither fantastic nor severely realistic, but sufficient unto itself, and in accord with Arthur's true, heroic character.

(iv) Justice
Enough has now been said to prove that the Arthur of peacetime is no idler, and that the burden of kingship does not crush him into nonentity. Nevertheless he has a king's regular duties, and many authors try to convey his fulfilment of them, largely in order to show that his world is not fantastic, but has an everyday solidity. This must be achieved without overburdening the work with humdrum detail. In some works, obsession with *chevalerie* means that Arthur's sole duty appears to be the maintenance of knights; but if more is required, justice can very conveniently serve as the emblem or quintessence of the king's tasks. Justice characterises the archetypal king, and it was the most popular attribute of the medieval king, one with which even his barons, justices within their own

fiefs, could identify even if they resented the application of royal justice to themselves. The problem of Arthur's justice is central to some works, notably the *Lanval* group and the alliterative *Morte*;[84] but in many more it features as a background datum – a datum, however, which may throw up unexpected excitements and complications.

The simplest way to introduce the theme of justice is by reference to Arthur's chronic itinerance. Although he has a favourite town (at first Caerleon, later Camelot), which from the Vulgate onwards reflects contemporary tendencies towards political centralisation and becomes his capital, he never entirely takes root in it. Now, regal itinerance partly meant the exercising of the king's *droit de gîte*, but it was also essential to the maintenance of royal justice, and to the demonstration of its availability to everyone in the realm.[85] The verse romances play on the reader's awareness of this: though they never show Arthur actually in court, the fact that he is seldom found twice running in the same place proves that his *eyre* is pursued with great energy. The prose romances are vaguer about Arthur's itinerance, and on the whole show no interest in everyday court justice, though a few sessions are briefly mentioned in the interests of realism. The rarity of such allusions may partly be explained by the contemporary tendency to deputise judicial functions to royal representatives; but conversely, at the same time provincial justice was increasingly brought under royal control.[86] The near-absence of the common people from the Arthurian world must largely explain this general indifference, but it undeniably undermines the solidity of the prose-romance secondary world.

More to aristocratic taste is the judicial duel, whose unflagging popularity in real life is amply mirrored in both Arthurian verse and prose. These duels are more than background data: they are exciting pieces of narrative, which often raise questions about judicial procedure and thus stir into life the theme of Arthurian justice. It is not so much that the romancers deny the validity of the judicial duel, either in real life or in the Arthurian world,[87] as that peculiar Arthurian circumstances can create complications. Favourite characters cannot be killed or – with the possible exception of Kay – defeated even in a wrongful quarrel. Arthur himself, in his enforced knight-orientation, must in this presidency of the duel uphold the demands of *chevalerie* even against those of abstract justice. Thus, in the duels between Gawain and Yvain, Gawain and Guiromelant, Kay and Bagomedes, Gawain and Galeron,[88] the duel proves useless not because the procedure is inherently unsound, but because Arthur does not or cannot allow it to take its natural course. In each instance save the third, Arthur dictates a settlement based on evidence rather than on the duel itself.[89] This makes the duel superfluous, but none of the authors suggest that it should have been dispensed with. In the third case, the duel is clearly about to produce the correct result – the death of the guilty Kay – when Arthur halts it. Thereafter there is no judicial settlement and the criminal escapes scot-free. Arthur's undeserving favourite cannot be eliminated by *any* judicial procedure.

More searching, but still not fundamental, criticisms occur in the prose. In TP Mark wins a duel, though he is patently in the wrong. His success is blamed on a technical hitch: he swore no oath beforehand. Arthur's reaction is therefore not to abolish or doubt the duel, but to amend its rules. Here, justice is eventually done by trial, but by an unofficial exercise of force in defiance of Arthur's judicial powers. Thus the author indicates that the Arthurian world is really ruled by violence, the only safeguard of justice being the stronger arm of the good knights. It seems unlikely that he intended this as a criticism of his own day; it is tied to Arthurian circumstances, though the limited criticism of the duel may well have wider applicability.

The forms of the duel are criticised again, on similar lines, in the *Prophécies*. Here, Arthur undergoes, instead of exercising, justice, and wins because he avoids the oath: 'ainsi con je vous ai conte se delivra le roi Artus de ce que il n'estoit sanz courpe' (f.136c). This may serve as an indication that the king himself is not exempt from justice, but if so it is strangely double-edged. Certainly Arthur's status as impeccable justiciar is turned to mockery. Once again, the *sen* is inseparable from its Arthurian context, being the last dismal legacy of Arthur's humiliating dependence on the False Guinevere.

Both duel and trial by jury are hilariously satirised in the thirteenth-century Anglo-Latin *Historia Meriadoci*. The criticisms are partly general – that the stronger always wins the judicial duel; partly Arthurian – that no court convened by Arthur to judge his own case is likely to be impartial (pp.17-19). Here, the entanglement is resolved by the free exercise of Arthur's magnanimity, implying that he has some discretion as to whether or not he fully submits to legal process. The inadequacy of both combat and trial are exposed once again in the False Guinevere story and its pendant in the Vulgate *Mort*.[90] Both works, like *Meriadoc*, expose the inadequacy of Arthur's court justice, not only in its fundamental procedures, but also in Arthur's involvement, which threatens his impartiality. In *Meriadoc* and the *Mort* he tries, with limited success, to be fair; in the False Guinevere affair he is patently not trying. The same partiality invalidates the judicial combats in *Yvain* and elsewhere. Thus criticism of the institution continually shades into criticism of the executor. These complications strongly and widely militate against the notion of Arthur as a supremely just king. Against this background his espousal, in pure expediency, of a wrongful cause in the *Suite* appears less startling, if not less shocking. In the end, Arthur once again dictates a settlement unconnected with the duel, but this scarcely excuses his earlier decision.

There is no consensus about Arthur's attitude to the judicial duel. Sometimes he is participant; sometimes – more normally for a king – president. Sometimes he is the prisoner of a faulty system; sometimes he manipulates the system to his advantage. Sometimes he overrides it – not always in the cause of ultimate justice. Criticism of judicial institutions, of Arthurianism, and of Arthur interweave. Also interwoven, of course, are the excitement of the combat and of immediate personal issues, which indeed usually take precedence. This attitude may explain why, despite the constant veiled criticism, Arthur retains his general reputation as a just king. Or perhaps it is the ubiquitous – particularly the chronicular – encomiums of Arthur which preserve that reputation. The 'good' king is necessarily just, and just 'good king Arthur' must always be.

It is equally hard to judge how far Arthur himself is considered to be *infra* or *supra legem*. Many times he himself is involved in legal disputes: authors find the resulting dilemmas particularly piquant. All in all it would seem that the issue, like that of Arthur's knighthood, is one of perpetual debate, but does not mirror the development of real-life institutions. Respect for sources and authorial opinion largely dictate the colour of any one treatment.

Arthur is never a tyrant, seeking power beyond that which the law gives him. In particular, he is eternally subject to the supreme Arthurian law, of knighthood. Defiance of this one law — even in obedience to abstract justice — is treason in Arthurian terms, as it is in the Mark of TP. Here is another explanation of Arthur's unflagging reputation for justice. What in the real world might seem arbitrary and unfair is supremely just in the *royaume aventureux*. Perhaps also that is why Arthur so seldom mediates outside his own kingdom: its laws are not valid outside, though knights from outside willingly come to subject themselves to it. Thus the theme of justice can divorce Arthur from real-life kings, instead of accentuating a resemblance.

The peacetime Arthur, then, strives to reconcile the demands of kingship, of knighthood and of individuality. The struggle can be made applicable to universal or particular real-life problems; it may brush the realms of heroic legend and even myth; but fundamentally it is inseparable from Arthur's own story. Fantasy and realism mingle strangely in his world, and he must adapt to both. Sometimes the results are surprising: a 'fantastic' adventure, like the killing of Ritho, may express a more realistic political message than does an apparently realistic trial-scene. The most successful Arthurian incidents satisfy the reader's expectations, whether based on real-life knowledge or on story tradition, but also startle him and lead him on.

VI

RELATIONSHIPS

Arthur, as the centre of the Arthurian universe, has to give it coherence by drawing everything in it into some relationship with himself. This process begins as soon as he appears. In the Nennian paragraph he is precisely, though puzzlingly, related to the British kings. In the *Mirabilia* he acquires a dog and a son. Early poetry and saints' lives give him companions, sometimes a couple, sometimes a host. The grave englynion, 'Trioedd y Meirch' and the Dumnonian king-lists attempt to fit him into an elaborate system of classification.[1] In the later developments, relationships evolve, become codified, and occasionally lapse, while new ones emerge. In this chapter we shall examine some of the more important and enlightening ones. They can be broadly divided into family and subject relationships.

Arthur is a classic case of the legendary figure who attracts previously unrelated characters into his orbit. Their proliferation gives his family tree a complication rivalled only by Perceval's. Few additions, however, are made altogether mechanically and without thought. Accurately defined family relationships are important in all 'primitive' societies. In the late prose romances Arthur's become excessively so, and dictate the action. Throughout the development they are a powerful shaping force in his life.

Arthur's remoter ancestry, whether Welsh- or Geoffrey-based, is less important than one might expect. The first is of no importance outside Wales, while in HRB Arthur's relationship to the earlier kings is actually very tenuous. Romance texts ignore most of Arthur's remoter HRB ancestry, without making much attempt to substitute another. This is not because they are uninterested in the remoter past, for the ancestries of Perceval, Lancelot and Tristan are, in the prose, painstakingly traced back to the Crucifixion. Arthur's ancestry, by contrast, is never traced further back than Constans, and there is confusion even there.[2] The tendency of the Grail-centred cycles is, indeed, progressively to isolate Arthur from the Grail past, and the virtual suppression of his ancestry is a means to this. Two late English chroniclers, Robert of Avebury and John of Glastonbury, do belatedly try to give him a Grail ancestry,[3] but they are too late to influence the main narrative development which insists on his secularity.

The identity of Arthur's parents, identified once and for all by Geoffrey, is extremely important to the shaping of his legend,[4] but there is hardly any direct contact between parents and child; their relationship — of destiny and blood — works on other levels. Arthur's family contacts are almost all with people of his own or a later generation — a fact which is partly explained by and partly conditions his oft-felt status as a father-figure.

Native Welsh tradition gives Arthur a motley assortment of brothers, sisters, uncles and cousins,[5] who can, however, be sorted into a tolerably coherent family tree, which orders itself around his mother. This coherence need not surprise us in the literature of a people famed for its passion for genealogy.[6] Genealogical clarity, indeed, preoccupies the Welsh authors far more than the human interest of the relationships, save in some cases of family obligation such as that to Culhwch or Illtud.[7] The most interesting aspect is that the most important relationship seems to be that of cousin. Whereas in the continental tradition incoming heroes are made into nephews, in the Welsh Culhwch and the rest are maternal cousins. This may be because Arthur, in becoming a grandson of Amlawdd Wledig, was slotted in amongst a crowd of pre-existent grandsons, but it does suggest that Welsh writers did not think the uncle relationships as significant as the continental ones did. This is surprising, as it is often assumed that it was important in the Celtic world. Conchobar and Cuchulainn, Finn and Diarmaid, Mark and Tristan, spring to mind as examples; but the first is suspect, it being widely reputed that Cuchulainn was Conchobar's son by incest. The Finn/Diarmaid link is made only in later texts, which may well have been influenced by the Tristan legend rather than vice versa. As for Mark and Tristan, there is no Celtic evidence for the nephewship earlier than the versions of Eilhart and Beroul.[8] The nephew relationship is not particularly prominent in early Welsh or Irish law. But we know that it was important in early Germanic society,[9] and it may well be that Germanic, continental beliefs influenced its introduction into both Arthurian and Tristan legends. I can point to no special significance of the cousin relationship in Celtic; but certainly the nephew idea was not strong enough to oust the genealogical importance of Amlawdd's grandsons. Arthur's Welsh cousins have the same status as his continental nephews: they are a comfort, a support — and a source of incessant clamours for aid both material and practical.

Arthur does have two Welsh nephews, Gwalchmai and Eliwlod. Neither is very prominent. Gwalchmai would scarcely attract attention from scholars were it not for his identification with the continental Gawain. It is likely that both Geoffrey and William of Malmesbury[10] singled out Gwalchmai precisely because his relationship to Arthur was significant in Norman eyes. Gwalchmai/Gawain is, indeed, the only member of Arthur's Welsh family to survive and prosper in continental literature. As for Eliwlod, his appearances are fleeting indeed;[11] and a dead nephew in the form of an eagle is hardly a consoling addition to the family circle.

Geoffrey, then, recreates Arthur's family almost from scratch, and later authors, as usual, build on him. From now on, human interest outweighs genealogical calculation and the simple fascination of names. Let us now examine the fortunes of Arthur's continental family relationships, dealing first with the minor figures. Some are of considerable interest, although they do not attain permanent stardom. One such is Hoel, Arthur's nephew (or cousin:[12] does the confusion indicate a 'transitional' attitude?) in HRB. In Arthur's early campaigns, Hoel has the status of nephew, favourite and right-hand man which the romances give to Gawain. His Breton nationality doubtless enhances his status in the author's, and perhaps Arthur's, eyes. But already in the later stages of HRB, Hoel begins to give place to Gawain. Perhaps this is because, to Geoffrey, Hoel symbolises the continuing glory of the Breton kingdom, and is thus dissociated from Arthur's fortunes and outlives him, which Gawain does not, and never will. Be that as it may, Hoel loses all significance in the romances, although – a tribute to Geoffrey's power – he does retain a shadowy existence throughout the romance development.

Other nephews have different destinies. A few, like Durmart, are important only in the romance which centres on them; outside it, they do not even earn mention in Arthur's retinue. Others, like Yvain and Caradoc, retain a toe-hold, but their nephewship may not be acknowledged, and is certainly not humanly significant, outside their own stories. Yet others, like Perceval and Lancelot, are at some stage given a nephewship to Arthur[13] which does not endure because, for both these characters, alienation from Arthur is a vital element in their mainline story. We see that nephewship is neither a certain passport to Arthurian prominence nor a *sine qua non* of it. Basically it is a cliché, a narrative convenience, which may gain meaning in the hands of a talented author.

Arthur's family tree does, indeed, shed leaves as fast as it acquires them, and some – by chance or by authorial decision – are scarcely glimpsed ere they fall. Some scarcely grow: he has, for instance, no brothers, save for his half-brother Cador in HRB, who is and remains a very shadowy character.

As for the plethora of sisters, their number and identity is never codified.[14] Only two, Morgain and Mordred's mother, develop enough individuality to secure a place in the legend; and in Morgain's case, this personality is largely an independent development.[15] The others, like all royal women in a male-dominated society, function as wives, mothers and political pawns. Inevitably, their marriages remove them from court and prohibit the development of a close relationship with Arthur. In the prose romances, this is all the more true as the sisters are half-sisters, much older than Arthur and certainly not brought up with him.

The minor sisters attain the peak of what importance they have in VM, when they communicate their sympathy with their brother to their sons, and so induce them to break with their fathers.[16] There is historical and psychological realism here: wives at a foreign court must often have sympathised with their families when the two realms were in conflict. The sisters' reaction is both touching and vital to the narrative, but it does not institute a permanent relationship with Arthur.

Mordred's mother is important in her own right in Gawain's birth tale – where she is certainly on good terms with Arthur[17] – but her relationship with Arthur is really important only in the incest story, and in that, it is the unknown blood-relationship, not a conscious brother-sister affection, which is vital. In VM, the sister is another Ygerne, completely innocent of criminal intent, taking the seducer for her husband. Her subsequent realisation of his identity might have made a splendid tale of Jocastan horror in the hands of a more leisured, or psychologically subtle, author. As it is, it is robbed of all meaning by its assimilation to the stereotyped reactions of her sisters. The horror is similarly missed in the *Suite*, where the sister is merely a pawn in Fate's hands – and a sex óbject. Later in the post-Vulgate, the incest is forgotten as far as the woman is concerned: Arthur feels for her the normal affection of a brother, and her eventual fate (*Folie Lancelot*, p.3) is in no way seen as punishment for her incest – as Arthur's is – although such a link would improve *sen* and *conjointure* and cries out to be made. Even Malory, in his own 'Sir Gareth', sees nothing between Morgawse and Arthur but a mild fraternal affection.

The complex role of Morgain has received much critical attention, and I shall not dilate on it.[18] Her fairy attributes set her apart from the normal world even in the Boron tradition, where they are acquired simply by study. She hovers elusively, malevolent or strangley benevolent, on the fringes of Arthur's story. One thing must be emphasised. Critics like to see in Morgain Arthur's fairy mistress.[19] Now, whatever may have happened in the murky world of surmised Arthurian origins, there is no hint of sexual relationship between Morgain and Arthur in any of our texts. The brother-sister relationship, codified from Chrétien onwards, invariably gives their behaviour perfect propriety, even in the tales of their after-life in Avalon.[20] It is true that Morgain has vast sexual appetites, and in Avalon she acts as 'fairy mistress' to Ogier and other visitors, but she has no such designs on Arthur. This propriety is particularly significant in view of the fact that Arthur in the prose does commit incest – but with another sister. If he and Morgain were known as lovers, it would be more natural to assume that the incest was with her; this would certainly lend point to her hostility, and to Arthur's destruction. But it would complicate Mordred's HRB affiliations, so perhaps we need not expect such a link. In its absence, Morgain remains peripheral, which is perhaps to her advantage, for the prose romancers have a fatal tendency towards over-explanation, and Morgain, by escaping it, keeps the fascination of enigma.

The relatives so far discussed are close to Arthur in blood, but not in personal contact. Few relations are 'close' to him in the latter sense, and the relationship is often hard to analyse. Some, however, span almost the entire literature, contributing both to its consistency and to its development. Of these, arguably the most important is Guinevere.

Guinevere has been claimed as Arthur's sovereignty-goddess.[21] The recurrent abduction story[22] obviously has mythological connotations, and although abductions occur in other mythologies – and in real life[23] – the absence of indications to the contrary allows the acceptance of a Celtic origin here. In the surviving texts, however, Arthur does not win his realm by marrying Guinevere, nor does he lose it to any of her abductors, save Mordred – to whom the 'abduction' is secondary. The *sen* of the legend develops away from the sovereignty belief.

Early Welsh gives us a few isolated and disconnected references to Guinevere in her formal role as consort and in her fatal role as abductee. None is developed for its psychological interest, though we may gather that Arthur values his wife at least as a prized possession — scarcely a startling discovery. The most interesting feature is perhaps the consensus that Guinevere was 'merch Ogran gawr'.[24] No extant legend explains this patronymic; but one wonders if one ever existed in which Arthur wooed the giant's daughter. I generally distrust the Lost Story, but there is some warrant for it here. Arthur is associated with giant-killing; the giant's daughter theme is widespread in Celtic;[25] and in *Culhwch* Arthur is more prominent in the winning of Olwen than is her real suitor. Such a story would explain Arthur's marriage without recourse to the sovereignty myth. Guinevere's unorthodox descent is unknown outside Wales, but then so are most of the Welsh data on Arthur's family.

Geoffrey, unaware of or revolted by Guinevere's giantish origin, gives her one of impeccable respectability. Respectability and dullness are, indeed, characteristics of Geoffrey's Guinevere until the dénouement, and even then Guinevere interests him no more in her unfaithfulness than in her years of marital fidelity. There is nothing in her to attract the later romantic and courtly authors, except the fact of her unfaithfulness. All interest in Arthur's marriage is therefore a back-formation from its breakdown. However, the irruption of Lancelot into romance stifles romance development of the actual Mordred intrigue. Chroniclers, on the other hand, will not touch the Lancelot story at any price, however imbued they may be with romance influence. This is not because chroniclers thought the Lancelot story untrue, but by its very nature, Arthur must take a back place if it be included, and this would seem absurd within the king-by-king structure affected by all chronicles. Mordred can destroy Arthur, as 'history' requires, without need to elaborate on either his or Lancelot's love for the queen.

While a few of the more talented chroniclers — Wace, Layamon, the alliterative *Morte* author — do take an embryonic interest in Guinevere, it is always necessary to the overall chronicle structure that she remain peripheral. In the romance world, however, Chrétien's seminally important introduction of the Lancelot theme ensures that he and Guinevere will eventually become the key to the whole Arthurian world and its tragedy. For the Lancelot story is essentially destructive and tragic. It is an Arthurian time-bomb; and before we go on to analyse its use in the great Chrétien-Grail-Malory sequence, it may be well to pause and consider how the lesser verse-romances attempt to defuse it. Most of them, indeed, simply refuse to consider Guinevere as anything other than a faithful consort. They even resist the attraction of Lancelot as a knightly paragon, continuing to prefer Gawain even after the prose romancers have hideously degraded him.

Rigomer does attempt to cash in on Lancelot's fame, but struggles to avoid the gravest implications of his devotion to the queen. The horn/mantle texts and the Lanval story, which turn on the queen's infidelity, betray their non-Arthurian origin by the authors' rigid avoidance of Mordred and Lancelot, and by the contortions which most perform in order to restore the *status quo*, and preserve something of Arthur's dignity, at the end. On the other hand, *Yder* heavily emphasises Guinevere's fidelity, as if deliberately refuting any aspersions on it which the reader may have heard. The favourable verse-romance view of Guinevere's fidelity extends to non-French works, even those which — like the Middle English *Auntyrs* — were written long after the great prose cycles and also show awareness of the Mordred story. In fact, Guinevere's resilience in the face of authorial criticism almost matches Arthur's own.

Even amongst the prose romancers, one is found to testify to Guinevere's fidelity, the individualistic author of *Perlesvaus*. He relates the Lancelot-Guinevere intrigue exclusively to Lancelot's spiritual state (I. 153, 166-8), and the love between Guinevere and Arthur is far more real to him. Guinevere remains Arthur's counsellor when all others desert him, displaying more than a purely sexual fidelity, while Arthur's feelings for her combine the chivalrous adoration of a lover with the trusting devotion of a husband. His misery at her death contributes greatly to the atmosphere of desolation and despair which enshrouds the closing scenes of *Perlesvaus*. Here, in fact, we find a tragedy of married love which is less exciting, but in some ways more moving, than the great Vulgate tragedy of infidelity. Arthur is exonerated from indifference as well as Guinevere from faithlessness, and human depth is given to the harmonious relationship widely assumed in the verse. Most important of all, Guinevere is wholly cleared of the charge of causing Arthur's downfall by her frailty.

Perlesvaus, however, remains peripheral to the main romance development, to which we must now turn.

It was clearly not Chrétien's intention, when he began his *Lancelot*, to narrate the destruction of Arthur's kingdom through the guilty lovers. It is, indeed, surely the dangers inherent in a settled intrigue between Lancelot and Guinevere which make Chrétien keep most of the action well away from Arthur and his court, and which make both him and Godefroi de Lagni unable to finish the story satisfactorily. Chrétien wished (or was compelled) only to analyse the classic courtly-love relationship within a significant social context – albeit one overlaid with mystery and magic. Nevertheless his Arthurian setting forced him at least to indicate something above the (later fatal) Arthur-Guinevere-Lancelot triangle.

The tale opens with Méléagant's challenge, which puts Arthur and the court in a strange state of paralysis and disarray, similar to that in which Perceval first sees them.[26] Whatever 'magical' explanation we find for Arthur's disarray (and Chrétien suggests none), it is clear that the glorious harmony between Arthur and his consort, so vividly portrayed in *Erec*, has melted away. Against Arthur's confusion and inaction, Lancelot's tumultuous arrival and furious dedication 'stick fiery off indeed'. It is a long time before we discover the mysterious pursuer's identity, and although he claims quite early on to be of Arthur's kingdom, he is not presented as one of Arthur's knights and his representative, as Gawain always is. From first to last he is fanatically dedicated to his lady; the profit which his actions bring to Logres, though important to the overall *sen* of the work,[27] is to him a mere corollary.

Chrétien does not pursue explicit criticism of Arthur beyond the opening scenes. Nor does either Lancelot or Guinevere express the least hostility or disrespect towards him: all such feelings are directed at Méléagant, the rival lover. Nevertheless, it is clear that, by the end of the romance, Arthur has irrevocably – and, on Chrétien's showing, deservedly – lost the fidelity of Guinevere, who in the climactic love-scene surrenders herself to her lover as completely as he to her. It is notable that in the fuss over Méléagant's ensuing detection, Arthur's honour is not called into question; but it would spring to the mind of any alert reader. Chrétien has doomed Arthur and wrested Guinevere from him: later writers have only to follow his lead.

Chrétien's intrigue, incomplete at both ends, cries out for further development. It is probable that that development began with a simple prosification of the *Charrete*;[28] and indeed, in both surviving versions of the prose story, the treatment of Arthur is similar to that in Chrétien: on the whole he retains his dignity. In the prose *Charrete* as we have it, embedded in LP, the night of love loses almost all its significance because it is not Guinevere's first infidelity (β omits it), and indeed, the whole *Charrete*, though still important, does not bulk enormously large in the complete LP. But its adoption was vital to the whole prose Arthurian development.

The early LP may have been intended from the first to work towards the *Charrete*. Even if it is not, its author is constantly aware of the Chrétien heritage. His task is to manoeuvre Arthur, Guinevere and Lancelot into their *Charrete* positions, while placing each on the appropriate register in the reader's sympathies. This is achieved by a long, carefully-controlled, but very definite degradation of Arthur to the profit of Lancelot. It proceeds in three stages: the Galehaut war, the Camille affair, the False Guinevere. Each is marked by a corresponding advance in Guinevere's commitment to Lancelot.

Before the Galehaut war, Lancelot and Guinevere are already strongly attracted to one another, but Guinevere has not faltered in her loyalty to Arthur, and he has done nothing to spoil their conjugal love. After the war, Arthur's moral castigation and political near-disaster, contrasting so sharply with Lancelot's success, indicate that he does not 'deserve' Guinevere's love. In strict courtly terms, perhaps, a husband was not required to 'deserve' as a lover was, but the contrast between Arthur and Lancelot is too obvious here to be inapplicable. Indeed, the author does not apply strict courtly rules to the Arthur-Guinevere-Lancelot triangle, but judges all three by a single moral standard. This emerges very strongly from the Camille affair, which is clearly introduced so that Arthur's marital infidelity may precede Guinevere's. Whatever excuse is made for Arthur by Camille's magical powers — and these are only very cursorily mentioned — the affair is clearly degrading and stupid, contrasting unpleasantly with the refined and exalted love of Lancelot and Guinevere. The author makes it clear that both affairs are to be judged by the same standard; Arthur fares very badly thereby.

The Camille affair destroys the royal marriage from within, but leaves the surface intact. The False Guinevere episode ruptures that surface so completely that only the author's fundamental concern for Arthurian stability and dignity (on which Lancelot's own credit partly depends) seems to compel him to restore the *status quo*.

Three versions of this episode exist.[29] The shortest (Micha's a) may represent the original author's intention, though its ending is both abrupt and confusing. The others, the Long Version and β, are close in context, but give differing impressions of the vital relationships. Both look forward to the rest of LP, and so have a vested interest in careful restoration of the Arthurian fabric.

Each of the three versions shows Arthur enmeshed in a cross-current of intrigues. He is worked on by the False Guinevere, by his own barons and advisers, by his own passions and by the demands of his kingly, judicial persona. Amidst this entanglement, the reader's feelings towards Arthur undergo constant alteration. In *a*, Arthur, in his judicial persona, deals impeccably with the first accusation, showing neither undue favour to Guinevere nor unjust suspicion of her. His cowardly surrender to his kidnappers makes a poor impression, but the insistence on the power of the potion with which the False Guinevere doses him may be taken as an excusing of all his subsequent actions: the more nauseating his behaviour, the more we are to believe it out of character. In particular we are struck by the fact that he actually resists the evil influence for some time. Nevertheless, in the Tarmelide scenes Arthur is clearly on the 'wrong' side, while all the reader's sympathy is evoked by the superb dignity and courage of Guinevere. Moreover, she, being unaware of Arthur's enchantment, cannot but be revolted and alienated by his attitude, and further drawn to her lover. Now, in *a* there is no open breach between Arthur and Guinevere, since the whole plot is revealed immediately after Lancelot's duel. Nevertheless the final effect is to soothe Guinevere's conscience over her love: 'car se toz li mondes savoit l'amor entr'aus deus, si li devroit l'an a bien jugier, tant l'a *deservi* en pluseurs leus'.

In the more complex Long Version, the possibility of a complete rupture is evoked from the beginning, and the interlace with Galehaut's story constantly reminds us that Guinevere can easily survive without Arthur (but not *vice versa*). Arthur is presented less sympathetically, being prejudiced against Guinevere from the start, before his kidnapping and enchantment; his judicial persona is much less in evidence, and he lets his own folly and lust sway him throughout. The potion is scarcely mentioned, so that, as in the Camille affair, Arthur is shown to have a degrading and shameful concept of love. The lengthy political and judicial manoeuvres which follow the kidnapping show Arthur in a consistently bad light (save in his continuing respect for Lancelot); and Guinevere's departure into exile bids fair to make the injustice permanent. The long separation is marked by a savage deterioration in the state of Arthur and his kingdom, and this implies that Guinevere is indispensable to Arthur's 'renommée'. Amustans, castigating Arthur, lays the blame wholly on him, and the seriousness of his lapse is emphasised by the fact that his passion for the False Guinevere outlasts even her exposure and death. Against Arthur's disgraceful behaviour, Guinevere's restraint, dignity, fidelity and dauntless courage contrast even more strikingly than in *a*. It is hard to believe that the Arthurian *status quo* can ever be truly restored. And yet Guinevere is haunted, during this episode, by the consciousness of her own sin. Thus a tension is created. On the one side, Arthur's behaviour justifies Lancelot and Guinevere; on the other, Guinevere's sin excuses Arthur. This tension fits very well into the overall pattern of the *Lancelot-Graal* cycle, in which the sins of all three protagonists are searchingly examined and finally, in the *Mort*, come home to roost. This may indicate that the Long Version represents a re-writing of *a* so as to fit the larger context; but it is not a cast-iron proof of such a relationship.

The β version contains still harsher criticisms of Arthur, particularly in Gawain's speeches; but it also allows him some lingering love and pity for Guinevere. He turns to the False Guinevere more out of a genuine – albeit misdirected – desire to do right than out of lust. Moreover, even the severe Amustans admits that Arthur had no means of identifying the true Guinevere, so that all in all Arthur appears to be more sinned against than sinning. Nevertheless, Guinevere, less conscience-stricken than in the Long Version, shows a spirited resentment of Arthur, and has to be coaxed to return; moreover, she has no hesitation in deceiving both Arthur and Galehaut in order to safeguard her own love.[30] Thus, once again, though in a different way, the balance of guilt and vindication is maintained.

The rest of the *Lancelot-Graal* maintains this basic equilibrium, but the reader's sympathies are progressively tipped on to Arthur's side. He commits no more adulteries, and is referred to as an excellent *preudom* unjustly betrayed by his wife. The False Guinevere story is forgotten – even in the *Mort*, whose central *matière* is modelled on it. Lancelot's failure in the *Queste* devalues the guilty love on this new plane, and the *Mort* itself takes special pains to demonstrate Arthur's worthiness as a husband, especially when the author makes it particularly clear that his heart is not in Guinevere's condemnation. Even his apparently savage determination to have her burned is motivated by frustration at Lancelot's escape. Was the glory of Lancelot's and Guinevere's love worth all the havoc it caused? Arthur's rehabilitation gives this final question an urgency which it would lack if he had remained a moral pygmy.

The *Lancelot-Graal*, then, presents an evolutionary study of Arthur's marriage, rather than a fixed opinion of the protagonists. Arthur, degraded in Part One, still emerges from the cycle with credit. Most important, however, the *Lancelot-Graal* converts Chrétien's Lancelot-Guinevere duo irretrievably into a triangle, in which not only Arthur's kingship, but also his personal character and feelings, are important.

Succeeding prose works inevitably take account of LP's presentation, but pick and choose freely among its varying shades of opinion. Thus VM accepts that Arthur's feelings are important, and undertakes to show how they developed before the beginning of LP, where – as we have seen – the couple dwell in unimpassioned harmony. According to Micha, VM enjoys the 'piquancy' of Guinevere's early infatuation for Arthur, and also wishes to show that Arthur, the universal paragon, can also be a courtly lover.[31] The piquancy and courtliness are, however, limited by the author's lack of delicacy and skill as well as a desire to accord with LP. In VM, the marriage is, in fact, basically a political alliance, arranged between Merlin and Leodegan without consulting the couple – a perfectly realistic account of a royal wedding. That the two are attracted to one another is simply a fortunate corollary. Arthur's knightly evolutions before the walls of Carmelide may partake of courtly 'deserving', but this author makes them savour of crude machismo rather than refined exaltation. A comparison of the first kiss of Arthur and Guinevere with its probable model, the first kiss of Lancelot and Guinevere in LP, will show how unrefined the former relationship is. Both kisses are encouraged by a third party, but there is a vast difference between Galehaut's exquisite sensibility and Merlin's heavy-handed paternalism towards two ignorant children. The VM affair belongs at best to the sentimental realm of *Floris and Blanchefor*: but it certainly initiates exactly the relationship found at the beginning of LP.

The *Livre d'Artus* also refers to the time before Lancelot's advent, but (probably because the author did not envisage a direct coupling with LP) it is far less anxious to accord with LP data. In fact, both Arthur and Guinevere, despite their practical co-operation, are light-heartedly unfaithful (VII. 132, 219), the latter idea being especially shocking in comparison with her adulterous faithfulness in the *Lancelot-Graal*. To accept the *Livre d'Artus* we must forget LP, and accept marital unfaithfulness as a light matter in this world of ten-minute seductions and swashbuckling adventure.

Utterly different is the attitude of the contemporary TP. For TP, the adultery is the *status quo*, and the author plays delicately on the tensions rising from Arthur's official awareness of it, and hostile attempts to enlighten him. He relies on readers' knowledge of the Vulgate *Mort* to produce excited awareness of the calamity attendant on full exposure. He also develops the LP idea that if the king is morally degraded, the love is vindicated; but he applies it to Mark, not Arthur. Tristan's love is even officially vindicated — in Arthur's court at least. Mark meets the fate which would have been Arthur's had not the later *Lancelot-Graal* rehabilitated him.

TP is intended to be read alongside LP; the post-Vulgate, on the other hand, may be held to replace it, and is not bound by LP *sen*. This applies particularly to Arthur's marriage, which loses much of its importance as the cause of the final tragedy, being replaced by the blood-feud theme; even Arthur's last war with Lancelot is seen in terms of family feud. It is not surprising, therefore, to find that the author devotes no subtlety to the Guinevere triangle, but falls back on the comfortable double standard whereby Arthur's adulteries are excusable, but Guinevere's damnable. The progress of the marital relationship is inconsistent. Arthur takes Guinevere in defiance of Merlin's warning. Defiance of Merlin always guarantees disaster, but at this stage the author is thinking of the Vulgate calamity, not that towards which he himself is working. Once Guinevere arrives, Arthur — surprisingly in view of his earlier determination — shows no interest in her; and yet shortly afterwards, in the Gué-la-Reine episode, he professes inseparable devotion to her. This is not to show the growth of love between the two; the author is thinking of the Vulgate reference which inspired that episode. The Vulgate says that Guinevere accompanied Arthur on this campaign, an unusual circumstance which demands explanation. The obvious explanation is that Arthur was devoted to her, but this confuses the *sen* of the author's own work. In the rest of the post-Vulgate he loses interest in the relationship, and when he does refer to it, he adapts the data to the episode in hand, being unconcerned to attain consistency in a secondary theme.

Differences among the prose romancers present a knotty problem to the eclectic Malory. If he did unify his materials, he succeeded in doing what no French author does, and gave a reasoned account of the Arthur-Guinevere relationship from beginning to end. Did he succeed? Edward Kennedy concludes from detailed source-study that Arthur in Malory passes from devotion to a final indifference which is politically laudable. To this end, Malory heightens Arthur's love in the first Tale, diminishing it thereafter until the Arthur of the last Tale appears much more unfeeling than his Vulgate counterpart.[32] I find it hard to accept this view. It is true that Arthur greets his bride with more enthusiasm in Malory than in the *Suite*. But the *Suite*, as we have seen, is inconsistent at this point, and Malory's alteration is surely made in the interest of improved consistency. At the other end of the development, Malory's Arthur is as concerned for Guinevere during the judicial duels as the Vulgate's is; and Malory invents a touching scene of the couple's relieved embrace. Arthur's stern maintenance of the law is not cruel in Malory. It is more impartial, less vindictive than in the source, and in any case Arthur's judicial pronouncements come from his kingly persona, not his human, suffering self. An independent reading of each text — as opposed to word-for-word comparison, which may induce critical myopia — gives much the same impression in both cases: that Arthur loves his wife but 'myght not be agyne the Ryght'.[33] The impression of indifference in Malory really hinges on the famous 'quenys I myght have enow . . .' remark. But we must remember that this is made at a moment of intense emotion; that the knights are dead, the queen merely missing; and that the maintenance of knights is Arthur's *raison d'être*. Moreover, other Arthurian males have the same order of priorities; Arthur is no sterner with his womenfolk than most.[34]

Malory's Arthur is faithful and loving throughout the book. He indulges in no extra-marital affairs — his momentary interest in Yseult[35] is not sexual, merely curious — and his fidelity to Guinevere is touchingly evoked in the Aunore episode, where it enables him to resist a magic stronger than Camille's or the False Guinevere's. He is an affectionate man who is torn by warring affections, but renounces none of them. Guinevere gives Arthur as much love as her passion for Lancelot will allow, and at the very last, her devotion to Arthur's memory outlives the passion. Her seemly burial beside Arthur's tomb sets the seal on the royal marriage. Malory's treatment of the relationship is handled more consistently than most of his inherited themes. It is also a fitting conclusion to the entire development. In it, Arthur may be kindly or indifferent, may be mocked or ennobled; but the central idea, the first, probably, to strike any Arthurian enthusiast, is that Arthur and Guinevere were a great king and queen who were driven by destiny into calamity, through no evil will in themselves. It is fitting that they should be reunited in death.

To verse romancers and chroniclers, Guinevere is the only woman in Arthur's world. In the prose romances — save *Perlesvaus* — he has other amours. These are not absolutely bound to shock. Authors must have been aware that most real kings kept mistresses or concubines as a matter of course. Arthur's affairs are a narrative resource of great potential significance.

Did Arthur have more than one wife? Fleeting Welsh evidences suggest that he did, referring puzzlingly to a double or triple Guinevere.[36] The significance of this can only be wildly surmised, and has no effect on the literary development — unless it inspires the False Guinevere story,[37] and in that it is made very clear that Arthur can have only one true wife. Only one other source suggests a second marriage. This is the Portuguese *Sagramor*,[38] which turns Arthur's liaison with Lisanor[39] into a marriage in order to legitimise its offspring, the hero of the romance. This liaison has nothing to do with the Welsh hints — it arrives at a similar conclusion by totally different, easily explicable means.

Though not widely promiscuous, Arthur is sometimes concupiscent. This appears first in the *Life of Cadog*, where Arthur is visited by a crude impulse to rape.[40] This is not paralleled in any early Welsh or continental Arthurian source, and it seems likely that the impulse to rape figured in the Cadog story before Arthur was incorporated. It is the prose cycles which determinedly turn Arthur into a philanderer, and they need no inspiration beyond their usual desire to downgrade the king.

Nowhere in the literature is Arthur an accomplished courtly lover. In the prose, he sticks to brief, well-spaced affairs, which he seems to consider pleasurable, therapeutic, and subject to no moral judgment. It is not, indeed, the immorality of the seductions which the authors hold up for our abhorrence, but their lack of refinement. Arthur in his affairs with Lisanor, Loth's wife, the girl in the *Livre d'Artus* and the mother of Artus le Petit[41] is about as subtle and considerate as a tank. It makes no odds whether the lady is willing, though in the first three cases she is. Arthur supremely lacks the elegant fidelity of Lancelot, the poetic delicacy of Tristan, the exalted melancholy of Palomides. He even lacks the light-heartedness of Gawain, who does at least take some care to please and flatter his partners. It is notable that his grossness in the prose romances is occasionally found also in the verse romances, applied to Guinevere.[42] There is a consensus that Arthur is no women's man.

Arthur does have genuine feeling for two mistresses: Camille and the False Guinevere. But this feeling is no saving grace. His subjection — particularly to the impostor — is the opposite of the 'obedience' of the courtly lover. The ennobling effect of true courtly love springs from the mistress, but it is the lover's responsibility to choose a worthy object for his love. If Arthur were 'courtly' disposed to the true Guinevere, the ennoblement would follow, for she is widely reputed to be a 'maintainer of good knights'. In some texts he may even have that ennoblement; but he gains none from his affairs.

Arthur's amours are, indeed, the least pleasant aspect of his personal relationships, contrasting sharply with the delicacy, warmth and devotion with which he treats his knights.[43] Though most authors applaud his knight-centredness, his treatment of women is one accusation which the hostile *prosateurs* are able to make stick.

The most lasting effect of Arthur's affairs is the offspring which they produce. All are sons. Lord Raglan calls it characteristic of the Hero that 'his children, if any, do not succeed him',[44] and this is true of Arthur everywhere save in *Sagramor* and the eccentric *Petit Bruit*;[45] but it is not true of every medieval hero. Alexander has no heir to succeed him, but Finn and Charlemagne have. The reasons for Arthur's lack of heirs are not mythic but literary. Probably Geoffrey, who makes Arthur childless, thinks of his reign as unique, ending in a void.

For post-HRB chroniclers, Arthur's death without issue is simply a matter of historical fact. In romance the matter is less simple. The Welsh supplied Arthur with sons — Anir, Gwydre and Llacheu —[46] before ever he gained a father or a crown. They did not, however, take any interest in the father-son relationship — which is in keeping with their general attitude to Arthur. Chrétien has exactly the same attitude in his two mentions of Arthur's son (*Erec* 1700, *Yvain* 663). He may have expected his readers to know, from Wace, that the child could not be Guinevere's; but the question does not much interest him. Neither Chrétien nor the Welsh consider any son as Arthur's possible heir, the latter because they did not consider Arthur biographically, the former because it would disturb the equilibrium. For Chrétien, the son certainly must not monopolise his father's affections, for this would detract from his status as 'father' to all the knights.

Lanzelet and *Perlesvaus* defy Wace by asserting that Loholt was Arthur's legitimate son.[47] *Perlesvaus'* treatment is, as usual, particularly interesting. The author bows to 'history' insofar as Loholt does not succeed Arthur; in fact, he turns this 'fact' to account in order to make of Loholt's death a scene of peculiar poignancy. By concentrating on this one scene, the author succeeds in making Loholt interesting without disturbing more familiar relationships. Loholt is also important in the narrative, by his death, which causes Guinevere's death, Kay's flight, and all their profound consequences, and also consummates the doomed Arthur's tragic loneliness by making him the last of his line. Within small compass, *Perlesvaus* gives deep significance to a normally shadowy and elusive figure.

Nowhere else is Loholt legitimate, and as a bastard it is generally accepted that he cannot be Arthur's heir. This fact dooms Loholt to obscurity, and he pursues a fleeting and eccentric course through the prose romances, untouched by the author's passion for expansion and codification. In LP and in the *Livre d'Artus*, as in *Perlesvaus*, he is notable chiefly through his death, and the former works do not equal *Perlesvaus'* moving account of it. In the *Livre d'Artus* he does briefly enjoy the status of acknowledged royal bastard, residing at court and commanding the affectionate esteem of his father, but this is the summit of his achievement. Once bastardy has disqualified him from the throne, there is no need for him to predecease Arthur; but no one bothers to keep him alive except Malory, in whose work he survives (under an altered name)[48] as a minor knight to the very last days. In *Sagramor* he even scores an odd and belated triumph, when Lisanor's son (the Vulgate Loholt) is conflated with Sagramor and, restored to legitimacy, ascends Arthur's throne, thereby outdoing even such a perennial favourite as Gawain. He achieves, in fact, a minor miracle of literary survival: in one way he is an Arthurian missed opportunity, but in another he is a permanent part of the Arthurian fabric.

In contrast, Artus le Petit exists only in the post-Vulgate, and is the deliberate creation of one author. He acquires importance through the degradation of Gawain, who loses his worthiness to monopolise Arthur's affections, and briefly comes closer to Arthur than any other son ever does. He also serves to counterbalance the evil Mordred, proving that Arthur's blood is not hereditarily tainted; and he is involved in the central tragedy of the blood-feud, which, indeed, culminates in his death.[49] His existence is a measure of the changes wrought by the post-Vulgate, in which alone a son of Arthur's can be more worthy than Gawain, more loyal than Lancelot.

106

Why do the romancers bother with these peripheral sons at all? Partly, perhaps, in deference to a vague tradition, partly to show that Arthur was capable of fatherhood. The bastards are not a reproach to Arthur; many other esteemed Arthurian kings, including Ban, Leodegan and Urien, have important bastards. The prose romancers consider Arthur's children important, but also find them rather hard to handle. The exception to this rule is Mordred, whose relationship with Arthur steadily gathers significance, while that with the other sons remains abortive. Not that any work describes a close personal relationship between the two, whether Mordred is considered as nephew or son — although any work in which Arthur makes Mordred regent must assume that he has good reason to trust him if Arthur is not to seem a complete fool. Nor does any work analyse fully the development of Mordred's evil character, for the anti-hero — with exceptions such as Raoul de Cambrai — was little to medieval taste. As in the case of Uther and Arthur, it is the fact of the blood-link, and its theological, philosophical and narrative significance, which preoccupies authors. Of course, Mordred's betrayal of Arthur has emotional impact even if he is only a nephew. That impact will be intensified, but not altered in kind, if Mordred is Arthur's son in any way other than by incest. We find such intensification in a few works, such as Boccaccio's *De casibus*, *Sagramor* and the Magdalen College chronicle,[50] which modestly suppresses the fact of the incest. In these works, Arthur's fall is not a punishment for fathering a bastard, which is no great crime in medieval story; the guilt is all on Mordred's side. Strikingly enough, the Vulgate *Mort*, which apparently invented the incest,[51] takes the same line, emphasising only the son's treachery. The incest is not used either to punish Arthur or to explain Mordred's wickedness. Nor is it invented, as Helen Adolf suggests, to stop Arthur becoming 'a national and political saint'.[52] No French prose author could consider Arthur any kind of a saint, while English chroniclers, in whom if anywhere lies the inclination to make him a 'saint', go on doing so undeterred by the incest-motif, which most ignore. No: the *Mort* author, like many another Arthurian contributor, has invented a theme the full implications of which he does not develop. Now, those implications are immense, for incest is universally abhorred, while unknowing incest, leading to horrid revelations and disaster, is widespread in mythology,[53] and, in general, the sin which comes home to roost is the neatest justification of God's ways to man. It is the post-Vulgate author who realises what a golden opportunity the incest gives to 'mythologise' Arthur's story; but even he, alas, fails to maintain the tragic intensity throughout his work. Indeed, almost all the significance is crammed into one dramatic conversation between Arthur and Mordred; but there it transcends the Arthurian legend itself, and, like all mythology, becomes the text of a discussion of the human condition.

By emphasising the incest, the *Suite* inverts the Vulgate *sen*, laying the initial guilt on Arthur. Now Arthur does not commit incest knowingly in either text: his is a material, not a formal sin, and is therefore not culpable in strict theology.[54] The Vulgate accepts this, but the *Suite* does not. There, the punishment for Arthur's sin springs from a deeper level than the Christian code, which offers forgiveness even for mortal sins. Arthur is judged by an ineluctable force which governs according to fundamentally moral, 'natural' principles.

The sin of incest is complicated by the intended sin of murdering the babies, which is discussed on a more narrowly theological basis. In all the great mainstream accounts, Arthur's tragedy is hedged around with 'if onlys', and this *Suite* conversation presents the most agonising one of all: if only Arthur, armed with foreknowledge, had slain Mordred at birth! Can it be right to do this small evil in order to save the realm? Merlin says not, invoking the doctrine of personal salvation: 'je voel mieus m'ame sauver que la terre'.[55] The author applies the same doctrine to Mordred. He does not assume that because Mordred is born of incest, he is necessarily wicked. Only Mordred himself can answer for his own character, and it is not permissible for anyone to end Mordred's life before he has sinned. This attitude is deeply significant to the whole post-Vulgate, which pivots on inherited blood-feud. Mordred's initial innocence proclaims that it is wrong to visit the sins of the fathers upon the children.

Arthur himself is willing to damn his soul in order to save the land. Pragmatically speaking, this is admirable, but it is theologically inadmissible, a spiritual suicide, rejection of God's supreme gift. The idea of balancing one life against many is meaningless in theological terms, for the value of each soul is absolute. Therefore, when Christ stops Arthur murdering the babies, he is saving Arthur's soul as well as their lives.

Notions of predestination further complicate the debate. If Arthur and Logres are destined to destruction by Mordred, then no striving of Arthur's can avert this in any case. The author here encounters an eternally insoluble problem. Can foreknowledge of the future enable us to alter it? Does destiny work under God, and does God intervene to change it? Such questions are the very stuff of myth. The myth here attached to Arthur is not intrinsic to him, or coeval with his Welsh origins. But it is ancient, and drags the thirteenth-century Arthur into depths which the Welsh Arthur, for all his surmised mythological origins, never plumbs. Its handling reveals in the *Suite* author a theologian (with perhaps a touch of Pelagianism!), a philosopher, and a writer of great power. He does not preach, as the *Queste* author does, but he involves the reader in a debate of timeless fascination.

However, in this supreme achievement the post-Vulgate author overreaches himself. Knowing and feeling what he does about Mordred, it is inconceivable that Arthur should welcome Mordred at his court, let alone entrust to him all he possesses. But 'history' and literary tradition demand that Arthur should do just that. This inhibits the *Suite* author from following through his own invention, and makes a mockery of a vital link in his tragedy.

Mordred's relationship to Arthur is, then, a theme of great power, which, although not fully realised by the authors, remains seminal to the legend and does much to shape it. It is the major development in the legend of the father-son relationship; but that relationship is nowhere central to Arthur's fate and character. It is always subordinated to his 'fatherhood' of his lineage, his knights and his kingdom.[56] In this matter, Arthur's public and kingly persona is, paradoxically, more 'human' than his private one. That is the profound consequence of the author's obsession with knights.

One character pinpoints this tension between Arthur's private and public personae: Gawain, who receives in full measure both the intense family affection denied to Arthur's sons and the fatherly love which Arthur gives to his knights. We have therefore placed the beloved nephew at the end of the family group in order that he may provide a transition to the wider world of subjects; he is indeed, in the eyes of many, Arthur's chief subject.

Arthur's adoration of Gawain falters but once in all the romance literature,[57] though Lancelot competes in later works for first place in Arthur's affections. Once again we have to thank Chrétien for establishing this Arthurian law, for the Welsh Gwalchmai, and even Geoffrey's Gawain, though important knights, have not the supreme place in Arthur's love. It is Chrétien, abetted by the later verse-romancers, who evolves the commonplace, much-repeated type-situations which exhibit Arthur's devotion: his concern for Gawain's danger, his persecution of the doctors when Gawain is wounded, his reliance on Gawain's counsel good or bad. Moreover, it is Chrétien who initiates the technique, of universal romance application, of using Gawain as a yardstick for Arthur's own credibility. At first, in *Erec*, *Cligès* or *Yvain*, Gawain's excellence justly evokes Arthur's love. Later, in *Lancelot* and *Perceval*, Gawain's character begins to deteriorate, and Arthur's love to seem myopic and prejudiced.

In post-Chrétien works, Arthur's love can seem foolish even when Gawain's knightly status is high, because Gawain often exploits the love quite ruthlessly in order to gain his own ends[58] — a procedure borrowed, perhaps, from Kay in Chrétien's *Lancelot*. An alternative criticism appears in the English *Dame Ragnell*, where Gawain is magnanimous but Arthur's crawling reliance on him is highly distasteful;[59] another alternative view is that of the Scots, for whom Gawain's loyalty to Arthur is a crime, not a virtue. The common thread in all these treatments is the subordination of king to knight. It is Gawain who, throughout the literature, expresses most effectively the baronial dream of control,[60] by using emotional pressure rather than political power.

In works which pursue Chrétien's late suggestions of a deterioration in Gawain's character, the *sen* of Arthur's love is changed. This is strikingly exhibited in the *Queste*, where Arthur's indictable reluctance to let the questers depart into new, spiritual realms is directed most of all at Gawain (p.21), and where the hermit's savage denunciation of Gawain's worldliness must reflect back on Arthur, who can see no flaw in him.

The *Mort* gives yet another twist to the relationship. There, Arthur does defy Gawain's will — when Gawain, acting the part of Dinas,[61] opposes Guinevere's condemnation. Ironically, obedience to Gawain here would avert the final tragedy, whereas Arthur's return to obedience later in the work produces a string of disasters. The *Mort*, in fact, uses the theme of Arthur's subjection sympathetically, as an element in a profoundly human tragedy, and so uses his talents to rejuvenate an old, and sour, *matière*. In the post-Vulgate and TP, however, a more profound change occurs. No longer does the author hymn, through the now unworthy Gawain, the superiority of knight to king; that theme is transferred to Lancelot. Instead, he laments the destructiveness of clan feeling. Both authors, like their successor, Malory, sympathise with Arthur's dilemma as his kingly person is brought into conflict with his private one and his love for Gawain runs counter to his love for knights, which it normally epitomises. Arthur recognises and is bound by the vengeance ethic which Gawain so murderously professes, and in the last instance source-respect forbids him to execute his beloved nephew — though at one point he goes as far as wishing that someone else would. At the same time it is brutally clear that Gawain's survival damages the security of the realm, and it contributes to the final collapse, so that Arthur's avuncular indulgence is — as in the Vulgate, but in a different way — largely to blame for his own downfall. His own noblest attributes, of love and truthfulness, betray him here in relation to Gawain, as they do elsewhere in relation to Mordred, Guinevere and Lancelot: these betrayals are perhaps the essence of Arthur's tragedy.

Arthur's love for Gawain is one of the greatest constants of Arthurian literature, but one work, the *De Ortu Walwanii*, appears to defy it, making Arthur exhibit an apparently gratuitous hostility towards Gawain. However, on closer examination the work proves not to be as exceptional as it seems. The hostility has been interpreted in psychological terms of rivalry between the father and the son over the mother.[62] I consider it unlikely that there ever was an 'original' tale of Arthur and Gawain in which this hostility was clear. In all our material, Gawain is Arthur's nephew, not his son, and there are absolutely no sexual overtones in the dutiful affection which Gawain pays to his aunt. The hostility-over-the-mother theme does exist in Arthur's legend, but it centres on Mordred, who does eventually become Arthur's (though never Guinevere's) son. If there is a psychological background to the *De Ortu* story, it is more likely to approximate to the 'atonement with the father' motif.[63] Now, the atonement motif — which is exceedingly widespread — requires that the son be severely tested before admission to the father's household. Every new knight undergoes such atonement through his first adventure. Arthur's kindliness to such knights is doubtless a courtly veneer over the essential motif, the father's roughness being transferred to Kay. The *De Ortu* restores something like the essential form. The myth is one of initiation, not of rivalry, and Gawain is chosen to act it out because he is well-known and normally close to Arthur, just as the famous Arthur is chosen in preference to Gawain's real father, Loth. Gawain stands for all Arthur's 'sons' — his knights. At the end he is firmly established in his usual position at the centre of Arthur's affections, and atonement is achieved.

Another point about Gawain deserves consideration. Often, he wields more power in the realm than Arthur.[64] But he does not seek kingship, remaining always the most knight-like of knights. His rejection of kingship, which is more emphatic even that Bohors', is curtly expressed in the English *Turke and Gowin*:

> For I never purposed to be noe king,
> never in all my livinge.   (ll.326-7)[65]

He is the king's eldest son, but even in texts like LP and the *Suite* which eliminate Loth many years before Gawain's death, there is no suggestion that he should take the Orkney crown. He is as bound to knighthood as Arthur to kingship. Tradition overcomes all impulses towards political realism. But there exists a lurking idea that Gawain ought to be *Arthur's* heir. The prominence of Gawain's position suggests it, especially where Arthur is childless. It is strong when, in *Rigomer*, Arthur makes Gawain regent, and overt when, in the False Guinevere episode, Gawain is chosen king by the barons. Arthur himself suggests it in extravagant self-abasement in the *Livre d'Artus* quarrel, and pronounces it most definitely in the alliterative *Morte*.[66] But Arthur never formally names Gawain his heir. He cares about the succession only in the chronicle tradition, and there the claim of Constantine – made only at the last minute – goes unchallenged. The universal belief that Gawain predeceased Arthur seems to work retrospectively to inhibit his acceptance as heir. The tentative elevations of Gawain to king express, rather, his indispensability to Arthur's kingship. But if the two roles are symbiotic, they are not interchangeable. Together they make the aggregate of effective kingship – as Arthur and Merlin do in VM. Moreover, Gawain by escaping heirship expresses every knight's desire for power without responsibility, adulation without restriction. He 'reigns' in the court as the archetypal knight.

Gawain completes the tale of Arthur's significant family relationships. We now pass to consideration of his subjects en masse; usually, though not always, this means his knights. Then we shall look at three important individuals: Kay, Merlin and Lancelot. Of course, others, such as Daguenet, Loth, Galehaut, Ban and Bohors, are of interest at various times; but they do not span enough works to contribute to a broad perspective.

> Com est riches de bial tresor
> qui bons chevaliers a o lui!
> . . . car rois ne puet onor avoir
> se de chevaliers ne liu vient.   (*Durmart* 8158-9, 8164-5)

Arthur's remark in *Durmart* encapsulates the attitude of almost every writer from the time when he first gathers two or three together in his name.[67] At first sight it is complimentary to Arthur. Geoffrey certainly considers it to be so: in *HRB* the knights are attracted by Arthur's personal excellence and the fame which he has won through the strength of his arm. But inseparable from it is the corollary that Arthur cannot survive without his suite; he is like a man who leans against a wall at such an angle that if the wall crumbles, he cannot stand alone. This view is emphasised more and more in the romances (in the chronicles Arthur retains control) until it seems that the knights can get along perfectly well without Arthur, but not *vice versa*. Geoffrey admiringly asserts that many who came to Arthur were foreigners, under no compulsion to serve him. This idea is all too easily turned against Arthur. It encourages the concept that all his knights are knights-errant, feudally bound to no lord and always ready to sell their swords to the highest bidder, whether he bid in excellence or in cash. We never see Arthur's knights as feudal barons, tied to him by the holding of lands which they fear to lose.[68] If he does grant lands to a knight (as Yder, Erec, Galeron, Gareth), that knight either vanishes from the story or reappears after gaily shedding his responsibilities. Arthur can keep them all only by personal charisma, or, when that fails, by cash payments. 'Tantum habes, tantum vales tantumque te diligo'!

It is a commonplace of medieval thought that gold — 'largesse'[70] — can buy loyalty which is sincere and lasting. This belief is woven into Arthur's legend and is sometimes openly put, as by the *preudom* of LP or by Merlin in the VM: 'vous ne poés avoir en nule maniere si bon los ne le cuer de vos gens comme par douner' (II. 111). The paradox works well for Arthur vis-à-vis the lower echelons of society — of which both the *preudom* and Merlin are thinking — but these people usually do not count in the Arthurian world. With the knights, who do count, the paradox does not work. Simple, personal loyalty which endures through misfortune and injustice unto death is not found in the Arthurian knight — with a few exceptions, such as Kay and Daguenet in the *Prophécies* — and both of these are generally considered to be fools. What loyalties the knights have work horizontally, not vertically. They may show devotion to the ideal of knighthood as exemplified in one another; they may have affection for one another; or they may align themselves with their own *lineage*. Lancelot sums up this horizontal feeling when he sets out for Arthur's court because 'l'en dist que tout li preudom sont en la maison le roi Artu' (III. 112). Arthur no longer has anything to do with the excellence of his court, which has become self-perpetuating.

Arthur is never allowed to resent the shallowness of his knights' feelings. Arthur's own attitude involves a reversal of the normal 'largesse' theory. According to this, calculated generosity in the donor should produce genuine affection in the recipient. But Arthur's generosity is backed by genuine feeling; it is the knights who are calculating. In the verse romances Arthur is a father-figure, kindly, reassuring, unchanging, protective, a refuge against the terrors of the outside, adolescent world. In the prose this feeling finds words: '. . . Il amoit tant tuz les compagnons de la table roonde cum se il les avoit tuz engendrés de sa char', says the author of the *Agravain* (V. 335), while in the *Queste*, presaging the dissolution of the fellowship, the idea is put more movingly: 'je les ai escreuz et alevez de tout mon pooir et les ai toz jors amez et encore les aim aussi com s'il fussent mi fil ou mi frere' (p.17). The post-Vulgate echoes the sentiment. Obviously this approach, too, soothes the baronial ego. Yet there is evidence that the prose romances, at least, were popular with royalty.[71] This is where Arthur's complex participation in 'chevalerie', discussed above,[72] comes into play. This allows the king, by a fresh paradox, to share in the very attitudes which his kingship makes possible for others.

Arthur's willing self-abasement has another corollary, unintended by the authors. It humanises him, giving him an affectionate, large-hearted, forgiving nature. If he is despised and rejected, is there not the noblest of precedents for such suffering? Authors do not deliberately present the forbearing Arthur as 'alter Christus', any more than they compare Mordred with Judas. But the lurking analogy comes readily to the mind of an unprejudiced reader. His knights — or knights in general — may not have found him lovable, but much of the original literary public probably did. The analogy may do something to explain the romances' continuing popularity.

Arthur nevertheless has resources to resist authorial and knightly spite; the entire structure would collapse if he did not.[73] Prominent among them is —

most surprisingly — the king's council. In theory, of course, the feudal baronial council ruled the king: 'debet rex omnia rite facere et per judicium procerum suorum'.[74] In practice, a king could often manage to circumvent or dominate his council; but we should not expect the romance Arthur to achieve this. Now the chronicle Arthur, created by Geoffrey, takes a Norman or Angevin king's pragmatic view of his council. He summons it when he feels inclined, or when he is fairly sure that its decision will accord with his desires, but on many occasions — most importantly, over Mordred's appointment as regent (HRB 468) — he acts independently. This portrayal of a virtually absolute monarch was kept alive by innumerable chroniclers, including the influential Wace, and was thus always available to romancers. Its influence seems to be discernible in the verse romances, whose authors may have been baronially idealistic while describing the king-knight relationship, but were often (perhaps unconsciously) realistic about practical politics. Chrétien's Arthur, like Geoffrey's, summons the council only when he wishes, often acts independently, and is never forced into a decision against his will. Even in *Cligès*, his obedience in the matter of Angrés' regency allows him to use the council as a scapegoat when Angrés proves false (l. 1064, 1066-7), and so preserves his own self-respect. Arthur serves his knights, certainly, but in his own way and of his own free will.

Chrétien's verse-romance successors show no progressive increase of interest or evolution of attitude as regards councils. Even though the barons frequently convene at court, especially on the great feast-days on which *magna concilia* were held in real life, they devote themselves to pleasure and to the hope of adventure, not to running the realm, while lesser *concilia* are convened only spasmodically. If Arthur accepts advice at all, it is usually from Gawain, who — like many a Norman or Capetian king's adviser[75] — holds no particular office, gives his advice informally and relies on the king's personal affection to maintain his position. Arthur's very deference to him is thus, in a way, a defiance of the notion of baronial control, making another Arthurian paradox.

The prose romancers are, in general, more acutely aware than the verse romancers of the importance of councils. This is particularly true of *Perlesvaus*, which, though still not binding Arthur by hard-and-fast rules, takes grave account of his duty of consultation. The *consilium* over Claudas, for instance, is more of a debate than any in the verse-romances, though its members still cannot dictate to the king. Later, Arthur's reliance on the evil counsellor[76] Brien causes councils to fall into desuetude, which is a criticism of both king and barons. A king may impose his will, but if he does not govern by consent of at least the majority of the barons he makes his own task impossible, while the barons have a duty to advise the king even when their advice is patently unwelcome. *Perlesvaus*, in fact, has a *thèse*: it acknowledges the king's freedom of action, but warns against its misuse.

The later prose romances are less critical. In them, Arthur retains his freedom of action, the council-bound Arthur of the Didot *Perceval* being quite exceptional.[77] Even the *Lancelot-Graal* prefers to criticise Arthur's independent decisions, and reliance on councils is conspicuously absent from the *preudom*'s recommendations despite his insistence on vassalic indispensability. Even in the

False Guinevere episode, with its entanglements of king's will, baronial resistance and legal obligation, Arthur imposes his own will even while professing meekness ('nus se doit si grant afere mener a chief sans le conseil de ses barons,' Micha I. 119) — just as real-life kings often did. The *Mort*, too, demonstrates the re-emergent dictum of 'quod principi placuit . . .'; in fact, the work is to a large extent the tragedy of a man who will not bow to counsel.[78]

In VM and the *Suite*, Arthur has an informal council, but it is not this but Merlin who rules — for Merlin, exactly like Arthur elsewhere, asks for advice and then does as he likes, and also reserves the right to overturn conciliar decisions. When Merlin disappears, Arthur steps into his shoes and wields the same power. We see him doing it in the *Livre d'Artus*, which makes it specifically clear that it is a virtue, not a necessity, for a king to consult his council. Only in the *Prophécies*, written in the late 1270s, is Arthur truly subjected to his council. Here, at last, the baronial power-dream is Arthurianised, at a time when in reality it was passing away for ever. Such is the irony of Arthurian 'realism'. Even in the late Middle-English, where mention of Parliament creeps into Arthuriana, it has no more control over the king than the baronial *consilia* — doubtless because in the romance world, with its chronic superabundance of resources, Arthur has no need to ask Parliament for money. In this matter we find that the 'secondary world' combines a limited realism with an essential autonomy and conservatism, a mixture which works to Arthur's advantage.

Why, if Arthur is so little trammelled by councils, does the knights' influence over him often strike one so forcibly? It is because the king and knights rule in different areas. The knights do not desire power with responsibility, but freedom, riches and flattery. Given those, they leave both the day-to-day government and the vital decisions to the king — like the aristocracy of Versailles. It is thus that Arthur can exist simultaneously in independence and in subjection.

Seldom if ever do Arthur's lowlier subjects meet him face to face. Those few authors who consider the matter generally agree that he treats them well, however. Wace benevolently considers the benefits which Arthur, who 'de povres homes ert amez', brings even to the lowliest villein. Layamon's far less affable monarch wins, like Richard I, the distant admiration of his people — to the improvement of his image. VM, the *Suite* and the early LP consider the 'menu pueple' worth cultivating, both in fulfilment of Arthur's coronation oath and because they have political weight: 'car li regnes ne puet estre maintenus se li communs des gens ne s'i acorde'. This recognition contrasts with the solid indifference of the verse romancers, and apparently acknowledges — albeit perfunctorily — the success of contemporary kings in allying themselves with the lower orders.[79] In the Vulgate *Mort*, the people's wrath at Guinevere's condemnation is a *calque* on Beroul's *Tristan*.[80] Their true opinion of Arthur emerges in a later remark: 'C'estoit li princes del monde qui plus estoit amez, car il leur avoit esté touz jours douz et deboneres' (p.172). The people remain loyal to Arthur when the barons, venal as ever,[81] defect to Mordred. The stanzaic *Mort* and Malory deny this and join the commons with the barons in infidelity to Arthur; but this change is surely made with an eye to contemporary English realities. In any case there remains the fundamental premiss that Arthur treats the commons well: it is, indeed, emotionally strengthened. It is overtly contradicted only once (apart from by the LP *preudom*), in the alliterative *Morte*, and even there, Arthur's 'tormenting' of the people is clearly an unnatural reversal of his habitual attitude, which is that nobly expressed through the giant-fight.

One may doubt whether Arthur, given the chronic chaos of his realm, really deserves his people's love. Authors engage in comfortable doublethink when they assure us that Arthur can content knights and people simultaneously: a doublethink which, for once, acts consistently to Arthur's credit.

In conclusion, we will examine Arthur's three most important extra-familial relationships.

Kay's association with Arthur is longer than any other. Its earlier stages are well-documented,[82] and I shall say little of them. Kay in the French verse romances stands in the same relation to Arthur as does the Gawain of TP and the post-Vulgate: a degenerate character for whom Arthur professes an undeserved affection, and whom the other knights tolerate for Arthur's sake. In *Yder* and *Perlesvaus* Kay — like Gawain in the post-Vulgate *Quest* — passes from unworthiness to criminality. *Perlesvaus*, iconoclastic as ever, allows this criminality to produce an irreversible breach between Kay and Arthur. *Yder* submits to the verse-romance equilibrium, allowing Kay to escape just retribution, as the later Gawain does, by appeal to Arthur. In the case of both Kay and Gawain, an originally deserved affection becomes an indictment of Arthur as the favourite deteriorates.

Doubtless because of the deterioration of Gawain from LP onwards, the same writers have a tendency to rehabilitate Kay. This operates on two fronts. In the verse (save in the Vulgate-influenced *Durmart*) there is no justification of Arthur's indulgence to Kay to replace the family affection of Gawain's case. Boron explains it, combining a virtual family connection with a chronic guilt-feeling on Arthur's part. Moreover, the explanation means that Kay — unlike Gawain — is not responsible for his own unpleasantness. Other works compound this by denying that Kay was excessively wicked or ineffectual: thus the First Continuation, LP, VM and the *Livre d'Artus*, though the latter is uneasy about Loholt's murder. In TP and the post-Vulgate, even Kay's role as buffoon is partly transferred to Daguenet. In the *Prophécies* Kay briefly becomes Arthur's sole defender. By then Kay and Gawain, the traditional opposites, have all but changed places. To sum up, Kay is never closely woven into Arthur's fate. His role is rather representational than active. He is indispensable to Arthur's world, and the partial evolution of his character is an indicator of the authors' view of that world and its inhabitants.

Merlin is scarcely a subject of Arthur's: rather the reverse, as Merlin claims in the *Baladro*: 'Yo hera senor de la Gran Bretana e de la Pequeña, e del rey Artur e de su fazienda toda, e quanta honrra me fazian todas las gentes, e creian quanto yo dezia, e guiavanse por consejo mio' (III. 71). The relationship, which is everywhere consistent, has three strands. Merlin combines the brusquely hectoring attitude of a king-maker to his puppet, the father's protective affection, and the firm governance of a teacher. To all three Arthur responds with meekness, affection, gratitude and obedience.

Boron's Merlin exults in his power, though he wields it selflessly for Arthur's benefit. Unavoidably, it appears that he 'unkings' Arthur. But there are mitigating factors. Merlin is as brusque to Uther and Pendragon – grown men both – as to the young Arthur. Neither escapes his tutelage till death, and they are as meek as Arthur. Merlin is more of a father to Arthur than are Uther or Antor; and obedience to one's father is a primary dictate of Christian morality. Merlin as teacher is to Arthur what Aristotle is to Alexander: a philosopher such as – according to at least one thirteenth-century theorist[83] – every prince should have to direct his education.

Above all, Merlin has God-given infallibility: therefore Arthur's deference to him is no foolish weakness but a most religious wisdom. He is a Good Counsellor, and might remind readers of Suger or the Archbishop of Canterbury.[84] And Arthur's very meekness is attractive: it brings out the humility and willingness to accept a rebuke which in many works appear to be typical of him.

A father and teacher must encourage his protégé to stand on his own feet. There is relatively little sign of Merlin's doing so. We may almost believe Malory's: 'for the most party dayes of hys lyff he (Arthur) was ruled by the counceille of Merlyon' (II. 97). However, Merlin's benevolent infallibility cannot be reconciled with Arthur's inevitable end. Even during the period of tutelage, Merlin has to be removed whenever Arthur takes a step towards his doom: during the incest, for example, or when Arthur resolves to marry in the *Suite*. In fact, Merlin's omnipotence is exercised selectively to keep Arthur on his predestined course. But the nearer one comes to the dénouement, the harder it is to imagine him standing aside – while Arthur entrusted the kingdom to Mordred, for instance. Therefore he must be removed at a fairly early stage. The removal can be given a powerful *sen* of its own, so that it appears to spring naturally from the intrigue:[85] thus is a virtue made of necessity. Merlin has his own destiny, and, like Morgain, can exist independently of Arthur's story. Nevertheless, and despite his final powerlessness to save Arthur, his disinterested benevolence contrasts with the attitude of most of the king's entourage. As well as shaping Arthur's destiny, he is important simply because he mitigates Arthur's terrible loneliness.

In the Vulgate and post-Vulgate cycles, Lancelot succeeds Merlin as the lynch-pin of Arthurian organisation. His role, however, is dual, since from his first appearances he is also marked as an eventual agent of Arthur's destruction. The verse romancers, realising this, avoid him, but the prose romancers delight in making Lancelot both more indispensable and more lethal. *Perlesvaus* is once again the exception; by removing Guinevere it is able to present a Lancelot utterly devoted to Arthur's interests, the William Marshal of the Arthurian world.[86] The contemporary and influential LP, however, vigorously presses the contrary, negative view, and so launches an irreversible trend.

Lancelot's relationship with Arthur is exceedingly complex throughout the *Lancelot-Graal*. Chrétien had assumed him to be a fellow-countryman and vassal of Arthur. Neither applies in Part One of LP. That Lancelot is *not* Arthur's vassal is Arthur's fault, because of his failure to avenge Lancelot's father, Ban. The result is that Lancelot has no legal or moral obligation to Arthur, and indeed has a moral stranglehold over him. This is, however, countered by his admiring acknowledgement of Arthur's glory. Both attitudes are then overlaid by the complexities of Lancelot's love for Guinevere.

The author, not desiring to rouse any sympathy for the wronged husband, insists throughout on Arthur's obligation to Lancelot, and his vindication of the latter reaches a climax in the False Guinevere episode, where Lancelot is even able – with much justification – to express open threats and hatred for the king. Lancelot's uneasy relationship with Arthur contrasts with his beautiful, though ultimately tragic, friendship with Galehaut. Both kings are seen to depend utterly on Lancelot[87] – Arthur politically, Galehaut emotionally – but only Galehaut really wins his love. Arthur gains no more than respect, and an admiration which by the end of Part One has largely evaporated.

Lancelot's relationship with Arthur remains cool, but courteous, throughout the later LP. The two (as in Chrétien) are seldom together, for Lancelot, quintessentially adventurous, is seldom at court. In the *Mort*, however, the relationship is tightened, ennobled, and enriched, becoming a moving study in reciprocal friendship doomed to destruction through human failings. At the same time, however, the *Mort* makes an alteration which has serious implications for Arthur in the later literature. Lancelot is not only politically essential in himself; he also leads a clan which is loyal to him, not Arthur,[88] so that the submission of most of the best knights to Arthur depends on Lancelot's personal loyalty. Thus Lancelot has a stranglehold on Logres, and the essential political tragedy of the *Mort* is not the breaking of the Round Table fellowship (as the stanzaic *Mort* and Malory believe), but the secession of the French Lancelot faction.

The post-Vulgate and TP are fascinated by this development in the *Mort*, and emphasise Lancelot's power to the point of obsessiveness. More and more, and more consciously, Arthur is politically and emotionally compelled to sacrifice all other considerations to the appeasement of the Ban faction. Evidences of this abound in both works, even to the point where people flock to Arthur's court not to see him, but to see Lancelot – a sad falling-off from the glories of HRB. The degeneration of Arthur's family further underlines the superiority of Lancelot's faction, until we actually discover Arthur planning to bequeath his kingdom to a Ban, in defiance of even the most basic family loyalty. Worst of all, the two *lineages* abhor one another, and Arthur, inescapably bound to both, is unable through the force of his own personality to prevent the fatal outbreak of this hostility in the final wars – whose *sen* is thus transformed. Only Lancelot's retirement to a monastery prevents him from becoming king of Logres, thus consummating his centrality to French Arthurian romance.

So powerful, indeed, has Lancelot's literary position now become that no later work even tries to topple him. Even the English authors, despite their continued affection for the more truly British figure of Gawain, unanimously accept Lancelot as the flower of chivalry. The English authors, however, avoid the slur on their national figure implied by the Ban and False Guinevere episodes or the post-Vulgate factionalising. Malory, most notably, reads back the noble friendship of the Vulgate *Mort* into the body of his work. What he loses thereby in complexity and excitement, he compensates for by his expression of human nature aspiring towards the highest ideals.

Throughout the literature, it is Arthur's fate to be betrayed or abandoned by those he loves. Every one of the relationships we have examined turns at some time to evil or sorrow. Those who have to do with royalty forever cry: 'Put not thy trust in Princes!' Arthur's career illustrates the opposite: let not princes put their trust in subjects! But there is a more universal message. Arthur relies too much on human support. He has no independent spiritual strength, and does not trust in God. It would be fitting if he, as well as Lancelot, were to end his days in a monastery, learning to draw strength from a source surer than the frail human beings who surrounded him in life.

VII

PERSONAL ATTRIBUTES

The 'biographer' of Arthur, unlike an ordinary biographer, does not have the comforting assurance that behind the sources, however scanty or misleading they may be, dwells a real person. There may be as many Arthurs as there are authors to write about him. However, the writers themselves *were* convinced that they were handling a genuine historical character. They respected their sources, and, while not shirking alteration, did not deliberately reject the 'truth'. If a large part of the resulting character *was* invented, is this not true also of many modern biographies?

It is therefore not wholly vain to seek for a basically consistent character of Arthur. Not all consistent traits will be moral: outward trappings like possessions may contribute largely to the portrayal. We go, then, in search not of the 'real' Arthur but of the 'essential' Arthur, the common property and creation of all the medieval authors.

The 'novelistic' analysis and development of character was little practised in the Middle Ages. Arthur exemplifies this, especially as it is hard to discern the man through the parade of typical regal virtues and vices. Nowhere is there a portrait of Arthur to match that of Claudas in LP. The strings of clichés, such as 'dous et deboneres', 'preus et courtois', express judgment on his character but do the opposite of individualising it. He does have a 'true' character, but it is built up from scattered hints and comments: 'Arthur wes wunsum þer he hafde his iwillen' (Layamon 1.11235); 'nus ne savoit si bien atraire gent a sa volenté comme il savoit' (Micha III. 111). Sometimes the 'real' man seems to emerge in spite of the author; it is then that he is most convincing.

Arthur emerges most often through relationships. As we have seen, authors mould him ruthlessly to fit the status of the current protagonist; nevertheless consistent traits emerge. He is affectionate, open-hearted, trusting, considerate and generous. When he does treat people harshly — the true Guinevere, Yder, the young Gawain, the Cote Maltaille — this strikes an experienced reader as exceptional. Either the author has an axe to grind, or he is trying to refresh an outworn motif. On the negative side, Arthur tends to be over-emotional and malleable, and to have favourites, some unworthy. The net result is a humanly attractive figure who normally retains sympathy. On the kingly level he is sometimes weak; but in medieval eyes a generous, trusting king was preferable

119

to a cold-hearted, suspicious tyrant. It is not surprising that the age of Machiavelli had no brief for Arthur, who even in Layamon distinctly lacks self-interested calculation.

A corollary of Arthur's affectionateness is forgivingness. Only in Layamon and the Huail story is he cruel or vindictive — and neither attained widespread circulation. He may thirst for some opponents' blood — Angrés, the *Suite* Morgain, Mordred — but in such cases justice, and outraged affection, are on his side. When he hates, he hates in hot blood, but more deeply 'characteristic' is the recurring scene of Arthur pardoning a defeated enemy and seating him at the Table. Vindictiveness is not one of his borrowings from the medieval Alexander.[1]

A further feature of Arthur's relationships is consistency, for he repeatedly expresses refusal to go back on his pledged word.[2] This normally laudable kingly characteristic can turn to ill, as in *Erec* or, more tragically, in the Vulgate *Mort*. It is not invariable: the LP *preudom* (II. 217), the *Suite* barons and the Scottish chroniclers accuse Arthur of faithbreaking. The accusations are justified in context, but are definitely exceptional. Like most trusting people, Arthur is trustworthy.

We may now pass to consideration of Arthur's 'moral' character. Medieval characterisation often involves moral, as against kingly, knightly or courtly norms; their nuancing helps to build up individuality. In Arthur's case, the moral dimension is particularly important. As the Grail theme increases its importance in the Arthurian mainstream, there is a growing tendency to judge the characters on a spiritual and religious, as well as a chivalrous, plane. Those who fail on this plane are debarred from realising their highest human potentialities; and on this plane the great king may fail utterly.

For convenience's sake I shall group my preliminary moral discussion around the Seven Deadly Sins — a system of character analysis well known and subtly used in the Middle Ages.[3] Let us see how much of a general picture emerges.

We may be quick to accuse Arthur of Lust and Pride. Lust, however, is confined to a few areas. The lustful Arthur of the *Life of Cadog*[4] is exposed for a saintly rebuke — which by a twist of narrative is administered by a layman. In LP, Arthur lusts for Camille; but although he is accused of lust also vis-à-vis the False Guinevere, the confusion of wives is scarcely his fault. The salacious *Livre d'Artus*[5] appears to consider lust indispensable to a knight-errant. In the Boron *Merlin* his incest with Loth's wife is totally damnable — but for its incestuousness, not its lust. The affair with Lisanor, which Merlin sanctions, can pass for the natural indulgence of a wifeless youth. In verse romances, the English, the Vulgate *Mort*, the chronicles, Arthur is a faithful husband. He never becomes an exemplum of lust. He cannot attain the rigid austerity of the Quest, or the adulterous fidelity of Lancelot or (usually) Tristan; but, then, he is never expected to. As for the 'daughter' sins of lust — blindness of mind, hardness of heart, inconstancy, cruelty — they are on the whole uncharacteristic of Arthur. Lust occasionally tempts, but does not govern him.

Pride is the defect of a kingly virtue, and all princes are prone to it. In Arthur it exists only in the chronicle and Middle English texts which present him as a conqueror, and even there is not always condemned. Geoffrey's and Layamon's Arthurs are splendid in their pride, and it is not blamed for their downfall; indeed, where pride is blamed, the blame comes in a package with the figure of Fortune,[6] and Arthur is unnaturally forced into a commonplace mould dear to the classifying mind of the late medieval moralist. Never is Arthur's pride nourished on the lies of flatterers, for like Alexander's it is based on solid success. It is never closely analysed, either in relation to Arthur's spiritual health or as an exemplum, save briefly in the alliterative *Morte*. LP analyses the sin of pride — but in relation to its new hero, the great conqueror Galehaut, not to Arthur.

The romance Arthur, indeed, more often evinces a becoming humility, which is none the less genuine for being forced on him by literary circumstances. It mitigates to some extent the humiliation of Arthur's dominance by his knights, for Arthur, being free from jealous resentment, almost invariably accepts his knights' triumphs as his own. It is they, indeed, who are more likely to suffer from vainglory.

'Daughters' of pride are presumption, hypocrisy, obstinacy, quarrelsomeness and disobedience. All, save perhaps obstinacy, are uncharacteristic of Arthur — and obstinacy may be an intensification of the virtue of consistency. In fact, Pride never roots deeply enough in Arthur to shape his whole character.

Closely allied to Pride is Covetousness. Again it is only as conqueror that Arthur exhibits it. He is never greedy of money or goods — quite the reverse. The only exceptions to this are the *Lives* of Cadog, Carannog and Padern,[7] and they are alien to the mainstream even in Wales. As for covetousness of land, there is a direct accusation only in *Auntyrs*. The connection with pride is strong: *Auntyrs* sees it as the root of all evil. The alliterative *Morte*, which probably inspired *Auntyrs*,[8] implies condemnation of Arthur's covetousness, as do texts like *Sagramor* (p.6), which castigate a greed for others' lands that involves neglect of one's own. We may conclude that Arthur's conquering career exposes him to the charge of covetousness, but that only a few morally-minded writers press it. Others expressly defend him, such as the author of *Golagros*,[9] and, even more notably, that of *Palamède*, in which Arthur indignantly rejects the idea of attacking Pharamond: '. . . et il fust . . . assiés plus miens hanemis qu'il n'est, ge lui donroie avant de ma terre que ge ne li taudroie de la soie' (Lathuillière p.194). This voluntary restraint is a relief from the normal prose-romance scepticism about Arthur's conquering abilities.

Arthur may, perhaps, suffer from the 'daughter' sins of covetousness, 'fear of loss' and 'worldly sorrow'. These are marks of an excessive preoccupation with earthly, unspiritual concerns, and point us forward to our consideration of Arthur's theological limitations.

Envy is totally uncharacteristic, and not the most hostile or moral author insinuates otherwise. When he is supreme in his world, he has none to envy. When he is not, he either takes prompt steps to make himself so, or generously recognises the other's superiority.

Sloth will strike some as very characteristic of Arthur. But, as we have sought to show, sloth does not equal *fainéantise*. It is when Arthur also neglects his *fainéant* duty of maintaining courtly *joie* that he can be accused of sloth. This occurs memorably in the first branch of *Perlesvaus*, but there the *volentez deslaianz* is imposed on Arthur from without, and is not a 'characteristic'. Real sloth occurs in the First Continuation (TVD 8760-8768), but still would not imply a characteristic were it not for Arthur's tendency, curiously recurrent in the verse romances and LP, towards fits of abstraction.[10] These build up a picture of a man very prone to fits of spiritual paralysis or *tristitia* from which he is powerless to emerge unaided, a man very prone, in fact, to the sin of sloth. This characteristic of Arthur's does not appear to be borrowed from any real king, though it faintly recalls Saul's possession, from which David roused him. There is no need, however, even for that inspiration, since the melancholy is always induced by concern for a missing knight, and that is universally typical of Arthur. The abstraction is not progressive, nor unique to Arthur; it is his personal manifestation of the cliché 'tristes et pensis'.[11] Successive imitation creates the impression of an individual quirk, such as a novelist might use to give a character life.

The daughter sins of sloth are relevant to Arthur: hatred of spiritual things, weakness in prayer, *accidia*, moral cowardice, despair. This again hints at the spiritual limitations which are so important to many authors.

Gluttony we may dismiss. We seldom hear details of the lavish fare provided in Arthur's hall,[12] and Arthur's custom of delaying the start of a feast argues a degree of self-control which many authors (and characters!) find excessive. The *Livre d'Artus* hints at over-indulgence in wine by young Arthur. But drunkenness in high places appears to be a pet hate of this author. The Scots, as often, reverse normal Arthurian trends to accuse Arthur of gluttony as yet another symptom of British degeneracy. Love of ease, a 'daughter' of gluttony, might attach to the *fainéant* Arthur, but his eagerness to perform, or at least hear of, adventure militates against this.

Anger, too, is uncharacteristic of Arthur: indeed his lack of it sometimes irritates the reader. His famous attack of royal rage in the alliterative *Morte* clearly delights the author, but belongs to genre, not to Arthur. Malory, realising this, tones it down to almost nothing.[13] Even in the *Morte* the anger is controlled, almost theatrical; not the 'deadly' anger which perverts will and judgment. Arthur exhibits that sort of anger only in the Vulgate *Mort*, against Mordred. Anger's daughter-sins are the vices of a tyrant: the TP Mark has them all, a fact which highlights his opposite number's general lack of them.

Through this survey Arthur emerges as a far from perfect character, but more white than black. He is spiritually limited, but can cut a deservedly good figure before the world. Except in some chronicles he is not conspicuously 'great'; rather is he disarmingly ordinary beneath his kingship. He is, as it were, humanised by long familiarity.

Let us now pass to the spiritual plane. A general survey of the material will convince us that Arthur seldom fails in conventional piety. As early as *Culhwch* he is the favoured of God. The pious correctness of Geoffrey's Arthur, with the influence of the Glastonbury legends,[14] ensures his wide acceptance as a Christian hero. Throughout the romance material he is meticulous in attendance at Mass, and he is fertile in good works: founding monasteries, reconstructing churches, distributing holy objects, sponsoring a crusade. Some texts, mainly chronicles, mention a special devotion to the Virgin.[15] In most contexts, Arthur is on good terms with the Church, and when he is not – as in the Welsh saints' lives, the Galehaut war or the Vulgate *Mort* – it is not deliberate provocation on his part. All in all, Arthur has just the right degree of public piety which is required of a king. But in the mainstream literature, this is judged to be insufficient for perfection in both the king and the man.

Once again, we may look at Chrétien as the initiator of this trend. As he moves from romance to romance, he takes an ever severer view of Arthur's spiritual limitations. Even in *Erec* his clumsy handling of the *Fier Baiser* custom provokes criticism. In *Cligès* he lacks Christian mercifulness, and on the occasion of Cligès' visit to England, Arthur presides over a court wholly devoted to rather pointless frivolity. In *Lancelot* Arthur has no spiritual resources to deal with the Méléagant crisis. The first scene of *Yvain* shows, as is often remarked, a slothful court with crumbling morale; and Yvain's later sojourn there, instead of glorifying him as it does Cligès, proves disastrous. Yvain has to grow spiritually *away* from his high renown at court before he becomes a 'complete' man. *Perceval* crowns this trend and takes it much further. Criticism of the chivalric and military code is felt from the beginning, and Perceval first sees Arthur in a most inglorious state. Perceval's own ambitions are rapidly directed away from Arthur, though neither the hero nor his instructors yet openly condemn the Arthurian ideal. But Gawain – already on the downgrade in *Lancelot* – exhibits in *Perceval* the limitations and absurdities of Arthurian success. His position at the end shows how the court's attitudes lead it up a spiritual blind alley.

The severity of *Perceval*'s judgement is mitigated by some of Chrétien's successors: worldly Arthurianism still has a long, glittering future. The *Perceval* continuations celebrate that future, but as they progress, Perceval becomes more and more distant from the court, so that Arthur remains totally cut off from the Grail world. In *Perlesvaus*, Arthur triumphantly overcomes one spiritual limitation, his 'volontez delainz', represents Christianity against the Old Law, and is even permitted himself to experience the Grail;[16] but still only Perlesvaus, the new Messiah, can in his mystic isolation attain to the highest spiritual experiences.

The *Lancelot-Graal*, however, continues Chrétien's trend. In Part One of LP, Arthur is still considered the favoured of God. But Arthur's defeat by Galehaut, followed by the long castigation of the *preudom*, reminds us that that favour must be earned – and Arthur has not done so. Far from attaining spiritual excellence, he is not even equipped for the ordinary duties of a king. So harshly is he judged that he must undergo the penance which, in real life, was deemed adequate for Henry II's implication in the murder of a saintly archbishop! Even after a full reform, he is still unable to overcome Galehaut, who would seem at this stage to have God's immanent approval. In Part One, Arthur, Claudas and Galehaut are all shown to be spiritually lacking. The author is saying that even kings are subject to God's laws – all the more so, indeed, for their position exposes them to greater temptations.

The author of Part One may not have the Grail theme in mind when he castigates Arthur. But his criticisms tie in very well with Chrétien's: both accuse the whole Arthurian system of spiritual sterility. Part One of LP thus points the way to the *Queste*, which takes Chrétien's view to the uttermost extremes. Arthur, his knights and their whole way of life are here *irrelevant* to the Grail, even if they are not blind to its importance. Far from being hallowed by the Grail, Arthur's kingdom only appears more evil for its presence. The logical working out of this theory appears, of course, in the Vulgate *Mort*, where the evils which the presence of the Grail, and the desire for it, have restrained break loose in total calamity. The *Mort* author is particularly conscious of Arthur's own spiritual limitations. Whereas Lancelot, Guinevere and even Gawain succeed before they die in attaining a personal understanding and love of God, Arthur continues to take refuge in conventional piety, cannot understand why this does not work, and dies in spiritually equivocal circumstances.[17]

Not all later authors judge Arthur, as a Christian, so severely; few accept the *Queste*'s scorn for the worldly chivalry which he admittedly represents. But the centrality of the Grail theme to the developing legend established a tragic equivocation at the centre of Arthur's story: his whole reign aspires towards a goal whose achievement will invalidate and destroy all he stands for. Arthur falls because of his spiritual inadequacy.

The contributions of many authors to Arthur's characterisation produce a remarkably self-consistent picture. Arthur is loyal and trusting; easily-led and affectionate; not piercingly intelligent, but capable of kingly tact and discretion; given to violent emotion and subject to depression; brave, proud in conquest, but somewhat lacking in moral fibre; pious, but lacking an entire spiritual dimension. This composite, cumulative portrait is convincing, as the rare and cliché-ridden direct descriptions of Arthur cannot be. It is not the 'real' Arthur, but it is an Arthur in whose historical reality it is possible to believe – and an Arthur whose character is his fate.

Most heroes are individualised partly by personal possessions. This is very true of Arthur, who is incomplete without his Round Table, his Excalibur, Camelot or (in Welsh) Celliwig and the hound Cabal. All authors acknowledge their importance; some authors make startlingly original use of them.

The Round Table is a case in point. Generally it is thought to seat all Arthur's knights; that its roundness equalises them all; that Arthur sat at it; that it was unique and made especially for him. In fact, all these ideas are seriously challenged in the material. Only in Layamon does the Table seat all the knights; elsewhere the number fluctuates enormously.[18] Normally it is for the select few. Seven authors consider all its occupants equal: Wace (though he contradicts himself elsewhere), Layamon, Thomas Gray, Vasconcellos, and the authors of *L'Atre périlleux*, *Arthur* and *The Grene Knight*.[19] Each of these could have conceived this highly sensible notion independently of the others. It is not part of the mainstream tradition, which abounds with squabbles over the relative merits of the knights and eventually sorts them out as neatly as a football league.[20]

As for Arthur, he usually sits at the *maistres dois* like any medieval baron. Only the *Suite* and the enthusiastic Hardyng seat him at the Table. Illustrators – including medieval ones – who put him there make an assumption unwarranted by most texts, and probably based on pictures of the Last Supper.[21] Never is Arthur a Christ-figure, although the occupant of the Siege Perilous certainly is. Arthur is both greater and lesser than the members of the Table, over whom he presides although they outstrip him in prowess.

As for the Table being made especially for Arthur, this is so only in the Wace tradition. Others deny it, for various reasons.[22] For Boron, the Table's roots are in a remote, mystical past, more significant than the petty squabbles of the Arthurian court. In LP, Arthur is belittled by the suggestion that his most familiar synechdochic possession is not really his at all, and that the best knights in the world go with the Table, not with Arthur. In *Perlesvaus*, Madaglan's demand for the return of the Table is a bombshell, part of the general disintegration of Arthurian organisation towards the end of the romance. Nevertheless the verse romancers and chroniclers continue to champion Arthur's rights in the Table, and even the late prose romances — TP and *Palamède* — assent to them. Nevertheless, his right to the Table is another belief held in the teeth of much Arthurian evidence.

The Table's uniqueness depends on its symbolic meaning. In the earlier material, that meaning depends on Arthur and his knights themselves, whose unique glory gives uniqueness to the Table. It is not The *Round* Table, it is *The* Round Table, Arthur's table. The religious symbolism developed by Boron militates against the Table's uniqueness, though the Three Tables echo and enrich one another's significance.[23] Other texts, which do not have Boron's enriching symbolism, also mention more than one Table. In the *Tavola Ritonda*, Arthur's Table is a mere copy of Uther's; in *Sagramor* Sagremor's is a copy of Arthur's.[24] Both inventions destroy the concept of the uniqueness of Arthur's whole reign and civilisation, as well as of his Table. In the ballad of *King Cornwall*,[25] excellent round tables seem to abound, to the ultimate loss of any meaning in Arthur's. It is really the Vulgate *Mort* and the post-Vulgate, with their fostering of the Ban faction, which shatter the concept of uniqueness, as the excellence of Ban and his followers cuts sheer across that of the Round Table fellowhsip, and the strife between factions finally obliterates the idea — never very strong — that the Tablers form an apostolic fellowship.

The Table does have a few interesting peculiarities. Chief of them is the Siege Perilous with its adaptable *sen*. Also interesting, however, is the post-Vulgate notion that each seat is labelled by God. This may rob Arthur of freedom of choice, but it also gives divine sanction to the fellowship — even if the divinity is little felt in the action, and is hard to reconcile with the presence of Agravain or Mordred. It produces a very interesting evolution. When a knight dies, his name fades. Therefore, the seats keep a check from afar on the knights' fortunes. The notion is thus assimilated to the common folktale motif of the sympathetic object which changes according to its owner's fortunes.[26] Most likely the author had heard such tales, and (perhaps subconsciously) altered his motif, inherited from the Vulgate, to conform to them. Here is an unusual demonstration of folklore's power to influence written literature.

Such peculiarities, however, are confined to a few texts. Overall the chief appeal of the Table lies in the excellence of the knights who adorn it. To

Arthurian imitators, a *table ronde* meant not an artefact but a tourney,[27] in fact an imitation of Arthur's paladins. The Table is the concrete expression of Arthur's knight-centredness.

I have little to add to previous studies of Arthur's sword.[28] We must note, however, that the way in which the French Excalibur shuttles between Arthur and Gawain[29] weakens its individualising significance for Arthur and throws its symbolism into confusion. Most absurd is VM, which, in order to justify Gawain's possession of Excalibur in LP, makes Arthur gradually lose interest in what, after Boron,[30] ought to be hallowed as the divine instrument of his kingship. In the post-Vulgate, degradation of Gawain justifies Arthur's retention of the sword — which in turn justifies his lamentations over it at the end, largely invalidated in the Vulgate *Mort* by the fact that it has for years not been his sword. The post-Vulgate author also eliminates much Vulgate incoherence with its new, parallel hand-in-the-lake scene.[31] But this invention produces a fresh complication. If Excalibur comes from the Lake, it cannot be the God-given sword in the stone. Therefore the latter must be eliminated. The author's method is even more untrue to the Boron *sen* than VM's. He castigates the sword's inferiority as a weapon, which quickly causes it to break. Thus all Boron's imagery is destroyed, while the new Excalibur has little significance, being indeed inferior to its own scabbard. As so often, the post-Vulgate author fails to think through what is basically a good idea.

In sum, Excalibur is often considered to be significant, though only Boron is sure of its meaning. It is not unique to Arthur, a fact which produces much confusion. It is nowhere vividly described; in the legend as a whole it takes a forlorn second place to the satisfyingly mysterious and ubiquitous Sword with the Strange Hangings. These negative findings comport a paradox. In the popular imagination, Excalibur is as famous a sword as Durendal. What makes it so is precisely that connection with Arthur which so many authors challenge. Once again, we find that general Arthurian beliefs are held in the teeth of much of the evidence.

No other possessions of Arthur's attain such general fame as the Sword and the Table. Others are occasionally mentioned, and may represent abortive attempts to individualise Arthur further. An example is the list of weapons in *Culhwch*, but these do not appear to have featured largely even in Welsh lore. Each has an obvious descriptive name: the sword 'Hard-notch', the spear 'Hewer-spear', the knife 'Pearl-handle'(?), the shield 'Face of the Evening'. None is obviously magical, and it is Arthur who individualises the weapons as much as vice versa. Geoffrey's ignorance of all save Ron and possibly Caledfwlch[32] consigns them to a rapid oblivion. All evidence principally the Welsh passion for names and clarifications.

In an age when detailed enthusiasm for weapons might be expected in many readers, it is rather surprising to find so little general interest in Arthur's. Only Layamon extends Geoffrey's largely conventional Arming of the Hero. There is one exception to this lack: Arthur's shield. This recurs almost as often as the Sword, though it did not so catch the popular imagination. The *Culhwch* name, Wynebgorucher, occurs nowhere else, but it may be significant that Geoffrey's

Pridwen (a name better suited to a shield than to the ship which bears it in Welsh)[33] has a similar meaning, 'fair face'. Both names may allude to the possibly ancient[34] idea that Arthur bore a portrait of the Virgin on his shield, a 'fair face' indeed.

Early sources[35] are much confused as to the nature of the image which Arthur bore on his shield. Wace and Giraldus take Geoffrey to mean that Arthur bore a portrait of the Virgin *inside* his shield as an object of private devotion, not outside as a blazon. This is the more likely as Geoffrey's allusion is apparently the first mention of a religious device being painted on a shield.[36] However, as interest in personal heraldic devices developed, from the late twelfth century onwards,[37] it became possible to consider Arthur's Virgin badge as such a device. William of Rennes seems to see it as such. At the least, if openly displayed it proclaims the wearer's allegiance to Christianity, and usefully identifies him in battle against the pagans.

However, after William's time a concatenation of circumstances prevented the general recognition of Arthur's Virgin badge. The verse romancers take little interest in the nascent heraldic art, and the prose romancers, who adopt it with ever-increasing enthusiasm, gain by a process whose nature can only be guessed the conviction that Arthur's device was three (or more) crowns.[38] This device never receives an explanation such as the prose romancers normally give, but it wholly ousts the HRB/Wace conception. Thus Arthur's Virgin shield, and with it the particularising − even spiritualising − notion of a special devotion to the Virgin, are thrust out of the mainstream development. It lingers, however, in byways, maintained by the quiet persistence of the chronicle tradition. Two 'explanations' of it exist. One is in the thirteenth-century Vatican Nennius, which sees it as a memento of Arthur's visit to Jerusalem.[39] Such mementos are so common that the story does not denote any special piety in Arthur. John of Glastonbury's explanation,[40] whereby the device commemorates Arthur's Glastonbury vision, connotes a more genuinely intense religious experience, through which the *sen* of shield and vision enrich one another. John has some interest in 'spiritualising' Arthur, as his record of his ancestry shows;[41] but he is too late and obscure to influence the mainstream conception.

The Virgin device survives into the late Middle English, despite general acceptance of the Three Crowns, but in a rather different form. Hardyng, the alliterative *Morte* and Boece all transfer it to Arthur's banner, indicating that it is no longer personal insignia, but a focus for allegiance, belonging to Arthur only insofar as he represents England, and proclaiming the whole nation's devotion to the Christian cause. This enlargement of meaning epitomises Arthur's transformation from Dark Age tribal warrior to fifteenth-century monarch.

Whatever its exact significance, the Three Crowns heraldry clearly celebrates Arthur's worldly kingship, and does more honour to it than the French prose romancers might wish; the English might see in it the emblem of dominion over England, Scotland and Wales. It figures in all representations of Arthur among the Nine Worthies,[42] which assures its popular acceptance; but it vanquishes the Virgin device by repetition, not by superior *sen*.

Neither Virgin nor Crowns are hereditary devices, but Arthur may have one such: the dragon which Geoffrey puts on his helmet and VM transfers to his banner. Geoffrey continually associates the dragon with the House of Constantine, and seems to see it as a true, hereditary heraldic device. VM, however, makes the *sen* of the dragon-banner uniquely and intensely personal to Arthur (see II. 264). Here, by a splendid piece of symbolic irony, Arthur unknowingly carries his fate and his nation's about with him wherever he goes. Moreover, in order to communicate the *sen*, the author has to describe the banner in considerable detail. It is a pity that this memorable device should be adopted only by VM's faithful follower, the *Livre d'Artus*. Battle-standards had great symbolic and practical importance in medieval warfare, and Arthurian war ought not to lack them. Also largely lacking is that other means of identification in the field, the war-cry. Charlemagne's 'Munjoie!' roused echoes in the breast of every Frenchman, while the Spaniards thrilled to El Cid's 'Santiago!'. What has Arthur to offer? Wace suggests 'Dius aie, Sainte Marie' (I. 8057). This excellently combines the Anglo-Norman traditional cry[43] with Arthur's special devotion, but unfortunately it does not catch on. LP substitutes the uninspiring 'Clarence!', which may be a pale imitation of 'Monjoie!' since both are place-names, but which certainly does not thrill us as does Charlemagne's cry. Only VM and the *Livre d'Artus* take up — in duty bound — LP's suggestion. Unintentionally they make it even more distasteful by the confusion induced by constant mention of the real place, Clarence. The cry particularises Arthur, but does him little honour. More inspiriting is the alliterative *Morte*, where Arthur's faithful followers simply cry his name.

Where Arthur's battle-accoutrements are concerned, many good opportunities are missed or rejected by the authors. Overall, however, he does little worse than other characters in the material. From this viewpoint, the authors would perhaps have done well to look *more* closely at real-life details.

The same could be said in connection with Arthur's residences and general peacetime possessions. Scattered descriptions of houses, council-rooms and tents[44] fail on the whole either to individualise Arthur or to draw him fully into the burgeoning world of medieval civilisation. The material generally is not lacking in descriptions of magnificent residence, but I do not think that the general vagueness over Arthur's residences is intended to insult him. It is simply assumed that he always has all of the best:

> Li plus bas jours de la semaine,
> quant plus priveement estoit,
> Pasques d'un autre roi sambloit. (*Deus espees* 34-6)

The reader is invited to imagine the most luxurious lifestyle he can conceive — whether it features 'hot peppered chops' or the tapestried magnificence of a fifteenth-century castle — intensify it ten times, and take it as a description of Arthur's lifestyle. He is particularised by superlatives rather than by distinct details.

Arthur's non-possession of magical objects generally is disappointing, but it has compensations. All the wonders and luxuries of the Arthurian universe belong to Arthur as the centre of that universe. The knights' tales, to which he

128

so avidly listens, offer to him in homage all the strangeness of his realm. Paraphrasing K. H. Göller,[45] we may say of Arthur: 'Seine Welt ist seine Persönlichkeit'. Everything which happens in the Arthurian world individualises Arthur: that is why his very name carries such magic.

VIII

DEATH AND AFTERMATH

With this chapter we can at last resume the chronological approach. We have no need, however, to tell the whole story of Arthur's death and survival legends, for their main lines have been exhaustively studied.[1] We shall therefore follow byways rather than highways, exploring some lesser-known features of Arthur's end and of the land he left behind.

The 'accepted' legend asserts that Arthur was betrayed by Mordred, and perished or departed after a final battle with the traitor. Major authors, from HRB/Wace to the prose romancers, work to make this end more significant and inevitable. Minor authors, however, are not all ready to fall in line. The verse romances envisage no end to Arthur's reign. Welsh vernacular tradition doubtless took a similar view. Most Welsh references to Camlann[2] are flippant and, even if they assume that it was fatal to Arthur, they do not take an elevatedly tragic view of the fact. Moreover, the combined references in Welsh are utterly contradictory, forbidding the reconstruction of an 'original' Welsh legend of Camlann.

Early Welsh literature does not definitely hold that Arthur perished at Camlann; conversely, there is no strong evidence of his survival. We have evidence[3] that Arthur's survival legend was current among the pre-Geoffrey Britons, but none that it featured in written – or even orally organised – Welsh literary tradition. The famous grave englyn[4] is the only possible surviving Welsh evidence of it, and that could bear other meanings to one not viewing it with hindsight. We know that the bards, for whom the Triads were devised, were taught to despise popular culture.[5] Welsh story seems to envisage an 'eternal' Arthur of the verse-romance type, rather than a surviving Vanished Hero, and this conclusion is supported by the fact that the Welsh *Bruts* add no details to Geoffrey's account of Arthur's passing.

It is, indeed, always hard to crush an idea of Geoffrey's. His account of Arthur's end is so welded into the mainstream tradition that later defiance of it might seem unthinkable. But it is defied, not by the meek Welsh, but by English and French writers. Three minor English chronicles hold that Arthur either defeated Mordred and lived peacefully for years after, or was never troubled by Mordred at all.[6] All three are Arthurian dead-ends, and their aberrations may be due simply to imperfect recollection of an orthodox source. Nonetheless they are a useful reminder that no Arthurian development is ever final, or universally recognised. Any author who wishes is entitled to set Arthur free from what may seem to be an inescapable tragic nexus. The three authors may indeed be quietly, but deliberately, refuting HRB. An Arthur who lives in peace and dies of old age will hardly make great literature, but he merits the biographer's consideration as another facet of Arthurian 'truth'.

The Cat legend, which enjoys a shadowy currency in French, can be used to bring Arthur to his end without recourse to Mordred. Not all versions that use it, however, assume that the Cat was fatal to Arthur, and even André, who mentions the belief, considers it foolish.[7] The legend is chiefly interesting as another defiance of HRB's canonicity.

Even those texts which accept that Arthur's career ended in battle with Mordred disagree widely over the circumstances – even if we exclude the Lancelot complication. The very name and location of the battle are, significantly, disputed. It is not certain that the Welsh thought Camlann to be in Cornwall, whereas the name certainly exists in Wales itself.[8] Geoffrey draws a satisfactory circle round Arthur's life by beginning and ending it in Cornwall,[9] but later writers obliterate it again. Cornwall is not, in fact, prominent in non-Welsh Arthurian literature. Often Tristan excludes Arthur from it, nor does Cornwall have for medieval Arthurians the romantic attraction it has for many moderns. It is therefore not surprising to find authors resiting the battle for their own purposes. The Didot *Perceval* puts it in Ireland, often in medieval times considered the haunt of barbarism and paganism.[10] Mordred's flight there emphasises his betrayal of Christianity and Arthurian civilisation. Arthur, in pursuing him, separates himself from his own world. The Vulgate *Mort* creates a new 'circle' by moving the battle to Salisbury Plain,[11] but does not have the last word. At least three widely-separated late authors under Vulgate influence move the location back to Cornwall: Gray, Jean de Waurin and the compiler of the Portuguese *Nobiliario*.[12] Each opts for the HRB location not because he prefers its *sen* to the Vulgate's, but because he thinks HRB to be more historically reliable. The Scots, for their part, move the battle to Humber: thus Mordred fights on his own borders, in defence of his legitimate rights, instead of being hounded to the uttermost end of Britain. Narrative truth and historical truth, as authors conceive them, prevent a consensus on the 'absolute' truth about the site. It exemplifies the shifting nature of Arthurian geography; nevertheless, accuracy is important, for identification of the site may mean much to Arthurian investigators and pilgrims – as Layamon and the post-Vulgate independently suggest.[13] Had the site been fixed, it might have become as popular a venue as Glastonbury.

Another variable is the fact – apparently indispensable – that Arthur and Mordred both fell in the battle. The story would seem to demand a culminating duel, but Geoffrey himself avoids this in the interests of verisimilitude, as in the cause of Lucius[14] – except that Arthur does *try* to kill Mordred. The first writer to alter Geoffrey's account is Henry of Huntingdon, whose dramatic sense – aided perhaps by memories of *chansons de geste* and of Hengest's death persuades him to adopt the duel in his 'summary'. It is not yet a mutual killing, for although Arthur clearly gets his death by his attack on Mordred, Mordred does not kill him – doubtless because it would be dishonourable for the traitor to slay the hero, as if Ganelon killed Roland. The relationship must be altered and intensified before that becomes acceptable. Nevertheless, Henry's version achieves the astonishing effect of ousting Geoffrey's in many chronicles.[15] Perhaps authors thought that Henry represented an alternative version of HRB (which is remotely possible); even so, they exercised artistic judgment in choosing him. In this light it is regrettable that the most talented imitators, like Wace and William of Rennes, ignored Henry's version, if they knew it.

Later versions of the duel need not derive from Henry's, for the idea is an obvious one. The alliterative *Morte*, for instance, motivates it in its own way through its development of Arthur's proud, passionate and revengeful character. It also humanises Mordred, so that it is no shame, but great increase in *sen*, if Arthur dies at his hands in a mighty duel, heroically isolated from the surrounding battle. The duel and its timing resemble, by convergent evolution, that in the Vulgate *Mort*, but the *sen* of the latter text is wholly different. It hinges on the father-son relationship, which indeed is important almost solely for the impact it gives to the duel. Of the three possible *sen* of the duel, the *Mort* rejects the 'Sohrab and Rustem' view, which requires the mutual non-recognition of the protagonists, and abrogates the Oedipal horror of the incest in favour of the Atrean horror of family hatred. That hatred gives maximum point to the savagery with which Arthur, from HRB onwards, always attacks Mordred; but, as in many Arthurian cases, we find that the inventor of the motif is not its best interpreter. The Vulgate author fails to convey the horror by his *pere/fils* opposition, which becomes mechanical; it is Malory who succeeds, in a scene which ranks supreme in all Arthurian literature. Here, Arthur's filicidal wrath, which turns precarious victory into calamity, is brilliantly conveyed in a short, sombre conversation, during which Destiny balances on a knife-edge. Mordred's more evil, patricidal wrath is compounded by political treachery, and both are encapsulated in the nightmarish final act: 'he threste hymselff . . . up to the burre of kyng Arthurs speare, and ryght so he smote hys fadir, kyng Arthure . . .' The image is of a wild beast, a boar, using his own death to encompass that of his slayer. Mordred has forfeited humanity. This is a magnificent transmutation of the Vulgate's tired chiasmus ('einsi ocist li peres le fil . . .') and revolting detail of the sun's ray.[16] The French and the English author combine to produce a work of genius which neither could have accomplished alone.

How fortunate that combination was becomes clear by contrast with the post-Vulgate, whose Oedipal tragedy ought to reach a tremendous climax in the duel. Unfortunately, a rival theme – the excellence of Ban's lineage – so dominates the author's mind at the end that he makes a monumental botch of the Arthur/ Mordred tragedy. The Vulgate wisely leaves the Lancelot theme in suspense during the last battle, leaving it as the confrontation of king and traitor. But the post-Vulgate is determined that nothing of significance shall be accomplished in Logres save by the Ban family, and so in the last battle Blioberis – perhaps the least interesting of the whole tribe – kills Mordred whilst Arthur stands idly by. Thus is the scene robbed of its proper significance, and the sense of an all-consuming fate destroyed. The author's obsessive nationalism makes him mean-spirited in this, the worst of his failures to live up to his own inventions. It is interesting to note that two imitators independently react against this meanness. Gray's English spirit revolts against the tyranny of the Bans: he entrusts the killing of Mordred to Ywain, an undistinguished but impeccably British figure and relative of Arthur's, who gains further importance by assuming Grifflet's role in the final scenes. Here is a valiant attempt at creative compromise. Salazar, who deeply admires the knight-king Arthur, restores the Vulgate duel, though reverting to the post-Vulgate immediately afterwards. Freer adaptors — Hardyng, Waurin, Vasconcellos[17] — unhesitatingly prefer the Vulgate. It was doubtless the staggeringly inept final scene which lost the post-Vulgate all chance of equalling the Vulgate's popularity.

Even so, two late medieval works outdo the post-Vulgate in betraying the last battle's intrinsic meaning. According to the *Tavola Ritonda*, Mordred defeats Arthur, and is himself slain by Lancelot.[18] Here, Arthur, even reinforced by the occasional Ban, cannot settle his own score against his ancient enemy. Surely a post-Vulgate source must lie behind this ultimate glorification of the genus Ban. It can never gain the force of the older story, though it may hold some meaning if Lancelot and Mordred personally hate one another. This they may do for the sake of Guinevere, whom, says the *Demanda*, Mordred loved 'tanto y mas que no Lanzarote'! In this case, Arthur would be ousted from his own tragedy, his death incidental. This all but happens in Jean d'Outremeuse. D'Outremeuse is not hostile to Arthur; but, inconsistent as ever, he picks the Lancelot story because it pleases his sense of the bizarre, which is far stronger than his sense of the tragic.

Often, French narrative development and Scottish prejudice produce similar results by convergent evolution. Thus, Mordred defeats Arthur in the Scots; neither survives the battle, but the Picts clearly win the victory, though a Pyrrhic one. The two change places; 'kind Mordred' is destroyed by treason and, perishing, he wins a moral (and technical) victory. The 'facts' about Arthur's end can, in fact, be stood on their heads by an ingenious and hostile author.

Much dispute rages over Arthur's end, even among those who accept the main facts of the battle. Texts even disagree, violently and in great detail, over the nature of his wounds.[19] Not that these are ever symbolic of Christ's wounds, for instance; the debate produces no intensification of *sen*. There is, however, a consensus that Arthur shows superhuman resistance to his injuries, whether or not he actually dies of them. It is also agreed that they are honourable: Arthur's death is not shameful like Alexander's or Merlin's. Whatever sins he commits in life are purged by his fall, and in death he can outdo the greatest worthies.

It was doubtless dispute over Arthur's wounds, as well as his survival, which produced the thirteenth-century *Vera Historia de Morte Arturii*.[20] This accepts the theory of many battle-wounds of which one appears fatal; but to this it adds the extraordinary story of the youth with the elm-spear, which defies explanation, from within or without the Arthurian legend. The youth is not from Arthur's past, or his *Doppelgänger*, or obviously supernatural; he is at any rate mortal. Elm-wood has no special significance in folklore; elder would be a different matter. As for the poison, it may suggest that Arthur is unkillable by ordinary wounds —

but then he is said already to have a fatal wound. Surely the author himself did not understand the story; but this does not help us to an explanation. A possible parallel is Odin's appearance to Sigmund in his last battle, and the same legend also provides Sigmund's killing of Gutthorm.[21] Neither parallel is close or wholly illuminating, and no obvious connection can be traced. There is one other account in which a poisoned weapon kills Arthur: this is a recently-collected Cornish tale, which also features a (magic?) storm associated with his death.[22] The *Vera Historia* may be traceable back to Cornwall,[23] but I know no Cornish or Celtic belief which would explain it. The *Historia* hints at mysterious forces attendant on Arthur's end, and intrigues the reader even while it baffles him. Arthurian dead ends may be as fascinating as the main development, and continual dispute over such details as the wounds may be fruitful.

The disputes extend to the question of Arthur's departure. There are three authorial alignments: those who hold that Arthur certainly survived; those convinced that he died; and those (the majority) who hover uneasily between the two. Often we find that what to one author is certain proof of a point, to another proves the opposite, or proves nothing.

Arthur's departure by ship is a case in point. To Geoffrey, writing as poet in the *Vita Merlini*,[24] the ship conveys Arthur to healing, but not to a magical place or to eternal life. To the Vulgate *Mort*, the boat is a funeral vessel, like those of Raguidel, Elaine or Perceval's sister. Here, Arthur expresses no hope of healing, but certainty of death, and Morgain is not expected to heal Arthur or convey him elsewhere than to his tomb. The boat figures in a very plain, though beautifully told, tale of Arthur's death. What to Layamon (ll.14277-82) means hope of life, to the *Mort* is certainty of death.

The same applies to the very tomb. In the exhumation story, investigation of the tomb proves Arthur's death. In *Perlesvaus* (I. 318) even the waiting tomb proves Arthur's eventual death. In the Vulgate *Mort*, the sealed tomb is sufficient proof. But the post-Vulgate author rejects this. Again he perverts his own *sen* by importing a contradictory motif. Throughout the work there is a clear expectation of Arthur's death: he exemplifies the common lot of man instead of escaping it. Yet Grifflet, investigating the tomb, 'no fallo sino el yelmo que traxo (Artur) en la dolorosa batalla'. This must throw doubt on Arthur's death, which is fatal to the overall *sen*. The detail of the helmet even hints that Arthur 'rises again', for it corresponds to Christ's empty grave-wrappings (John 30. 6-7). The author in fact recognises the Messianic nature of the Briton Hope, but is probably overawed by the implications. Both his ideas — exemplary death and Christological survival — are good, but irreconcilable in his own context.

Malory, too, reacts against the Vulgate's crushing of hope.[25] He knows that ideas of noble death and healing voyage are incompatible, but he obscures the clash with a veil of semi-judicial, semi-poetic language which has bamboozled most readers ever since. Malory preserves a cautious silence about the exhumation. It occurs to no author to doubt that the bones exhumed were actually Arthur's; indeed, it is still hard to convince a believer that the bones were probably 'planted'. The *Vera Historia*, like Malory, takes the sealed tomb to allow doubt as to whether Arthur is in it. Both authors stress that no one actually saw Arthur interred. Apparently one can use sealed graves, like statistics, to prove what one likes.

Avalon itself can be used to prove or disprove Arthur's death. If Avalon is Glastonbury, it proves death; if it is the Island Paradise, it proves life and healing. Italian authors, ignorant of Glastonbury, even manage to combine the notions by asserting that Arthur went to the island paradise of Avalon only to die.[26] Gray identifies Avalon with Glastonbury, but his Arthur sets sail thence once again to his paradise. Thus the reasoning 'Avalon = Glastonbury, therefore Arthur died in Avalon' becomes 'Avalon = Glastonbury, therefore Arthur, who did not die, went somewhere else'.

Arthur's survival takes, of course, many different forms, approximating to every available folk-belief. But there is dispute also within the 'death' party. Indeed, Arthur in the Wild Hunt and Crow legends[27] may have 'died', returning to earth via a process which takes no real account of Christian beliefs. The twelfth-century *Draco Normannicus*[28] contains hints that Arthur, like Lazarus, has died, and returned in some unhallowed state. Certainly, Arthur's assimilation to fairy kind casts doubt on his spiritual state, and Henry, the hero, contrasts Arthur's perennial life with his own hope of Heaven. In fact, Arthur's death and survival stories may interact in curious ways.

The empty tomb in the post-Vulgate suggests death and resurrection; how God's judgement fits in we cannot tell. The 'rex quondam' epitaph[29] similarly suggests resurrection. Possibly Arthur's second reign was expected in the Millennium, a theologically acceptable time for the resurrection of the blessed dead.[30] This idea might find more favour than the more direct Christology of a Second Coming. It is radically different from the Briton Hope, which does not involve death or Christian judgement, so that the return may occur at any time. The two beliefs are confused by Malory — who tries to christianise the hope — but are really separate.

If Arthur is to reign in the Millennium he must have won favour at the particular judgement — which he escapes if he does not die, as Merlin does by retirement to his 'esplumoir'.[31] Other authors are more doubtful of his chances: so in the Vulgate *Mort*, which allows him Christian burial but no such certainty of bliss as Lancelot's or Gawain's. Nor is there any hint that he expires in a proper frame of mind,[32] like Gawain or Galehaut. Arthur is an ordinary soul, not greatly good or bad, and the author consequently hazards no guess at his soul's fate. Some English works are more definite. Arthur's end in the alliterative *Morte* is edifying, his sins are purged by his fall, and as the first Christian worthy he must have good hope of heaven. In the *Vera Historia*, too, his end is conventionally edifying, and the echo of John 14. 2 in 'rex enim raptus est ad paratam sibi mansionem' (fol. 61r) hints at a speedy transition to heaven. Even more definite is the Hailes version, which ends with four unique hexameters stating that Arthur went to heaven *living*, like Enoch and Eli — these being safer comparisons than Christ, though the author surely has the Ascension in mind. Finally, in Hardyng, there is a strong, though not explicit, expectation that Arthur will gain the saint's, or even the martyr's, crown. Thus does chroniclers' English partisanship for Arthur find its most emphatic expression through Arthur's death.

Some authors, then, doubt Arthur's immediate salvation, whereas patriotic enthusiasts actually imagine him as a great Christian soul, a reputation which he scarcely deserves in life. Even the most hostile author does not actually consign him to Hell or even Purgatory.

Turning to the survival legend, we are immediately struck by the cleavage between works dealing with Arthur's earthly career and his 'after-life'. No one doubts that Arthur of Britain and Arthur of Avalon are the same person, but the two become progressively more distant. Nowhere — even in *Culhwch* or *Preiddeu Annwfn* — does the first Arthur have any magical powers. Works in the broad HRB tradition treat him so fundamentally realistically that they shrink from following him to Avalon. We must look for Avalon in notes, allusions and scraps of folklore. One treatment of it produces an interesting sub-literature, only remotely connected with the mainstream but remarkably self-consistent, the consistency deriving from source-respect and approximation to widespread folkloric belief. This is the story of Arthur's life in the island paradise, which I now propose briefly to examine.

Arthur in Avalon acquires the status of fairy king which he never has in his 'first' life. In that life his realm may be 'filled with faerie', but he and his knights are always the mortals who venture into fairyland, not the fairies themselves. In his 'second' life he crosses the divide and is lost to mortal existence. This does not happen instantaneously. Although Arthur in *Vita Merlini* is treated much more fancifully than in HRB, he does not change his nature. His sojourn in the Fortunate Isle is strictly temporary, and his followers, like Christ's apostles, expect a rapid second coming. The island is not other-worldly; it is not until Arthur's refuge is equated with some pre-existent notion of Paradise that he can become immortal. This happens in William of Rennes, whose paradise combines notions of the classical Golden Age and the Christian earthly paradise, and independently in *Draco Normannicus*, where Arthur's antipodal residence may well be equated with the terrestrial paradise.[33] Even then he may not be immortal. It is universally believed that time in the Otherworld flows differently, so that a few hours there may be equivalent to many years outside. A mortal there may live an apparent eternity — but if he returns, he will fall once more victim to mortality. This tyranny does not apply to true fays, who freely visit mortal lands. Now, in William, Arthur's return is not expected. Stephen's Arthur seems able, like a fay, to return; but Henry II's scorn for Arthur's threats suggest that they are empty, because he really is still bound by fairy time.

In the later sub-literature, the hold of Arthur's mortality is slackened. His blood-relationship to Morgain helps, making a fay of him in his second life, just as it makes a human of Morgain in the mainstream development.[34] Also important is the assimilation of the universal story of the visiting mortal, the visitor being a man of later days to whom Arthur is the fairy king. The most interesting occurrences of this belief occur in the fourteenth-century French epic, especially in *remaniements* containing substantial injections of romance material. The works concerned are *La Bataille Loquifer*, *Le Bâtard de Bouillon* (ll.3291-3689), *Ogier le Danois* (f.149a-154c), *Tristan de Nanteuil* (ll.8526-8788), *Brun de la Montaigne* (ll.5626, 3237-3925), and *Huon de Bordeaux* (pp.598-606).[35] They borrow extensively from one another. The first three agree that Arthur dwells on a luxuriously-appointed Mediterranean island, together with Morgain (whose authority may be greater than his); his subjects may all be women. Arthur is well-disposed to mortal visitors and needs their help in his wars, but does not visit mortal lands. His land uses fairy time, and mortals can find it only by chance. All these elements belong to international folklore, and some may have been derived from Celtic originals – though not from a coherent Celtic legend of Arthur in Avalon. This approximation to general beliefs encourages Arthur's recognition as the king of *all* Faërie. Now, Faërie is not always thought of as an island: more often it is shifting, unlocated.[36] As the Avalon/Glastonbury identification becomes more widely known, it may be easier to imagine the fairy Arthur as belonging to such an ubiquitous fairyland. *Tristan de Nanteuil* begins to do so. Arthur's dwelling-place there is in a vague 'Armenia', but its location shifts, and some of its inhabitants (though still not Arthur) pass freely into mortal lands. In *Brun de la Montaigne*, Arthur's possession of ubiquitous fairy kingship is plainly stated: 'tout cil lieu faë sont Artus de Bretaigne' (1.567). He still has a fairy castle, but his land is not geographically cut off from ordinary places, into which he can now freely pass.

Arthur being firmly established in fairy lordship, other former mortals are encouraged to try their luck. Hence in *Huon de Bordeaux*, Oberon and Huon accede to fairy kingship via the path first trodden by Arthur. This occasions a transference to Arthur's second life of the French attack on his glory: in *Huon* fairyland is given a 'realistic' political organisation in order that Arthur may be ousted. This idea seems to have repelled English writers; at least, Lydgate mentions (among other, incompatible beliefs) Arthur's reception as *sole* king of Faërie,[37] and the recent Cornish legend already referred to tells the same tale. Even in his second life, Arthur is not secure from foreign detraction – but he has defenders.

The idea that Faërie has a named king and a definite political organisation belongs to literature rather than folklore. Hence it is understandable that oral lore claims neither Arthur, Oberon nor Huon as fairy king. Indeed, in recorded lore Arthur is not a fairy at all, but a giant, a man or a cave-sleeper. The sole exception to this, from any period, seems to be the tale in the Chronicle of Lanercost.[38] Basically, this is a straightforward visit to fairyland. There is only a general resemblance to the fay Arthur of the bastard epic, and this is probably due to convergent evolution, the Lanercost author having dignified his common-place tale with the famous name of Arthur. Quite possibly he saw him as a *revenant* rather than a fairy – though the distinction is often hard to draw, and *Loquifer* speaks of 'la gent faë/ qui sont du siecle venus et trespassé' (p.256). It is possible that the Chronicle draws on a lost tradition that Arthur was a fairy king, but I think it unlikely. His acceptance as such is, rather, a literary, and largely a French development. A combination of source-respect with the absorption of international motifs defines this new Arthur, and also cuts him sharply off from the Arthur of the primary literature.

Here we must leave the fascination of Arthur's survival and return to the Britain which he left behind. Only in some 'secondary' contexts does Arthur's mesnie accompany him to fairyland;[39] in the primary literature they remain to mourn him. What is this aftermath like?

For the chroniclers, of course, the record continues, often to their own day. Inevitably Arthur's reign, however glorious, bulks small in such a tale of years, so that the 'aftermath' is more important than anything Arthurian. To the verse romancers, there is strictly no 'aftermath'; but even they frequently lament the degeneracy of their own day, and thus suggest an aftermath of change and decay, much as the HRB tradition speaks of defeat and loss. As for the prose romances, all nominally centre on the Grail, and so should care little for events after its passing; but few authors can resist the desire to trace Arthur's downfall, and to cast at least a glance at even later events. All view Arthur politically rather than poetically; and as politics do not die with their exponents, Logres' fate outlives Arthur. The huge group of *chansons de geste* dealing with the aftermath of Charlemagne's reign shows the same attitude. A great man changes the world by leaving it, and those changes are part of his story.

In many texts, Arthur's followers find it hard to accept his loss. *Vita Merlini*, Wace, the Didot *Perceval*, Bocaccio and Vasconcellos,[40] in their different ways, record the hope of a speedy return, while Layamon and Gray[41] variously try to rationalise this expectation. As with Christ, such authors witness a hope which becomes less and less immediate and passes eventually into myth — in fact, consciously or unconsciously, they 'explain' the Briton Hope. They also express Arthur's domination of his world, since his followers are so lost without him that they prefer to await him rather than begin the thankless task of rebuilding.

Life must go on, however — and the first requirement is a new king, even if he be considered a trustee. Geoffrey's Constantine[42] is almost universally accepted, obscure though he be. To Geoffrey, indeed, his obscurity is important, because it implies the minimum continuance of Arthurian glories. Geoffrey carefully eliminates all the familiar figures, down to the Arthurian bishops, who cannot be removed by battle, but all die in the paragraph after Camlann. *Vita Merlini*, with its dismal catalogue of Constantine's troubles, again emphasises how little Arthurianism has been preserved.

Most of Geoffrey's successors imitate his reticence, and pessimism, over Constantine, but there are exceptions. Layamon, for instance, emphasises Arthur's eagerness to preserve as much as possible when he administers to his designee a sort of coronation oath to maintain the status quo. And Constantine briefly succeeds in doing so, indicating that Arthurian regeneration might be possible were it not for the remorseless pressure of Destiny.

Long after, Malory greatly outdoes Layamon in optimism. Not being a chronicler and therefore bound to trace Britain's downfall, he can afford to do so. 'Than syr Constantyn . . . was chosyn kyng of England . . . and worshypfully he rulyd this royame' (III. 1259). Now, in Malory, as in the French prose, Arthur does not designate Constantine or take any interest in the future of the realm; but the barons attempt to preserve the Arthurian inheritance. And they largely succeed. Constantine, related to Arthur and reared since the Roman expedition in Arthurian traditions, is well fitted for the task. Malory fully develops the tragedy in human terms, but his robust patriotism encourages him to mitigate the political collapse.

138

Even more optimistic, but different, is Vasconcellos. Now, the original Peninsular romances of chivalry[43] do not usually have an Arthurian setting. Rather do they appeal to Spanish readers by introducing new characters, often in a Spanish setting. This is what Vasconcellos ingeniously does. By conflating Constantine with Sagremor he produces a successor versed in Arthurian tradition, who regulates his 'new' world so well that 'não ouve inveja ao tempo del rey Artur' (p.21). Thus Vasconcellos combines tradition with innovation and, incidentally, denies the uniqueness and tragic transience of Arthurian civilisation. It becomes but one manifestation of an unbroken tradition of Chivalry which began with Bacchus. This is an old idea,[44] but Vasconcellos' use of it is new. He comes very late in our period, but is no less innovatory for that.

The Scottish tradition envisages a struggle for the succession, which begins in Arthur's lifetime. As Arthur has no heir of his body, his nomination is very important. It occasions a factional struggle between the supporters of Mordred and of Constantine, the latter being fanatically racialist. Boece, inventing this struggle, suppresses Constantine's relationship to Arthur in order to compound the villainy of the British party. The last battle becomes the resolution of the struggle for the succession, which Constantine wins – but it is an empty triumph. Arthur gets death as the reward of his weak submission to the Constantine faction, and in the aftermath the Britons are punished with swift and dreadful disaster. Nowhere in the literature is Constantine's succession so important, or does it so dictate events both during Arthur's reign and after.

Mordred's claim is vindicated only by the Scots, but it is important elsewhere as well. Indeed, it could be said that the whole tragedy, from HRB onwards, hinges on the succession. If Arthur had had a legitimate son, or compelled universal recognition of a designee, then Mordred's rebellion might never have happened. Much of medieval history is shaped round struggles for the succession, so this aspect of the tragedy must have had wide and compelling interest. HRB leaves no time for Mordred to justify his rebellion, but more leisurely authors do give him some opportunity, without necessarily sanctioning him. In the Vulgate *Mort*, Mordred can justly claim the barons' choice – though it is based on the lie that Arthur nominated him – and also the fact that (since the other nephews are dead, and Constantine does not feature in the Vulgate) he is Arthur's nearest surviving relation. His claims are very successful in the narrative, and the author himself does not wholly discount them. Imitators of the Vulgate eliminate these details but, on the other hand, the stanzaic *Mort*, Malory and some Spanish chronicles[45] substitute the apparently stronger claim of Arthur's nomination. In the English works, however, this is wholly specious, for Arthur is playing for time in order that Lancelot may come to his aid.[46] In every case, too, the recognition is forced on Arthur and does not mitigate the traitor's villainy. Development of his claims enriches the political tragedy, but even in the Vulgate it can do nothing to vindicate him.

Other shadowy claimants exist. Gawain we have mentioned.[47] Lancelot has a strong notional claim in the French prose,[48] but the iron hand of HRB fact restrains him. Nonetheless it is significant that neither the Vulgate nor the post-Vulgate mentions Constantine: if Lancelot cannot be king, then no one will be.

Generally, however, Mordred is the most important claimant, Constantine the eventual successor, and the various *sen* develop round these two 'facts'.

The first task of the successor is widely thought to be the 'Venjance Artu', the avenging of a medieval hero being widely thought a vital part of his story. Arthur's is universally held to be conducted through vendetta, not law, a fact which, in the HRB tradition, produces some discussion of the morality of sanctuarising murder.[49] Always the feud is pursued until Mordred's line is exterminated. The passage of time brings no mitigation of this 'primitive' law, which is stronger, even, in the alliterative *Morte* than in HRB. In the Scots, this extermination merely continues the Mordred/Constantine factional struggle, Arthur's avenging being a secondary consideration. The vengeance ethic is again toned down, wholly differently, by Vasconcellos, for whose hero the sons of Mordred constitute a political threat. Nevertheless, the fact that Vasconcellos, so far removed from HRB itself, should retain the struggle shows how deep-rooted vengeance was in the medieval mind, and in Arthur's story.

The same rootedness ensures the sons' survival into the prose cycles, although Constantine himself does not survive beyond Wace. In the Vulgate *Mort*, the sons reign unchallenged after Salisbury, for none remains to oppose them. In fact, Mordred's blood is victor at Salisbury if anyone is, and Lancelot, the Frenchman, is needed to save England from its own evil offspring. There is fine irony in the sight of Arthur's destroyer acting as his avenger. Lancelot's motives are noble and altruistic, but to the reader his very success put the last full stop to the tale of Arthurian and British collapse. The post-Vulgate tells the same story, but gives it less weight. Here, three separate vengeances are worked out in the aftermath, and the other two — Artus le Petit's attack on Blioberis and Mark's razzia — belong to themes more prominent in the cycle as a whole. The author — undiscriminating once again — would have done better to jettison the whole complication of Mordred's sons.

Lancelot's vengeance persists in late works. D'Outremeuse disconnects it from the enmity with Arthur, while Waurin makes of it a chillingly modern political pogrom extending to all Mordred's supporters. In Malory, however, we find a transformation. He eliminates the sons, not Constantine, so that when Lancelot, bent on vengeance, comes over, he finds no one to slay. Between the last battle and Lancelot's advent there is an interregnum of strange peace. It is unrealistic, of course, but by introducing it Malory implies that England, in spite of all, has a stability which will permit regeneration without French assistance — which happens in Constantine's reign. The last battle purges the realm, and there is no vengeance because there is no bitterness or enmity left. This new view adds to the sublimity of Malory's concluding pages. They are the work neither of a political realist nor of a nationalist, but of a magnanimous poet.

We will conclude our discussion of the Arthurian aftermath with brief remarks on commemoration. From HRB through the verse romances and into the prose, the need to authenticate Arthurian 'truths' produces an extraordinary mass of inventions and ratiocinations, in which the earnest claims to honesty on the authors' part complement their invention of an intense desire in the Arthurians themselves that a record might remain.[50] Side by side with the concept of

140

written records, however, there is the idea of 'archaeological' evidence, the survival of relics. This begins early, with the ruins of Caerleon and Caradoc's horn, and continues via Hardyng and Caxton to the present day. It is most sophisticated, however, in the post-Vulgate.[51] This insists particularly on commemorative statuary – which is curious, as real-life thirteenth-century sculpture was almost exclusively religious in inspiration and subject.[52] The post-Vulgate author may have been inspired by Roman statuary, or extrapolated from the religious; in either case he remarkably anticipates 'real' developments, proving once again that life imitates art – even, perhaps, in matters of Art.

The post-Vulgate, in fact, carries to a high pitch the creation of 'contemporary' evidence for the Arthurian period – a sort of literary Piltdown Man. It also, however, produces a counter-tendency. Against Arthur's desire for commemoration are enemy forces trying to obliterate all memory of him. These are not blind Chance and Destiny, but human enemies: Mordred's sons and Mark, who work to eliminate 'les proves et remembrances des proesces que le lignage le roy Artus avoit fait' (*Die Abenteuer*, p.124). Mark is the more effective. Like a latter-day Caracalla, he practises with fearsome efficiency the technique of 'damnatio memoriae'. Ironically, it is not Arthur's removal but Lancelot's that encourages Mark,[53] so that the Bans' power, which builds up Arthur's fame, is also indirectly responsible for its destruction.

The post-Vulgate contradicts itself (once again), however, in order to introduce a last innovation. This is the TP/post-Vulgate story of Charlemagne's tour of Arthurian Britain,[54] which assumes that relics do survive. The survival, however, does little to bolster Arthur's fame, since each reference to Charlemagne's visit involves a disparagement of Arthur. Now, this visit does not seem to be independently attested in Charlemagne literature. It is a post-Vulgate or TP invention intended to consummate the attack on Arthur begun by the Bans – as emerges very clearly when TP claims Charlemagne as a descendant of Ban. It is often asserted that the HRB/Wace Arthur is the Norman challenge to Charlemagne.[55] Here, a hundred years later, we find the challenge clearly recognised – and countered.

Our study of the byways of Arthur's death-tale has shown us many points of authorial dispute. Some disputes cause fragmentation, each author finding a solution which appeals to no one else, so that his version becomes a dead end. Sometimes intelligent consideration produces new stories, or even transformation of the mainline story. In a story as widely important as this, no tiny deviation is wholly devoid of significance. Whether the author seeks historical fact, poetic truth or philosophical truth, he is unlikely to set down any detail without some meditation.

Arthur's fame is imperishable: on that, at least, all medieval writers are agreed. And yet the overall impression given by the death-tale, in all its complexities, is not cheerful or triumphant. However great Arthur's achievements in any sphere, they pass away after his end. Relics cannot re-create the Arthurian age, and even enthusiasts who act out Arthurian scenes know that they are looking back on a lost Golden Age. Arthur's 'survival' is no comfort, because the 'surviving' Arthur is out of reach of mankind and its troubles. Nor does the dead Arthur attain that spiritual glory to which all the deepest medieval thinkers aspire — that glory which Galehaut, Lancelot and even Guinevere witness in their latest hour. Literary story development can only postpone, not fundamentally change, Arthur's final doom, and his story — like Alexander's — is fundamentally one of Mortality. He undergoes the ordinary lot of man, a struggle through the complications of earthly life towards an uncertain, and yet inevitable end; yet it is by re-enacting the tragedy of Everyman that he wins a permanent place in the human heart.

NOTES

Introduction

1 This sentence is based on an oral communication from Derek Brewer.
2 F. Bogdanow, *The Romance of the Grail* (Manchester, 1965), 10. Hereafter RG.
3 J. Weston, *The Legend of Sir Gawain* (London, 1897), 10-11; J. Markale, *Le Roi Arthur et la société celtique* (Paris, 1976), 146-7.
4 Markale, 305-42.
5 R. Barber, *The Figure of Arthur* (London, 1972), 108.
6 Point developed from an oral communication from Derek Brewer.
7 On this term see J. R. R. Tolkien, *Tree and Leaf* (London, 1964), 37-63.

Chapter I Antecedents

1 Gildas, *De Excidio et Conquestu Britanniae*, ed. H. Williams, Cymmrodorion Record Series, 3 (London, 1899-1901). For basic information on Gildas see ALMA, 1-3 and references there cited. See also T. Jones, 'The Early Evolution of the Legend of Arthur', NMS 8 (1964), 3-21.
2 *De Excidio*, 60.
3 Fletcher, *Arthurian Material*, 9.
4 I use the name 'Nennius' for convenience in reference, though his authorship of the *Historia Brittonum* is disputed: see D. Dumville, '"Nennius" and the *Historia Brittonum*', SC X (1975), 78-94. References to the text are to F. Lot, *Nennius et l'Historia Brittonum*, BEHE 263 (Paris, 1934).
5 Ranulf Higden, *Polychronicon*, ed. C. Babington et al., 9 vols (London, 1865-86), V, 306.
6 See R. Hanning, *The Vision of History in Early Britain* (New York, 1966), 45-62.
7 Ibid. 50-2.
8 Nennius, 170-96.
9 Ibid. 183-5. On Vortimer see R. Bromwich, *Trioedd Ynys Prydein* (Cardiff, 1961), 386-8.
10 On Germanus see I. Williams, 'Hen Chwedlau' THSC 1 (1946), 28-57 (38-40).
11 Geoffrey of Monmouth, *Historia Regum Britanniae*, ed. Acton Griscom (London, 1929), 370-3.
12 Hanning, 108-10.
13 Ibid. 3-43; B. Smalley, *Historians in the Middle Ages* (London, 1974),

passim, especially 18-63.

14　Hanning, 101-6, 123-9.

15　On this legend see E. Faral, *La Légende arthurienne*, BEHE 255-7 (Paris, 1929), I, 263-93.

16　HRB, 219.

17　On Henry and William see Fletcher, 38-44. I assume the non-existence of Geoffrey's 'vetustissimus liber'; on Geoffrey's sources see ALMA, 81-5 and references there cited.

18　Henry of Huntingdon, *Historia Regum Anglorum*, ed. T. Arnold, RS (London, 1879), 48.

19　William of Malmesbury, *Gesta Regum Anglorum*, ed. W. Stubbs, RS (London, 1887-9), I, 11-12.

20　Ibid. 12. On the survival legend generally see ALMA, 64-71, with references.

21　See especially Hanning, 121-71; J. S. P. Tatlock, *The Legendary History of Britain* (Berkeley and Los Angeles, 1950) (hereafter LHB), passim.

22　Hanning, 145.

23　ALMA, 85.

24　On this theme in Geoffrey see B. Roberts, 'Geoffrey of Monmouth and Welsh Historical Tradition', NMS XX (1976), 30-9 (33).

25　On the Welsh background to Uther, see TYP, 520-2.

26　On Merlin see LHB, 171-7; A. O. H. Jarman, *The Legend of Merlin* (Cardiff, 1960).

27　R. W. Southern, 'History as Prophecy', TRHS New Series 22 (1972), 159-78.

28　On recurrence see Hanning, 136-40.

29　To whom William of Rennes, a twelfth-century Latin imitator of HRB, compares Arthur: *Gesta Regum Britanniae*, ed. F. Michel, Cambrian Archaeological Association (Bordeaux, 1862), l. 2979.

30　B. Roberts, 'Testunau hanes Cymraeg canol', in *Y Traddodiad Rhyddiaith yn yr Oesau Canol*, ed. Geraint Bowen (Llandysul, 1974), 274-301 (298-9).

31　Cf. Lathuillière, 126, n. 31.

32　Below, pp. 76-80.

33　*Perceval*, ed. W. Roach, TLF 71 (Geneva, 1959), ll. 6169-70.

34　Ed. J. R. R. Tolkien and E. V. Gordon (2nd edition revised by N. Davis, Oxford, 1967), ll. 1-35; also ll. 2525-6, an echo at the close of the poem.

35　*Historia Meriadoci and De Ortu Walwanii*, ed. J. D. Bruce (Göttingen, 1913), 1.

36　E. Köhler thinks that Chrétien intended to end the Arthurian world in *Perceval*: *Ideal und Wirklichkeit in der höfischen Epik*, Beihefte zur ZRP, 97 (2nd ed., Tübingen, 1970), 207-8, 211. I consider it unlikely that Chrétien would have gone so far, but there is certainly a feeling of foreboding.

37　*Cligès*, ed. M. Roques, CFMA (Paris, 1970); L. D. Wolfgang, *Bliocadran*, Beihefte zur ZRP, 150 (Tübingen, 1976).

38　*Historia Regum Anglicarum*, in R. Howlett (ed.), *Chronicles of the Reign of Stephen*, RS (London, 1884-9), I, 11-18. See also J. E. Houseman, 'Higden, Trevisa, Caxton and the Beginnings of Arthurian Criticism', RES 23 (1947), 209-17 (209).

39　*Polychronicon*, V, 337, 339; Thomas Gray, *Scalacronica* in M. L. Meneghetti, *I fatti di Bretagna* (Padua, 1979), 69-71. See also Houseman, 211; Fletcher, 182, 225.

40　Boece, *Scotorum Historiae* (Paris, 1574), ff. 154v-166r. On the Scots chroniclers generally see Fletcher, 241-8; K. H. Göller, 'König Arthur in den schottischen Chroniken', *Anglia* 80 (1962), 390-404; F. Alexander, 'Late Scottish Medieval Attitudes to the Figure of King Arthur: a Reassessment', *Anglia* 93 (1975), 19-28.

41 *Scalacronica*, in Meneghetti, *I fatti*, 70.
42 Cf. Fletcher, 241.
43 W. Ferguson, *Scotland's Relations with England* (Edinburgh, 1977), 17-73, passim.
44 Boece, f. 158r.
45 W. Entwistle, *The Arthurian Legend in the Literature of the Spanish Peninsula* (London, 1925), 37; E. G. Gardner, *The Arthurian Legend in Italian Literature* (London, 1930), 6.
46 *Chronicon Monasterii de Hales* (British Library MS Cotton Cleopatra D III), ff. 7r-8r; *Scalacronica* (Corpus MS), f. 820; John of Glastonbury, *Historia de Rebus Glastoniensibus*, ed. J. P. Carley, British Archaeological Reports 47 (1978).
47 LHB, 262.
48 *The Historia Regum Britanniae: A Variant Version*, ed. J. Hammer (Cambridge, Mass., 1951); Wace, *Roman de Brut*, ed. I. Arnold, 2 vols, SATF (Paris, 1938). See also ALMA, 94-103, with references.
49 Smalley, 27ff.
50 Ed. W. A. Nitze, CFMA (Paris, 1971). See ALMA, 251-9, with references.
51 On the generation problems in Perceval's ancestry, see Wolfgang, *Bliocadran*, 1-37 passim.
52 ALMA, 254-6.
53 Ibid. 320-1.
54 Ed. W. A. Nitze and T. A. Jenkins (New York, 1922).
55 Vol. I of Sommer. See ALMA, 313-15, with references.
56 Vol. VII of Sommer. See ALMA, 336-8.
57 Analysed in Löseth, 423-35, 487-91. See ALMA, 350-2.
58 Lathuillière, 393-4.
59 Köhler, 39-43.
60 Löseth, 423-6.
61 John of Glastonbury, 89-92, 98-9.
62 See Meneghetti, *I fatti*, 70-1.
63 *Mer des histoires*, ed. A. Borgnet and S. Bormans (Brussels, 1864-87). See also Fletcher, 222-4.

Chapter II Conception and Birth

1 LHB, 312-19.
2 Ibid. 317, n. 52.
3 See B. Roberts, *Brut y Brenhinedd*, DIAS, MMW, 5 (Dublin, 1971), xiv-xv.
4 W. Schmidt, *Untersuchungen zum 'Geta' des Vitalis Blesensis* (Ratingen, 1975), 16. *Geta*, ed. C. Müller (Bern, 1840).
5 Hyginus, *Fabulae*, ed. M. Grant (Lawrence, Kansas U.P., 1960), 47.
6 LHB, 317.
7 Grant, 7.
8 *Gesta*, ll. 2924-7.

9 LHB, 317, n.49.
10 Ibid. 313-14.
11 Cf. LHB, 318.
12 Hammer, 221.
13 As Tatlock does: LHB, 316, n.45.
14 'The Concept of Sin in Medieval Romance', in *Studies in Honour of M. Schlauch*, ed. M. Brahmer et al. (Warsaw, 1966), 21-30 (21-8).
15 Hanning, 153-4.
16 See e.g. Gautier de Châtillon, *Alexandreis*, PL, vol. 209 (Paris, 1855), col. 465; *The Old French 'Roman d'Alexandre'*, ed. E. Armstrong, et al., Eliott Monographs 36-8 (Princeton, 1937), 2, ll. 145-84.
17 C. B. Lewis suggests in *Classical Mythology and Arthurian Romance* (Oxford, 1932), 253-6, that the Atrean legend influenced the Arthurian. His evidence is flimsy, however: the resemblance is surely generic.
18 Malory, *Works*, ed. Eugène Vinaver (Oxford, 1947).
19 An important point: see below p.30.
20 Ed. W. Roach (Philadelphia, 1941). On its relationship to Boron's work, 15-130, passim. Merlin expects salvation: 278.
21 *El Baladro des Sabio Merlin*, ed. P. Bohigas, Selecciones Bibliofilas, vols 2, 14, 15 (Barcelona, 1957-62), II. 184. See also E. Brugger, 'L'Enserement Merlin IV', ZFSL, 35 (1909), 1-55 (31-2).
22 E. Brugger, 'L'Enserement Merlin II', ZFSL, 30 (1906), 169-239, (173-86); *Perlesvaus*, I. 281-2, II. 321.
23 See J. W. C. Turner, *Russell on Crime*, 2 vols (London, 1950), I. 806.
24 Cf. T. Wright, 'The Tale of King Arthur', in *Malory's Originality*, ed. R. M. Lumiansky (Baltimore, 1964), 12-66 (25).
25 Below pp.41-5.
26 F. Pollock and F. W. Maitland, *The History of English Law*, 2nd edn, reissued by S. F. C. Milsom, 2 vols (Cambridge, 1968), II. 396-9; S. M. Cretney, *Principles of Family Law* (London, 1974), 309-11.
27 Pollock and Maitland, II. 397; Beaumanoir, *Coutumes de Beauvais*, ed. A. Salmon (Paris, 1899-1900), I. 295.
28 Beaumanoir, I. 295, note.
29 As he well may: for possible English affiliations of Boron see W. A. Nitze, 'Robert de Boron, Enquiry and Summary', S 28 (1953), 279-96 (280-5).
30 Below pp.41-3. H. Micha, in 'Reflets du monde contemporain dans le *Merlin* de Robert de Boron', RLR 81 (1975), 395-430 (409-11), says that Boron considers Arthur a true bastard; but this is surely mistaken.
31 *Of Arthur and of Merlin*, ed. O. D. Macrae-Gibson, EETS no. 268 (Oxford U.P., 1973), I, ll. 3154-9. Hereafter AoM.
32 *Arthur*, ed. F. J. Furnivall, EETS, Original Series, 2 (Oxford U.P., 1864).
33 Fletcher, 182, 184-5. L. M. Keeler, *Geoffrey of Monmouth and the Late Latin Chroniclers 1300-1500* (Berkley and Los Angeles, 1946), 9; *Nobiliaro (Os Libros de Lingagens)*, ed. A. Herculano, Portugaliae Monumenta Historica (Lisbon, 1856), I. 243.
34 Göller, 'Schottischen Chroniken', 398-9.
35 See e.g. ALMA, 108, with references.
36 Layamon, *Brut*, ed. G. L. Brook and R. F. Leslie, EETS 250-77 (Oxford, 1973, 1978), ll. 9607-15; Roach, *Continuations*, IV, ll. 31792-31858. How these two authors came to tell the same story is a problem which we cannot go into here.

37 *Pedeir Keinc y Mabinogi*, ed. I. Williams (Reprint, Cardiff, 1964), 20 (hereafter PKM); Sommer, III. 13-19.
38 John of Glastonbury, 89.
39 Lord Raglan, *The Hero* (London, 1936), 190-294, passim.
40 On Macghnimhartha generally, and Cochulainn's in particular, see P. I. Mac Cana, *Celtic Mythology* (3rd impression, London, 1975), 101-5.
41 *De Ortu*, 54-5; D'Outremeuse II. 182-4; Boece, f. 155r.
42 Cf. R. Imelmann, *Layamon's Brut: Versuch über seine Quellen* (Berlin, 1906), 60-2.

Chapter III   Accession

1 There is a useful summary of Arthur's early Welsh appearances in J. M. Williams, 'Y Darlun o Arthur ym Mhucheddau'r Saint ac yn Englynion Arthur a'r Eryr' (Unpublished M. A. thesis, University College of Wales, Aberystwyth, 1969), 1-31; on Arthur in the lives see pp. 48-142. See also R. Barber, *King Arthur in Legend and History* (London, 1973), 25-56; ALMA, 12-51.
2 *Owein*, ed. R. L. Thomson, DIAS, MMW 4 (Dublin, 1968); *Peredur*, ed. G. W. Goetinck (Cardiff, 1976), 13; *Geraint*, in *Llyfr Gwyn Rhydderch*, ed. J. G. Evans (2nd edn with preface by R. M. Jones, Cardiff, 1973), col. 386.
3 I disagree with J. Markale, who in *Le Roi Arthur et la société celtique* (Paris, 1976), 221-38, connects Arthur with Irish notions of kingship. There is no real warrant in even the Welsh material for such a connection.
4 K. H. Shepherd, 'The Presentation of King Arthur in Medieval Romance' (Unpublished M. A. thesis, London University, 1907), 245.
5 On whom see L. K. Born, 'The Perfect Prince', R 3 (1928), 470-504 (494).
6 On such theories in LP, see E. Kennedy, 'Social and Political Ideas in the First Part of the French Prose *Lancelot*', MA 26 (1957), 90-106.
7 On all such see R. M. Woolley, *Coronation Rites* (Cambridge, 1915).
8 On Pepin see E. Peters, *The Shadow King* (New Haven and London, 1970), 34-8; on William, D. C. Douglas, *William the Conqueror* (London, 1964), 181-9; on Philip, E. Perroy, *La Guerre de Cent Ans* (Paris, 1945), 54-6. The example of Guy was suggested to me by Dr Morgan.
9 LHB, 290-1.
10 Ibid. 304.
11 E. Kantorowicz, *The King's Two Bodies* (Princeton, 1957), 312-20.
12 R. Fawtier, *The Capetian Kings of France*, trans. L. Botter and R. J. Adam (London, 1960), 48-50; Kantorowicz, 313-36 and passim.
13 A loaded word: see Peters, 39-45, and compare HRB, 364 (Constans and Vortigern, *dignus/indignus*).
14 C. Petit-Dutaillis, *La Monarchie féodale en France et en Angleterre, X^e -XIIIe siècle* (Paris, 1933), 27.
15 HRB, 455-8. This is not a coronation as P. E. Schramm (*History of the English Coronation*, Oxford, 1937, 64) implies.
16 M. Bloch, *Les Rois thaumaturges* (Strasbourg and Paris, 1924), 186-223.

17   Often the case: cf. Michel's introduction, xvii.

18   L. D. Wickham Legg, *English Coronation Rites* (Westminster, 1901), 30-1.

19   Legg, 30, mentions only one MS.

20   A slightly fuller version is found in the Didot *Perceval*, 299-300.

21   R. Imelmann, *Layamon's Brut: Versuch über seine Quellen* (Berlin, 1906) considers the possibility (61-2), but draws no conclusions.

22   See below pp.46-8.

23   Kantorowicz, 42-96.

24   On origins and analogues to this motif, see A. Micha, 'L'Epreuve de l'épee', R 70 (1948-9), 37-50.

25   AoM, ll.2088-90. For the Welsh see J. H. Davies, 'A Welsh Version of the Birth of Arthur', YC 24 (1913), 247-64 (253). For Salazar see H. L. Sharrer, 'The Legendary History of Britain in Lope Garcia de Salazar's Libro de las bienandanzas e fortunas' (Unpublished PhD thesis, University of California, Los Angeles, 1970), 115.

26   See e.g. Born, passim.

27   M. A. Klenke, 'Some Medieval Concepts of King Arthur', KFLQ V (1958), 191-7, argues that Arthur was widely seen as *Alter Christus*, but her evidence is largely iconographical, and seems flimsy to me. Boron's parallelism works on different lines.

28   See e.g. R. S. Loomis, *Celtic Myth and Arthurian Romance* (Columbia, 1927), passim.

29   Stith Thompson, *Motif Index of Folk Literature* (Copenhagen, 1955), H.1242. The motif figures in the legend of Niall's accession — see F. J. Byrne, *Irish Kings and High Kings* (London, 1973), 73-6 — but a direct Irish connection with Boron is highly unlikely.

30   Compare St Alexis, and the child in Chaucer's *Prioress' Tale*.

31   For basic information on Malory's use of sources in this Tale, see *Works*, 1265-1359.

32   M. Bloch, 218-22.

33   See e.g. Petit-Dutaillis, 262-3.

34   Detailed comparison in K. H. Göller, *König Arthur in der englischen Litteratur des späten Mittelalters*, Palaestra 268 (Göttingen, 1963), 52-4. (Hereafter KA.)

35   Below pp.80-90.

36   On Augustus and Christ, see Hanning, 26-7.

37   On this attitude see H. Levy, 'As myn auctor seyeth', MA XII (1943), 26-38.

38   ALMA, 319-22, 325-8.

39   Davis, 252, 253, 256, 'Lord, remember me when thou comest into thy kingdom', cf. Luke 23.42.

40   Kantorowicz, 317-36.

41   As Göller says, KA, 51.

42   M. Keen, *The Laws of War in the Later Middle Ages* (Oxford, 1965), 68.

43   Shepherd, 69-71.

44   E. Pochoda, *Arthurian Propaganda* (Chapel Hill, 1971), 46-52, interprets the oath in detail in terms of contemporary theory.

45   Not in his predecessor's reign, as Vinaver says (*Works* III. 1285).

46   Kantorowicz, 328-30.

Chapter IV   Arthur at War

1   Keen, 64.
2   Köhler, 106-8.
3   On warfare in the epic, see R. Bloch, *Medieval French Literature and Law* (California U.P., 1977), 63-106.
4   TYP, 88.
5   'Culhwch ac Olwen', in *Llyfr Gwyn Rhydderch*, cols 452-507.
6   *Cligès*, ed. A. Micha, CFMA 84 (Paris, 1957), ll.6583-4. *Erec et Enide*, ed. M. Roques, CFMA 80 (Paris, 1970), ll.1884-1954. Renart de Beaujeu, *Le Bel inconnu*, ed. G. P. Williams, CFMA 38 (Paris, 1965), ll.5334-5592. *L'Atre périlleux*, ed. B. Woledge, CFMA 76 (Paris, 1936), ll.10-11. *Yder*, ed. H. Gelzer, GRL 31 (Dresden, 1913), ll.2496-9. *Hunbaut*, ed. J. Stürzinger and H. Breuer, GRL 35 (Dresden, 1914), ll.92-7. *Li Chevaliers as deus espees*, ed. W. Förster (Halle, 1877), ll.75-110. *Les Merveilles de Rigomer*, ed. W. Förster and H. Breuer, GRL 19 and 39 (Dresden, 1908, 1914), ll.14795-8. *Floriant et Floriete*, ed. H. Williams, UMPLL 23 (Michigan, 1947), ll.2637-66. *Durmart li Galois*, ed. J. Gildea (Villanova, 1965), ll.12760-4 (less definite).
7   Keen, 67.
8   A. M. Hocart, *Kingship* (Oxford, 1927), 20-32.
9   Keen, 66-7.
10   F. H. Russell, *The Just War in the Middle Ages* (Cambridge, 1975), passim.
11   Below pp.131-40.
12   T. Turville-Petre, *The Alliterative Revival* (Ipswich, 1977), 103.
13   Keen, passim.
14   See R. Barber, *The Figure of Arthur* (London, 1972). The latter view was suggested to me by Mr Oliver Padell.
15   Barber, *Figure of Arthur*, 54-104.
16   Ibid. 101-4.
17   A. Micha, 'Les Sources de la Vulgate du Merlin', R 72 (1952), 299-345 (301-4).
18   Below pp.62-3.
19   Kantorowicz, 261.
20   Below p.100.
21   'Aspects of Celtic Mythology', PBA 20 (1954), 207-42.
22   Mac Cana, 119-20.
23   Russell, 298.
24   M. Pelan, *L'Influence du Brut de Wace sur les romanciers de son temps* (Paris, 1933), 41-50.
25   Ibid. 43.
26   *Roman d'Alexandre*, ll.1963-2006; compare l.112. J. R. Hamilton, *Alexander the Great* (London, 1973), 120-7.
27   *Syr Percyvelle of Galles*, ed. F. Holthausen and J. Campion, AMT 5 (Heidelberg, 1913), ll.240-446, passim.
28   *Durmart*, l.6064; *Deus espées*, ll.209-93.
29   F. Lot, *Étude sur le Lancelot en Prose*, BEHE 226 (Paris, 1918), 356-8. Roach's textual notes (463n., 464n.) show that scribes did not recognise the name Claudas, which they would if it were familiar from LP.
30   See E. Sandoz, 'Tourneys in the Arthurian Tradition', S 19 (1944), 389-404 (402).

31 Russell, 44.
32 See E. Vinaver, *The Rise of Romance* (Oxford, 1971), 129-38.
33 H. Adolf, 'Studies in the *Perlesvaus*', SP 62 (1945), 723-40; J. N. Carman, 'South Welsh Geography and British History in the *Perlesvaus*', in *A Medieval Miscellany*, ed. N. J. Lacy (Lawrence, 1972), 37-57 (51-7).
34 This evolution of Arthur's career is being studied by Dr Kennedy.
35 On which see RG, 76-8, 170-4.
36 On Anglo-French nationalistic rivalry at this time, see R. W. Southern, 'England's First Entry into Europe', in *Medieval Humanism* (Oxford, 1970), 135-56; J. C. Holt, 'The End of the Anglo-Norman Realm', PBA LXI (1975), 223-64.
37 See ALMA, 485-8: AoM, Lovelich's *Merlin*, the prose *Merlin*.
38 F. Alexander (27-8) says that the Scots romance is less hostile than its source; but the selection is still significant. Edition by W. Skeat, EETS OS 6 (Reprint Oxford U.P., 1965).
39 See e.g. Fawtier, 86.
40 Translated K. G. Webster (New York, 1951), 134.
41 E.g. Sommer III. 335; Micha I. 85, III. 37; Lathuillière, 200; *La Folie Lancelot*, ed. F. Bogdanow, ZRP Beiheft 109 (Tübingen, 1965), 119.
42 Lot, *Etude*, 184-5.
43 This was a recurrent theoretical point: see J. Riley-Smith, *What Were the Crusades?* (London, 1978), 24-8.
44 Lot, *Nennius*, 195, n.8; D'Outremeuse II. 203-17; Add. 25434, fol. 150-152a; *Golagros and Gawain*, ed. F. J. Amours, in *Scottish Alliterative Poems*, STS (1897), ll. 302-4.
45 Though Frederick II was excommunicate at the time of his crusade. This may have inspired the *Prophécies* author, who was certainly interested in Italian affairs: see ALMA, 352.
46 On the False Guinevere see below pp. 100-2.
47 Lot, *Nennius*, 195 n.8.
48 Alliterative *Morte Arthure*, ed. E. Brock, EETS OS 8 (reprinted 1967). On the *Morte*'s influence on *Golagros*, see W. Matthews, The *Tragedy of Arthur* (Pennsylvania, 1960), 163-70.
49 G. Cary, *The Medieval Alexander* (Cambridge, 1956), 77-end, especially 94-7, 101, 146-8. Matthews, 70-112, compares the Middle English Arthur with Alexander in this light; he exaggerates the condemnatory implications of the resemblance for Arthur.
50 Cf. LHB, 305.
51 See Walter Ullmann, 'On the Influence of Geoffrey of Monmouth on English History', SH (1965), 257-76.
52 See especially Boece, fol. 163b.
53 'Lai de Melion', in P. Tobin, *Les Lais anonymes des XIIe et XIIIe siècles*, PRF 143 (Geneva, 1976), 289-318.
54 P. Meyer, *Alexandre le Grand dans la littérature française du Moyen Age* (Paris, 1886), II. 190.
55 The MS tradition of the First Continuation is complex: see Roach, *Continuations*, I. xxxiv-xli. I normally follow the mixed redaction (vol. I, MSS TVD).
56 Comparison in KA, 121-4.
57 Typically 'romance': see e.g. J. Finlayson, *Morte Arthure*, YMT (London, 1962), 84n.

58 Especially Matthews, passim; see also KA, 142-3.
59 *The Auntyrs of Arthure at the Tarne Wathelyne*, ed. R. Hanna (Manchester, 1974).
60 KA, 123; Matthews, 170-1.
61 Micha I. 61.
62 See Roberts, *Brut y Brenhinedd*, xxiv-xxxi.
63 *Vita Gildae*, ed. T. Mommsen, in MGH, Auct. antiq. XIII, part I.
64 T. Jones, 'Chwedl Huail ap Caw ac Arthur', in *Astudiaethau Amrywiol a gyflwynir i Syr Thomas Parry-Williams*, ed. T. Jones (Cardiff, 1968), 48-64.
65 Above, p. 11.
66 See M. J. Wilkes, *The Problem of Sovereignty in the Later Middle Ages* (Cambridge, 1963).
67 Hanning, 169.
68 Leo of Naples, *Alexander*, ed. F. Pfister, SMT 6 (Heidelberg, 1913), 59-98, passim.
69 Howlett, *Chronicles*, IV. 65-75. See Fletcher, 120-1.
70 Vinaver, *Rise of Romance*, 60-7.
71 As A. Micha suggests on the basis of source-study: 'La Guerre contre les Romains dans la Vulgate du Merlin', R 72 (1951), 310-13.
72 Fawtier, 83-7.
73 Matthews: Turville-Petre, 102-3; R. M. Lumiansky, 'The Alliterative *Morte Arthure*, the Concept of Medieval Tragedy and the Cardinal Virtue Fortitude', MRS 3 (1968), 98-117, with references.
74 John Hardyng, *Chronicle*, Facsimile, English Experience 80 (Amsterdam, 1976), f. lxxvi recto. See KA, 34-9.
75 On Malory and the *Mort* see M. E. Dichmann in *Malory's Originality*, 71-89; on Hardyng, Benson, 69.
76 Usual tactics for a medieval commander: see C. Oman, *The Art of War in the Middle Ages* (London, 1899), vol. 2, passim.

Chapter V Peacetime

1 Title of study by J. Campbell (2nd edn, Princeton, 1968).
2 G. Jones, *Kings, Beasts and Heroes* (London, 1972), passim, especially 112-17. On literary hunts see P. Thiebaux, *The Stag of Love* (Ithaca, N.Y., 1944).
3 Freymond, *Artus' Kampf.*
4 A. de Vries, *Dictionary of Symbols and Imagery* (Amsterdam and London, 1974), 85-6.
5 See I. Foster, 'Astudiaeth o chwedl *Culhwch ac Olwen*' (Unpublished M.A. thesis, U.C.W. Aberystwyth, 1935), 197-241.
6 In 'The Avowyng of Arthur', ed. C. Brookhouse, A xv (1968), ll. 161-273. See KA, 81-3. There is no need to postulate direct Celtic influence on 'The Avowyng', though it is possible.
7 J. M. Williams, 68.
8 On Chrétien's sources and his use of them, see R. Bromwich, 'Celtic Dynastic Themes and the Breton Lays', ET 9 (1960-1), 439-73. On stags in Celtic

belief, see A. Ross, *Pagan Celtic Britain* (London, 1974), 175-201.

9   As in C. Luttrell's study *The Creation of the First Arthurian Romance* (London, 1974).
10 On Dinadan see E. Baumgartner, *Le Tristan en prose*, PRF 133 (Geneva, 1975), 253-9, with references.
11 As in *Perlesvaus* I. 48-51; Huth I. 150-2.
12 *Avowyng*, ll. 257-62; 'Dame Ragnell', in D. B. Sands, *Middle English Metrical Romances* (New York, 1966), ll. 13-50; cf. *Auntyrs*, ll. 33-9 and Hanna's remarks, 45-6.
13 J. Bruce, 'Arthur and the Wild Hunt', RR 3 (1912), 192-7; also A. Taylor, RR 12 (1921), 285-9.
14 Sandoz, 401; Löseth, 400.
15 On early evidence for Tristan see R. Bromwich, 'Some Remarks on the Celtic Sources of *Tristan*', THSC (1955), 32-60.
16 PKM, 1.
17 A famous story to this effect is told of Philip Augustus: see A. Luchaire, *Philippe-Auguste* (Paris, 1881), 8-10.
18 E.g. *Elucidation*, ll. 402-35; *Perlesvaus*, I. 310-13; Sommer, III. 164.
19 I. Williams, 'Englynion Arthur a'r Eryr', BBCS (1925), 269-86. See also J. M. Williams, 143-70.
20 I. Williams, 'Englynion . . .', 280.
21 PKM, 1, 89.
22 On the two versions of this story, see Lot, *Etude*, 372-7; A. Micha, 'Etudes sur le Lancelot en Prose', R 76 (1935), 334-41.
23 Cf. C. Pickford, *L'Evolution du roman arthurien en prose* (Paris, 1960), 221-3.
24 Stith Thompson F. 331.
25 Above p. 25.
26 William of Newburgh, 16.
27 On this process see e.g. T. Jones, 'Y Stori Werin yng Nghymru', THSC (1970), 16-32 (16).
28 H. Owen, 'Peniarth MS 118', YC 27 (1917), 115-49 (129).
29 Barber, *Figure of Arthur*, 119; H. Pilch, 'Galfrids Historia', GRM Neue Folge 7 (1951), 254-73 (262).
30 Giraldus Cambrensis, 'Descriptio Cambriae', in *Opera*, ed. J. S. Brewer et al. (London, 1861-91), VI. 185.
31 *Culhwch* bears marks of reworking: Foster, 'Astudiaeth', 19-22.
32 Cf. T. Jones and G. Jones, *The Mabinogion*, Everyman's Library 97 (Reprint, London, 1968), xxv. It is not necessarily a Celtic trait.
33 Cf. Shepherd, 15.
34 Cf. M. C. Blanchet, 'Le Double visage d'Arthur chez Layamon', in *Studi in Onore di Italo Siciliano* (Florence, 1969), I. 71-82 (71).
35 On whom see J. Finlaysson, 'Arthur and the Giant of St Michael's Mount', MA 33 (1964), 112-20.
36 *Aeneid*, III. ll. 613-61; *Metamorphoses*, XIV. ll. 167-220.
37 On which see Finlaysson, 'Arthur and the Giant . . .', 116-17.
38 Larousse Encyclopedia, 90; Genesis 6.4.
39 Shades of *Beowulf* are often suspected in Layamon: see e.g. Wyld, 14.
40 Blanchet, 'Le double visage d'Arthur'.
41 See below.
42 B. Blakey, 'The Harley *Brut*', R 82 (1965), 44-67 (55, l. 150-1).

43 See ALMA, 376.
44 T. Gwynn Jones, *Welsh Folklore and Folk-Custom* (London, 1930), 78-80. No-Man: Stith Thompson K 602. See also A. Taylor, 'King Arthur and the Tale of the Three Truths', RP 17 (1963-4), 586-94.
45 Story of Arthur's chair and Arthur's oven: see E. Faral, 'Un des plus anciens textes relatifs à Arthur', *Arthuriana* I (1928), 22-8.
46 Above p.53.
47 Matthews, 24, 129.
48 Foster, *Astudiaeth*, 284-5.
49 See e.g. Köhler, 67-88.
50 *Lai du Mantel*, ed. F. Wulff, R 14 (1885), 364, 1.242-3; *La Vengeance Raguidel*, ed. M. Friedwagner in *Raoul de Houdenc: Sämtliche Werke* (Halle, 1909), II, ll.42-60; Gardner, 246 (on the romance of *Gismirante*, where the treatment reaches the zenith of absurdity).
51 Jones and Jones, *Mabinogion*, xxvii.
52 See Roach, *Didot Perceval*, 44 n.1; RG, passim.
53 On which see e.g. Köhler, 22-3.
54 E.g. Löseth, 326.
55 KA, 35.
56 See e.g. Gerbert de Montreuil, *Perceval*, ed. M. Williams and M. Oswald, 3 vols, CFMA 28, 50, 101 (Paris, 1922, 1925, 1975), I. 1460-4; Sommer, V. 319-20.
57 C. T. Erickson, *Le Lai du cor*, ANTS 24 (Oxford, 1973), 3-22.
58 As he always does, save in *Diu Krône*: Erickson, 4.
59 On this episode see M. Lambert, *Style and Vision in the Mort d'Arthure* (Yale U.P., 1975), 56-63.
60 F. Bogdanow, *La Folie Lancelot*, ZRP Beiheft 109 (Tübingen, 1965), 80.
61 R. Bloch, 63-4, 77-81.
62 First Continuation, TVD 3332-3447; GGK passim. On the motif see E. Brewer, *From Cuchulainn to Gawain* (Cambridge, 1973), 1-34.
63 Cf. Shepherd, 6.
64 Löseth, 423-6; *Tristan de Loenis*, ed. A. Bonilla (Madrid, 1912), 302-13; Gardner, 44-63, 90.
65 Cf. above p.22.
66 Vulgate *Mort: La Mort le roi Artu*, ed. J. Frappier, TLF (3rd edn, 1964). On the motif generally see *Perlesvaus* II. 92-5.
67 Ed. M. Roques, CFMA 89 (Paris, 1972).
68 *Li Chevaliers du papegau*, ed. F. Hackenkamp (Halle, 1896); see ALMA, 335. In prose, but accepts all the verse-romance conventions.
69 *Arthur and Gorlagon*, ed. G. Kittredge (New York, 1966).
70 Ed. M. Mills, EETS 261 (Oxford, 1969).
71 On which see Peters, 175-81.
72 See Peters, 199-202.
73 Above p.44.
74 On knighting ceremony, see R. Barber, *The Knight and Chivalry* (London, 1964), 38-40.
75 Ibid. 292.
76 Cf. RG, 215-16.
77 *Die Abenteuer Gawains, Ywains und Le Morholts mit den drei Jungfrauen*, ed. O. Sommer, ZRP, Beiheft 47 (Halle, 1913), 94.
78 The exact relationship of TP to the post-Vulgate is disputed. For a recent

consideration, see Baumgartner, 40-62.
79 Cf. Pickford, *Evolution*, 223.
80 Bonilla, *Tristan*, 204-6; Malory II. 490-1; Gardner, 81-2, 184, 298.
81 Below p. 141.
82 On such imitation see L. Benson, *Malory's Mort d'Arthure* (Harvard U.P., 1976), 162-85.
83 Lambert, 57-109 passim.
84 Pochoda, passim, especially 44-52; R. Bloch, 14-61; G. Keiser, 'The Theme of Justice in the Alliterative Mort Arthur', AM (1975), 94-109. On the Lanval theme, see e.g. KA, 92-4, with references.
85 Jolliffe, *Angevin Kingship* (London, 1955), 139-65.
86 R. Bloch, 128-37.
87 Cf. R. Bloch, 14-61 passim.
88 *Yvain*, ll. 5985-6358; First Continuation, TVD, ll. 656-1076; Second Continuation, ll. 28670-28976; *Awntyrs*, ll. 469-624.
89 On the Yvain settlement see Hanning, 'The Social Significance of Twelfth-Century Chivalric Romance', MH New Series III, (1972), 1-25 (19).
90 On the relationship, see Frappier, *Etude*, 211-12.

Chapter VI   Relationships

1   Lot, *Nennius*, 194, 216 and notes; ALMA, 12-19; TYP, 97-121; S. M. Pearce, *The Kingdom of Dumnonia* (Padstow, 1978), 139-52, passim.
2   ALMA, 319-20.
3   Fletcher, 189; John of Glastonbury, 68, 89.
4   Above pp. 26-9.
5   See M. Blaess, 'Arthur's Sisters', BBSIA 8 (1956), 69-77.
6   Giraldus Cambrensis, VI. 200.
7   *Culhwch*, cols 459-60; Wade-Evans, 196.
8   Mac Cana, 101; R. J. Cormier, 'Open Contrast: Tristan and Diarmaid', S 51 (1975), 589-601; Bromwich, 'Some Remarks . . .'
9   T. P. Ellis, *Welsh Tribal Law and Custom in the Middle Ages* (Oxford, 1926), I. 382-5; Tacitus, *Germania* XX; T. A. Gorbaty, 'The Uncle-Nephew Relationship: Origin and Development', F 88 (1977), 221-35.
10 William of Malmesbury, 42.
11 J. M. Williams, 158-9.
12 Blaess, 71.
13 W. G. Harris, 'Peredur nai Arthur', BBCS (1975), 311-14; *Lanzelet*, 92.
14 Blaess, 72-7.
15 On Morgain, see L. A. Paton, *The Fairy Mythology of Arthurian Romance*, (2nd edn, New York, 1960).
16 Sommer II. 127, 130, 167.
17 P. Meyer, *Les Enfances Gavain*, R 39 (1910), 5, 11, 193-208.
18 Paton, *Fairy Mythology*, passim. Loomis, *Celtic Myth*, 191-4.
19 Paton, I. 29-33, II. 136-43, and passim.
20 On this see Paton, 39-47.
21 E.g. Markale, 236-68.

22   K. T. Webster, *Guinevere: A Study of her Abductions*, ed. D. T. Webster (Milton, Mass., 1951).

23   Cf. LHB, 310-11.

24   TYP, 155. 'Cawr' can occasionally mean simply 'hero'.

25   Forster, 114-21.

26   See above p. 56.

27   On which see e.g. D. Kelly, *'Sens' and 'Conjointure' in 'The Chevalier de la charette'* (The Hague, Paris, 1966).

28   Though G. Hutchings assumes that it was incorporated into the design: *Le Roman en Prose de Lancelot* (Paris, 1930), lii-lv.

29   See A. Micha, 'Les Episodes du voyage en Sorelois et de la fausse Guenièvre', R 76 (1955), 334-41; E. Kennedy, 'The Two Versions of the False Guinevere Episode in the Old French prose Lancelot', R 77 (1956), 94-104.

30   Cf. A. Micha, 'La Tradition manuscrite du *Lancelot* en prose', R 85 (1964), 478-504 (488).

31   A. Micha, 'La Suite Vulgate du Merlin: étude littéraire', ZRP 71 (1955), 33-58 (33).

32   'King Arthur and King Mark', 190-234.

33   Stanzaic *Mort Arthure*, ed. H. Bruce, EETS Extra Series 88 (Oxford, 1959), l. 912.

34   Compare Sommer, III. 389; *Folie Lancelot*, 17; Malory, I. 442.

35   III. 143. See E. Kennedy, 'The Arthur-Guinevere Relationship in Malory's Mort d'Arthur', SL 14 (1971), 29-40 (30).

36   TYP, 155-6.

37   Ibid. 156.

38   Jorge Ferreira de Vasconcellos, *Sagramor* (Memorial das Proezas da Segunda Table Redonda) (Lisbon, 1897), 14.

39   See below.

40   Wade-Evans, 26-7.

41   Sommer, II. 124; Huth, I. 147; Sommer, VII. 219; *Demanda*, 232-5.

42   *Lai du Cor*, ll. 298-306; *Rigomer*, ll. 16235-43.

43   Shepherd, 186.

44   *The Hero*, 180.

45   *I fatti*, 57-8; Fletcher, 211.

46   Lot, *Nennius*, 216; *Culhwch*, col. 499; TYP, 416; J. Bruce, 'Arthur's son Loholt', RR 3 (1912), 179-89.

47   Bruce, 'Arthur's son'.

48   Malory, III. 1150. Cambridge Add. 7071, f. 225d, has 'Booze' for 'Laholt', and this MS may, I suspect, have been Malory's actual source.

49   RG, 193.

50   Fletcher, 188; Gardner, 233; *Sagramor*, 5.

51   Frappier, *Etude*, 32-7.

52   'Concept of Sin . . .', 29.

53   E.g. Oedipus, Kullervo, Philomela, Apollonius.

54   H. Rondet, *Notes sur la théologie du péché* (Paris, 1957), 77-8.

55   Cf. *Queste*, 181; *Measure for Measure*, Act III, Scene 1.

56   On this 'fatherhood', see below p. 112.

57   Below p. 110.

58   E.g. *Rigomer*, ll. 16299-16302; First Continuation TVD 14077f; *Livre d'Artus*, VII. 47-56.

59   Sands, 324.

60 Köhler, 21-4.
61 Frappier, *Etude*, 191.
62 R. Thompson, 'Gawain against Arthur', F 85 (1974), 113-21.
63 Campbell, 130-48.
64 Especially in the Vulgate *Mort*. H. Blake, 'Etude sur les structures narratives dans la *Mort Artu*', RBPH (1972), 733-43.
65 J. W. Hales and F. J. Furnivall, *Bishop Percy's Folio Manuscript* (London, 1867-8), I. 88-102.
66 Cf. Matthews, 137.
67 See B. Roberts, 'Rhai o gerddi ymddiddan Llyfr du Caerfyrddin', in *Astudiaethau ar yr Hengerdd*, (Festschrift I. Foster), ed. R. Bromwich and R. Jones (Cardiff, 1978), 280-325 (p.300): 'guir goreu im bid'.
68 For this arrangement see Joliffe, 39-52 et passim.
69 See HRB 264.
70 Köhler, 22-30.
71 See e.g. Pickford, 273-85.
72 Above pp. 80-90.
73 Cf. E. Kennedy, 'King Arthur in the First Part of the Prose *Lancelot*', in *Medieval Miscellany* (Festschrift E. Vinaver), ed. F. Whitehead et al. (Manchester, 1965), 186-95 (190).
74 'Leges Anglorum', quoted in Joliffe, 32.
75 See e.g. Petit-Dutaillis, 258-60.
76 A favourite persona in medieval narrative.
77 Above p. 67.
78 Cf. Frappier, *Etude*, 282.
79 On this alliance see e.g. Köhler, 11-18.
80 Frappier, *Etude*, 191.
81 Though they have done homage to Mordred: 173.
82 TYP, 303-6; J. Haupt, *Der Truchsess Keie im Artusroman*, PSQ 57 (Berlin, 1971).
83 Born, 487.
84 The latter being primary counsellor to the English king: Petit-Dutaillis, 161-6.
85 Above p. 28.
86 J. N. Carman ('South Welsh Geography ...', 56) and H. Adolf ('Studies', 738) say that Lancelot is modelled on William, but this is needless: both are types.
87 A point made by Dr Kennedy.
88 Frappier, *Etude*, 328.

Chapter VII   Personal Attributes

1 On Alexander's vindictiveness see Cory, 101, 107, 110 and passim.
2 E.g. *Erec*, ll. 61-2; *Lancelot*, I. 181; Vulgate *Mort*, 227; Malory, I. 297; *Lybeaus Desconus*, ll. 218-21.
3 See K. E. Kirk, *Some Principles of Moral Theology* (London, 1921), 265-8.
4 Above p. 105.
5 On this salaciousness, cf. ALMA, 338.

6　See K. Höltgen, 'König Arthur und Fortuna', Anglia 75 (1957), 35-54.
7　J. M. Williams, 63-93.
8　Cf. Matthews, 154-61.
9　See above p.65.
10　E. Kennedy, 'Royal Broodings and Lovers' Trances in the First Part of the Prose *Lancelot*' in *Mélanges Jeanne Wathelet-Willem* (Liège, 1978), 301-13.
11　On which see Köhler, 177.
12　Except in the alliterative *Morte*, ll.176-215: such detail is typical of the alliterative genre (Turville-Petre, 69-73).
13　Dichmann, 85.
14　Faral, *Légende arthurienne*, II. 103-451.
15　See Huth II. 163; Löseth, 180; HRB, 444; *Perlesvaus* I. 328; *Prophécies*, f.150d; and below p.127.
16　On Arthur's spiritual role in *Perlesvaus*, see T. E. Kelly, *Perlesvaus: A Structural Study* (Geneva, 1974), 158-69.
17　Frappier, *Etude*, 249-51.
18　L. H. Loomis, 'Arthur's Round Table', PMLA 41 (1926), 771-84 (775n).
19　Respectively: ll.2747-62 (but compare 10461-2); ll.11446-50; fol.71c; p.5; ll.63-5; ll.47-8; Hales and Furnivall, II. 56-77, ll.6-15.
20　See the lists in Sandoz, 403-4.
21　L. H. Loomis, 'Arthur's Round Table'.
22　For details see *Perlesvaus* II. 335-6, with references.
23　ALMA, 257, with references.
24　Gardner, 155; *Sagramor*, 3.
25　Hales and Furnivall, I. 59-73.
26　Stith Thompson, E. 761.
27　ALMA, 554.
28　E. Vinaver, 'King Arthur's Sword . . .'; RG, 174-6.
29　E. Vinaver, 'King Arthur's Sword', 517-20.
30　Above pp.42-3.
31　Vinaver, 'King Arthur's Sword', 523.
32　'King Arthur's Sword', 515. 'Ron' simply means 'spear', and Geoffrey's choice of this name might be coincidental, independent of *Culhwch* and Welsh tradition.
33　LHB, 203.
34　Barber, *Figure of Arthur*, 101-4.
35　T. Jones, 'Early Evolution . . .', 7-8; HRB, 438; Wace, ll.9293-6; Giraldus Cambrensis, VIII. 126.
36　G. J. Brault, *Early Blazon* (Oxford, 1972), 23.
37　A. Fox-Davies, *Complete Guide to Heraldry* (Revised ed., London, 1969), 10-11.
38　Brault, 44-5, with references.
39　Lot, *Nennius*, 195.
40　See *Perlesvaus* II. 104-20.
41　Above p.22.
42　R. S. Loomis, *Arthurian Legends in Medieval Art* (New York, 1938), 37-40.
43　Wace, *Roman de Rou*, ed. A. J. Holden, SATF (1970-3), l.13193.
44　E.g. HRB, 450-2; Sommer, III. 203; Didot *Perceval*, 258; *Baladro* I. 239; Harley *Brut*, ll.105-19; *Golagros*, ll.312-13.
45　KA, 163.

Chapter VIII   Death and Aftermath

1   See ALMA, 307-13, 325-35 and notes; and for an excellent recent interpret-
     ation of Malory's account, Lambert, 138-221. On survival see M. Scanlan,
     'The Legend of Arthur's Survival' (Unpublished PhD thesis, Columbia
     University, 1961).
2   TYP, 160-2.
3   Scanlan, 23-30.
4   T. Jones, 'The Black Book of Carmarthen "Stanzas of the Graves" ', PBA 58
     (1967), 97-137 (127).
5   T. Gwynn Jones, 'Bardism and Romance', THSC (1913-14), 232-305.
6   Fletcher, 198-9, 211, 254.
7   TYP, 486.
8   G. Melville Richards, 'Arthurian Onomastics', THSC (1969), 250-64 (253).
9   LHB, 56-8.
10   Rickard, 221.
11   Frappier, *Etude*, 175-7.
12   Respectively: Cambridge Corpus Christi College MS 133, f.80b; Jean
     de Waurin, *Recueil des Chroniques*, ed. Ward E. Hardy, RS (London,
     1864-91), I. 445; *Nobiliario*, 243.
13   *Brut*, l.14239; *Demanda*, 326.
14   Above p.68.
15   Fletcher, 120.
16   Frappier calls this 'grande poésie' (*Mort*, xixn) – I cannot imagine why.
17   Respectively: f.lxxvii; 447; 9-10.
18   Gardner, 190.
19   Wace, l.4210; Layamon, l.14266; Giraldus, VIII. 129; Vulgate *Mort*, 245;
     Didot *Perceval*, 277; *Demanda*, 326; *Nobiliario*, 243; Salazar, 134.
20   See the articles and edition by M. Lapidge and R. Barber in *Arthurian
     Literature* (Woodbridge, 1981), I. 62-93; and Appendix 2 of my thesis,
     'The Development of the Figure of King Arthur' (University of Cambridge,
     1981).
21   *The Saga of the Volsungs*, trans. M. Schlauch, Scandinavian Classics 35
     (2nd ed., New York, 1949), 77, 144.
22   M. Courtney, *Cornish Feasts and Festivals* (Penzance, 1890), 58 (originally
     in Folklore Journal, V, 1886, 87).
23   Cotton Cleopatra D. III is a Hales MS, and Hales had dependencies at Paul
     and Breage: D. Knowles and R. Hadcock, *Medieval Religious Houses:
     England and Wales* (2nd ed., London, 1971), 120.
24   Ed. Basil Clarke (Cardiff, 1973).
25   On this passage see S. Lappert, 'Malory's Treatment of the Legend of Arthur's
     Survival', MLQ 36 (1975), 354-68.
26   Gardner, 234.
27   Scanlan, 200-17.
28   *Chronicles of the Reign of Stephen*, II. 696-707. See J. S. P. Tatlock, 'King
     Arthur in *Normannicus Draco*', MP 31 (1933), 1-18, 114-22.
29   Chambers, 125.
30   F. L. Cross, *The Oxford Dictionary of the Christian Church*, 2nd ed., revised
     F. L. Cross and T. A. Livingstone (Oxford, 1974), 916.
31   Didot *Perceval*, 278-9.
32   Frappier, *Etude*, 250-1.

33 See J. Wright, *The Geographical Lore of the Time of the Crusades* (New York, 1965), 262.
34 Above p. 97.
35 Edited, respectively: R. Leroux de Lincy, *Le Livre des Légendes* (Paris, 1836), 247-56 (extracts); R. F. Cook, TLF 187 (Geneva, 1972); unpublished text in British Library Royal 15-E-VI; K. V. Sinclair (Assen, 1971); P. Meyer, SATF 1 (1875); S. Lee, EETS 40 (1882) (Lord Berners' translation).
36 See H. R. Patch, *The Otherworld According to Descriptions in Medieval Literature* (Reprint, New York, 1970), passim.
37 *Fall of Princes*, ed. H. Bergen (Washington, 1923-7), III. 1.3111.
38 Keeler, 65-6.
39 Scanlan, 30-2.
40 Respectively: ll. 956-7; l. 13298; 277; Gardner, 234; 14.
41 *Brut*, l. 14297 ('*an* Arthur'); *I fatti*, 68.
42 Above p. 111.
43 On which see H. Thomas, *Spanish and Portuguese Romances of Chivalry* (Cambridge, 1920).
44 See Chapter 1, n. 63.
45 *Mort*, ll. 3232-3320; Malory, III. 1235; *Nobiliario*, 243; R. Menéndez Pidal, 'La Crónica general de 1404', RABM (1903, 2), 34-55 (39). On source-relationship see K. Jones, 'Versions of Arthur's Last Battle', BBSIA 26 (1974), 197-205.
46 A fact missed by P. McCaffrey, 'The Adder at Malory's Battle of Salisbury', TSL 22 (1977), 17-27.
47 Above pp. 110-11.
48 See particularly Micha, I. 111; Vulgate *Mort*, 247.
49 502-3. Sanctuary did not generally extend to high treason: see ODCC, 1233.
50 See, e.g., *Folie Lancelot*, xxi-xxvii; Baumgartner, 88-96; R. Bloch, 199-208.
51 Huth I. 234; *Die Abenteuer*, 124; *Folie Lancelot*, 134; *Demanda*, 326 (more of a charnel-house!)
52 See e.g., Fowler, *History of Sculpture* (London, 1916), 197-9.
53 RG, 266.
54 Löseth, 302, 371; *Demanda*, 269-70, 326; Lathullière, 133, 187. Noted in L. Muir, 'King Arthur, Style Louis XVI', in *Studies in Eighteenth-Century French Literature Presented to Robert Niklaus*, ed. J. Fox (Exeter, 1975), 163-8 (164).
55 E.g., G. Gerould, 'King Arthur and Politics', S 2 (1927), 33-51.

BIBLIOGRAPHY

1 TEXTS

A *Latin*

Arnold, T., *Henry of Huntingdon: Historia Regum Anglorum*, RS (London, 1879).

Babington, C., et al., *Ranulf Higden: Polychronicon*, 9 vols, RS (London, 1865-86).

Hector Boece: *Scotorum Historiae* (Paris, 1574).

Brewer, J. S., et al., Giraldus Cambrensis: Opera, 8 vols, RS (London, 1861-91).

Bruce, J. D., *Historia Meriadoci and De Ortu Walwanii* (Göttingen, 1913).

Carley, J. P., *John of Glastonbury: 'Cronica'*, British Archaeological Reports 48 (1978).

Clarke, B., *Vita Merlini* (Cardiff, 1973).

Grant, M., *Hyginus: Fabulae* (Lawrence, Kansas U.P., 1960).

Griscom, A., *Geoffrey of Monmouth: Historia Regum Britanniae* (London, 1929).

Hammer, J., *Historia Regum Britanniae, a Variant Version* (Cambridge, Mass., 1951).

Howlett, R., *Chronicles of the Reign of Stephen*, 4 vols, RS (London, 1884-9).

Kittredge, G., *Arthur and Gorlagon* (Reprint, New York, 1966).

Lapidge, M., 'The Vera Historia de Morte Arthuri: *an edition and translation*', in *Arthurian Literature I*, ed. R. Barber (Woodbridge, 1981), 79-93.

Lot, F., *Nennius et L'Historia Brittonum*, BEHE, 263 (Paris, 1934).

Meneghetti, M. L., *I Fatti di Bretagna* (Padua, 1979).

Michel, F., *William of Rennes: Gesta Regum Britanniae*, Cambrian Archaeological Association (Bordeaux, 1862).

Migne, A., *Gottfried of Viterbo: Pantheon*, in PL, 198 (Paris, 1885).
Gautier de Châtillon: Alexandreis, in PL, 209 (Paris, 1855).

Mommsen, T., *Vita Gildae*, in MGH, Auct. Antiq. XIII, part I (Berlin, 1894).

Müller, C., *Vitalis Blesensis Geta* (Bern, 1840).

Pfister, F., *Der Alexanderroman des Archipresbyters Leo*, SMT 6 (Heidelberg, 1913).

Stubbs, W., *William of Malmesbury: Gesta Regum Anglorum*, 2 vols, RS (London, 1887-89).

Williams, H., *Gildas: De Excidio et Conquestu Britanniae*, Cymmrodorion Record Series, 3 (London, 1889-1901).

Bibliography

B   Welsh

Bromwich, R. (ed.),   Trioedd Ynys Prydein (Cardiff, 1961).
Evans, J. G. (ed.),   Llyfr Gwyn Rhydderch: Y Chwedlau a'r Rhamantau,
    2nd edn, with preface by R. M. Jones (Cardiff, 1973).
Goctinck, G. W.,   Peredur (Cardiff, 1976).
Lewis, H.,   Brut Dingestow (Reprint, Cardiff, 1974).
Parry, J. J.,   Brut y Brenhinedd, Medieval Academy of America (Cambridge,
    Mass., 1937).
Richards, G. Melville,   Breudwyt Ronabwy (Cardiff, 1948).
Roberts, B.,   Brut y Brenhinedd, DIAS, MMW 5 (Dublin, 1971).
Thomson, R. L.,   Owein, DIAS, MMW 4 (Dublin, 1968).
Williams, I.,   Pedeir Keinc y Mabinogi (Reprint, Cardiff, 1964).

C   French

Armstrong, E. et al.,   The Old French Roman d'Alexandre, 3 vols, Eliott
    Monographs, 36-8 (Princeton, 1937).
Arnold, I.,   Le Roman de Brut de Wace, 2 vols, SATF (Paris, 1938).
Blanchard, J.,   Les Deux Captivités Tristan, BFR, B15 (Paris, 1976).
Bogdanow, F.,   Le Folie Lancelot, Beihefte zur ZRP, 109 (Tübingen, 1965).
Borgnet, A. and Bonmans, S.,   Jean d'Outremeuse: Mer (Myreur) des
    Histoires, 7 vols (Brussels, 1864-87).
Cook, R. F.,   Le Batârd de Bouillon, TLF 187 (Geneva, 1972).
Curtis, R.,   Le Tristan en prose, 2 vols (Munich, 1963; Leiden, 1976).
Erickson, C. T.,   Robert Biket: Le Lai du Cor, ANTS (Oxford, 1973).
Ewert, A.,   Marie de France: Lais (Oxford, 1944).
Förster, W.,   Li Chevaliers as deus espees (Halle, 1877).
Förster, W. and Breuer, H.,   Les Merveilles de Rigomer, 2 vols, GRL 19 and
    39 (Dresden, 1908, 1914).
Frappier, J.,   La Mort le roi Artu, TLF (3rd edn, 1964).
Friedwagner, M.,   Raoul de Houdenc: Sämtliche Werke, 2 vols (Halle,
    1897-1909).
Gelzer, H.,   Das Altfranzösische Yderroman, GRL 31 (Dresden, 1913).
Gildea, J.,   Durmart li Galois, 2 vols (Villanova Press, 1966).
Hardy, W. and Hardy, E.,   Jean de Waurin: Recueil des Chroniques, 5 vols,
    RS (London, 1864-91).
Heuckenkamp, F.,   Li Chevaliers du papegau (Hallen, 1896).
Hutchings, G.,   Le Roman en prose de Lancelot (Paris, 1930).
Leroux de Lincy, R.,   Le Livre des légendes (Paris, 1836).
Martin, E.,   Fergus (Hallen, 1872).
Meyer, P.,   Brun de la Montaigne, SATF 1 (Paris, 1875).
Micha, A.,   Chrétien de Troyes: Cligès, CFMA 84 (Paris, 1957).
    Lancelot, 6 vols, TLF 187, 247, 262, 278, 283, 286 (Geneva, 1978-80).
Nitze, W.,   L'Estoire dou Saint Graal (Joseph), CFMA 57 (Paris, 1971).
Nitze, W. and Jenkins, T. A.,   Perlesvaus, 2 vols (New York, 1922).
Paris, G. and Ulrich, J.,   Merlin, 2 vols, SATF (Paris, 1886).
Paton, L. A.,   Les Prophécies de Merlin (New York and London, 1927).
Pauphilet, A.,   La Queste del Saint Graal, CFMA 33 (Paris, 1972).
Potvin, A.,   Perceval le Gallois, 6 vols (Mons, 1865-71).

Bibliography

Roach, W., *Continuations of the Old French Perceval*, 4 vols (Philadelphia, 1965-71).

The Didot Perceval (Philadelphia, 1941).

Perceval, ou le conte du Graal, TLF 71 (Geneva, 1959).

Roques, M., *Erec et Enide*, CFMA 80 (Paris, 1970).

Yvain, ou le Chevalier au Lion, CFMA 89 (Paris, 1971).

Lancelot, ou le Chevalier de la Charrette, CFMA 86 (Paris, 1972).

Sommer, H. O., *Arthurian Romances*, 7 vols (Washington, 1908-13): 1. *Lestoire del Saint Graal*; 2. *Lestoire de Merlin*; 3-5. *Le livre de Lancelot del Lac*; 6. *Les aventures ou la queste del Saint Graal. La mort le roi Artus*; 7. Supplement, *Le livre d'Artus*.

Die Abenteuer Gawains, Yuains und die Morholts mit den drei Jungfrauen, Beihefte zur ZRP, 47 (Halle, 1913).

Sinclair, K. A., *Tristan de Nanteuil* (Assen, 1971).

Stürzinger and Breuer, *Hunbaut*, GRL 35 (Dresden, 1914).

Thompson, A. W., *The Elucidation* (New York, 1931).

Tobin, P. M. O., *Lais anonymes des xiie et xiiie siècles*, PRF 143 (Geneva, 1976).

Williams, G. P., *Renaut de Beaujeu: Le Bel inconnu*, CFMA 38, (Paris, 1964).

Williams, H., *Floriant et Floriete*, UMPLL 23 (Michigan, 1947).

Williams, M. and Oswald, M., Gerbert de Montreuil: *Perceval*, 3 vols, CFMA 28, 50, 101 (Paris, 1922, 1925, 1975).

Woledge, B., *L'Atre périlleux*, CFMA (Paris, 1936).

Wolfgang, L., *Bliocadran*, Beihefte zur ZRP, 150 (Tübingen, 1976).

D *English*

Amours, F. J., *Scottish Alliterative Poems*, STS (Edinburgh, 1897).

Bergen, Lydgate: *Fall of Princes*, 4 vols (Washington, 1923-7).

Brock, E., *Morte Arthure*, EETS, Original Series 8 (Oxford U.P., Reprint, 1967).

Brook, G. L. and Leslie, R. F., Layamon: *Brut*, 2 vols, EETS 250, 277 (Oxford U.P., 1963, 1978).

Bruce, J. D., *Le Morte Arthur*, EETS, Extra Series 88 (Oxford U.P., Reprint, 1959).

Furnivall, F. J., *Arthur*, EETS, Original Series 2 (Oxford U.P., Reprint, 1965).

Hales, C. B. and French, W. H., *Middle English Metrical Romances* (Reissue, New York, 1964).

Hales, J. W. and Furnivall, F. J., *Bishop Percy's Folio Manuscript*, 3 vols (London, 1867-8).

Hanna, R. W., *The Auntyrs off Arthure at the Terne Wathelyn* (Manchester, 1974).

Hardyng, J., *Chronicle* (Facsimile) English Experience, 805 (Amsterdam, 1976).

Holthausen, F. and Campion, J., *Sir Percyvalle of Galles*, AMT V (Heidelberg, 1913).

Kurvinen, A., *Sir Gawain and the Carl of Carlisle*, Annales Academiae Scientiarium Fennicae, Series B, Vol. 71^2 (Helsinki, 1951).

163

Lee, S. L., *Duke Huon of Bordeaux, by Lord Berners, Part 1*, EETS 40 (Oxford U.P., 1882).

Macrae-Gibson, O. D., *Of Arthour and of Merlin*, EETS 263 (Oxford U.P., 1973).

Mills, M., *Lybeaus Desconus*, EETS 261 (Oxford U.P., 1969).

Sands, D. B., *Middle English Metrical Romances* (New York, 1966).

Skeat, W., *Lancelot of the Laik*, EETS, Original Series 6, (Oxford U.P., Reprint, 1965).

Tolkien, J. R. R. and Gordon, E. V., *Sir Gawain and the Green Knight* (2nd edn, Revised by N. Davis, Oxford, 1972).

Turnbull, W. B., *Stewart's Metrical Chronicle of Scotland*, 2 vols, RS (London, 1858).

E *Spanish and Portuguese*

Bohigas, P., *El Baladro del Sabio Merlin*, 3 vols, Selecciones bibliófil as, 2, 14, 15 (Barcelona, 1957-62).

Bonilla y San Martin, A., *Libros de Caballerias*, 2 vols (Madrid, 1907-8). *Don Tristan de Loenis* (Madrid, 1912).

Herculano, A., *Portugaliae Monumenta Historica: Scriptores*, Vol. 1 (Lisbon, 1856).

Magne, A., *A Demanda do Santo Graal*, 3 vols (Rio de Janeiro, 1944).

Vasconcellos, J. Ferreira de, *Sagramor: Memorial das Proezas da Segunda Tabla Redonda* (Reprint, Lisbon, 1897).

2 LITERARY STUDIES

Barber, R., *King Arthur in Legend and History* (Cardinal, London, 1973). *The Figure of Arthur* (London, 1972).

Baumgartner, E., *Le Tristan en prose*, PRF (Geneva, 1975).

Benson, L., *Malory's Mort d'Arthur* (Harvard U.P., 1976).

Bezzola, R., *Le Sens de l'aventure et de l'amour* (Paris, 1947).

Bloch, R., *Medieval French Literature and Law* (California U.P., 1977).

Bogdanow, F., *The Romance of the Grail* (Manchester, 1965).

Bowen, G. (ed.), *Y Traddodiad Rhyddiaith yn yr Oesau Canol* (Llandysul, 1974).

Brewer, E., *From Cuchulainn to Gawain* (Cambridge, 1973).

Cary, G., *The Medieval Alexander* (Cambridge, 1956).

Chambers, E. K., *Arthur of Britain* (London, 1927).

Comfort, W. W., *Chrétien de Troyes: Arthurian Romances*, Everyman's Library, 698 (Reprint, London, 1967).

Entwistle, E., *The Arthurian Legend in the Literatures of the Spanish Peninsula* (London, 1925).

Evans, D. S., *A Grammar of Middle Welsh*, DIAS, MMW (Dublin, 1970).

Faral, E., *La Légende Arthurienne*, 2 vols, BEH 8, 255-7 (Paris, 1929).

Finlayson, J., *Morte Arthure*, YMT (London, 1967) (for introduction and notes).

Fletcher, R. H., *The Arthurian Material in the Chronicles* (Boston, 1910;

Reprinted, New York, 1958).

Frappier, J., *Etude sur La Mort le roi Artu*, PRF 70 (2nd edn, Geneva, 1961).

Gardner, E. G., *The Arthurian Legend in Italian Literature* (London, 1930).

Göller, K. H., *König Arthur in der englischen Litteratur des Spätens Mittelalters*, Palaestra 268 (Göttingen, 1963).

Hanning, R., *The Vision of History in Early Britain from Gildas to Geoffrey of Monmouth* (New York, 1966).

Haupt, J., *Der Truchsess Keie im Artusroman*, PSQ 57 (Berlin, 1971).

Imelmann, R., *Layamon's Brut: Versuch über seine Quellen* (Berlin, 1906).

Jarman, A. O. H., *The Legend of Merlin* (Cardiff, 1960).

Jones, G., *Kings, Beasts and Heroes* (London, 1972).

Jones, G. and Jones, T., *The Mabinogion*, Everyman's Library 97 (Reprint, London, 1968) (for introduction).

Keeler, L., *Geoffrey of Monmouth and the Late Latin Chroniclers* (Berkeley and Los Angeles, 1946).

Kelly, D., *'Sens' and 'Conjointure' in 'The Chevalier de la Charette'* (The Hague, Paris, 1966).

Kelly, T. F., *Perlesvaus: A Structural Study* (Geneva, 1974).

Ker, N., *Medieval Manuscripts in British Libraries*, 2 vols (Oxford, 1969).

Köhler, E., *Ideal und Wirklichkeit in der höfischen Epik*, Beihefte zur ZRP 97 (2nd edn, Tübingen, 1970).

Lacy, N. J., *A Medieval Miscellany* (Lawrence, 1972).

Lambert, M., *Style and Vision in Malory's Mort d'Arthur* (Yale U.P., 1975).

Lathuillière, R., *Guiron le Courtois*, PRF 86 (Geneva, 1966).

Lewis, C. B., *Classical Mythology and Arthurian Romance* (Oxford, 1932).

Lods, J., *Le Roman de Perceforest* (Geneva, 1951).

Loomis, R. S., *Celtic Myth and Arthurian Romance* (Columbia U.P., 1927).

Loomis, R. S. (ed.), *Arthurian Literature in the Middle Ages* (Oxford, 1959).

Löseth, E., *Le Roman en prose de Tristan* (Paris, 1891).

Lot, F., *Etudes sur le Lancelot en prose*, BEHE 226 (Paris, 1918).

Lumiansky, R. (ed.), *Malory's Originality* (Baltimore, 1964).

Luttrell, C., *The Creation of the First Arthurian Romance* (London, 1974).

Markale, J., *Le Roi Arthur et la société celtique* (Paris, 1976).

Matthews, W., *The Tragedy of Arthur* (Pennsylvania, 1960).

Meyer, P., *Alexandre dans la litterature française du Moyen Age*, 2 vols (Paris, 1886).

Murphy, G. and MacNeill, E., *Duanaire Finn*, 3 vols, ITS 8, 25, 43 (1904, 1933, 1953).

Paton, L. A., *The Fairy Mythology of Arthurian Romance*, 2 vols (2nd edn, New York, 1960).

Patch, H. R., *The Otherworld According to Descriptions in Medieval Literature* (Reprint, New York, 1970).

Pauphilet, A., *Etude sur la Queste du Saint Graal* (Paris, 1921).

Pelan, M., *L'Influence de Wace sur les romanciers de son temps* (Paris, 1931).

Pickford, C., *L'Evolution du roman arthurien en prose* (Paris, 1959).

Pochoda, E., *Arthurian Propaganda* (Chapel Hill, 1971).

Rickard, P., *Britain in Medieval French Literature* (Cambridge, 1956).

Schmidt, W., *Untersuchungen zum Geta des Vitalis Blesensis* (Ratingen, 1975).

Tatlock, J. S. P., *The Legendary History of Britain* (Berkeley and Los Angeles, 1950).

Thiebaux, P., *The Stag of Love* (Ithaca, New York, 1974).

Thomas, H., *Spanish and Portuguese Romances of Chivalry* (Cambridge, 1920).

Turville-Petre, T., *The Alliterative Revival* (Ipswich, 1977).

Tolkien, J. R. R., *Tree and Leaf* (London, 1964).

Vinavier, E., *The Rise of Romance* (Oxford, 1971).

Webster, K. T., *Guinevere: A Study of her Abductions*, ed. D. C. Webster (Milton, Mass., 1951).

Webster, K. T. (trans.), *Ulrich von Zatzikhoven: Lanzelet* (New York, 1951).

Weston, J., *The Legend of Sir Gawain* (London, 1897).

3   REFERENCE AND GENERAL

Barber, R., *The Knight and Chivalry* (Cardinal, London, 1974).

Bloch, M., *Les Rois thaumaturges* (Strasbourg and Paris, 1924).

Brault, G. J., *Early Blazon* (Oxford, 1972).

Byrne, F. J., *Irish Kings and High Kings* (London, 1973).

Campbell, J., *The Hero with a Thousand Faces* (Princeton, 1968).

Courtney, M., *Cornish Feasts and Festivals* (Penzance, 1890).

Cretney, S. M., *Principles of Family Law* (London, 1974).

Cross, F. L., *The Oxford Dictionary of the Christian Church* (2nd edn, revised by F. L. Cross and T. A. Livingstone, Oxford, 1974).

Douglas, D. C., *William the Conqueror* (London, 1964).

Ellis, T. P., *Welsh Tribal Law and Custom in the Middle Ages*, 2 vols (Oxford, 1976).

Fawtier, R., *The Capetian Kings of France*, trans. R. Butler and R. J. Adam (London, 1960).

Ferguson, W., *Scotland's Relations with England* (Edinburgh, 1977).

Fowler, H. N., *A History of Sculpture* (London, 1916).

Fox-Davies, A., *Complete Guide to Heraldry* (Revised edn, London, 1969).

Hamilton, J. R., *Alexander the Great* (London, 1973).

Harvey, J., *The Plantagenets* (Fontana, London, 1967).

Hocart, A., *Kingship* (Oxford, 1927).

Huizinga, J., *The Waning of the Middle Ages*, trans. F. Hopman, (Penguin Books, Reissue, 1972).

Jolliffe, J., *Angevin Kingship* (London, 1955).

Jones, T. Gwynn, *Welsh Folklore and Folk-Custom* (London, 1930, reprinted Ipswich, 1978).

Kantorowicz, E., *The King's Two Bodies* (Princeton, 1957).

Keen, M., *The Laws of War in the Later Middle Ages* (Oxford, 1965).

Kirk, K. E., *Some Principles of Moral Theology* (London, 1921).

Knowles, D. and Hadcock, R., *Religious Houses: England and Wales* (2nd edn, London, 1971).

Legg, L. D. W., *English Coronation Rites* (Westminster, 1901).

Loomis, R. S., *Arthurian Legends in Medieval Art* (New York, 1938).

Lloyd, J. E., *A History of Wales to 1284*, 2 vols (2nd edn, Cardiff, 1912).

Mac Cana, P., *Celtic Mythology* (3rd Impression, London, 1975).

Morris, J. R., *The Age of Arthur* (London, 1973).

Nicholson, R., *Scotland: The Later Middle Ages* (Edinburgh, 1974).

O'Callaghan, J. F., *A History of Medieval Spain* (Cornell U.P., 1977).

Oman, C., *History of the Art of War*, 2 vols (London, 1924).

Pearce, S. M., *The Kingdom of Dumnonia* (Padstow, 1978).

Perroy, E., *La Guerre de cent ans* (Paris, 1945).

Peters, E., *The Shadow King* (New Haven and London, 1970).

Petit-Dutaillis, *La Monarchie féodale en France et en Angleterre, x^e -xiiie siècle*, Evolution de l'humanité, 4 (Paris, 1933).

Pollock, F. and Maitland, F. W., *The History of English Law*, 2 vols, 2nd edn reissued by S. C. Millsom (Cambridge, 1968).

Raglan, Lord, *The Hero* (London, 1936).

Riley-Smith, J., *What were the Crusades?* (London, 1977).

Rondet, H., *Notes sur la théologie du péché* (Paris, 1957).

Ross, A., *Pagan Celtic Britain* (Cardinal, London, 1974).

Russell, H., *The Just War in the Middle Ages* (Cambridge, 1975).

Salmon, A. (ed.), *Beaumanoir: Coutumes du Beauvaisis*, 2 vols (Paris, 1899-1900).

Schlauch, M. (trans.), *The Saga of the Volsungs*, Scandinavian Chronicles, 35 (2nd edn, New York, 1947).

Schramm, P. E., *A History of the English Coronation* (Oxford, 1937).

Smalley, B., *Historians in the Middle Ages* (London, 1974).

Southern, R. W., *Medieval Humanism* (Oxford, 1970).

Stith Thompson, *Motif-Index of Folk-Literature*, 6 vols (Copenhagen, 1955-8).

de Vries, A., *Dictionary of Symbols and Imagery* (Amsterdam and London, 1974).

Wilks, M. K., *The Problem of Sovereignty in the Later Middle Ages* (Cambridge, 1963).

Woolley, R. M., *Coronation Rites* (Cambridge, 1915).

Wright, J., *The Geographical Lore of the Time of the Crusades* (New York, 1965).

4 MANUSCRIPTS

London, British Library: Harley 902; Additional 25434; Royal 15-E-VI.
Cambridge, Corpus Christi College 133.
Cambridge University Library, Additional 7071.
Edinburgh, National Library of Scotland, Advocates 19-1-5.

5 THESES

Foster, Idris, *Astudiaeth o chwedl Culhwch ac Olwen*, MA, University College of Wales, Aberystwyth, 1935.

Scanlan, Honora, *The Legend of Arthur's Survival*, PhD, University of Columbia, 1961.

Sharrer, Harvey, *The Legendary History of Britain in Lope Garcia de Salazar's Libro de las bienandanzas y fortunas*, PhD, University of California, Los Angeles, 1970.
Shepherd, K. H., *The Presentation of King Arthur in Medieval Romance*, MA, University of London, 1907.
Williams, J. Mary, *Y Darlun o Arthur ym Mhucheddau'r Saint ag yn Englynion Arthur a'r Eryr*, MA, University College of Wales, Aberystwyth, 1969.

6 FESTSCHRIFTEN

Bromwich, R. and Jones, R. (eds), *Astudiaethau ar yr Hengerdd* (Presented to Idris Foster) (Cardiff, 1978).
Festschrift für Gustau Gröber (Halle, 1899).
Mélanges d'Histoire du Moyen Age offerts à F. Lot, (Paris, 1925).
Fox, J. (ed.), *Studies in Eighteenth-Century French Literature presented to Robert Niklaus* (Exeter, 1975).
Jones, T. (ed.), *Astudiaethau Amrywiol a gyflwynir i Syr Thomas Parry-Williams* (Cardiff, 1968).
Brahmer, M. et al. (eds), *Studies in Honour of M. Schlauch* (Warsaw, 1966).
Studi in onore di Italo Siciliano, 2 vols (Florence, 1967).
Whitehead, F. et al., *A Medieval Miscellany* (Presented to E. Vinaver) (Manchester, 1965).
Mélanges de Philologie et de littératures romanes offerts à Jeanne Wathelet-Willem (Liège, 1978).

7 PERIODICALS

	Anglia
A	Anglistica
AB	Annales de Bretagne
AM	Annuale Medievale
	Arthuriana
ASNS	Archiv für das Studium der Neueren Sprachen
BBSIA	Bulletin Bibliographique de la Société Internationale Arthurienne
BBCS	Bulletin of the Board of Celtic Studies
BJRL	Bulletin of the John Rylands Library
ET	Etudes Celtiques
F	Folklore
GRM	Germanisch-Romanische Monatsschrift
H	History
JEGP	Journal of English and Germanic Philology
KFLQ	Kentucky Foreign Language Quarterly
MH	Medievalia et Humanistica
MRS	Medieval and Renaissance Studies
MS	Medieval Studies
MA	Medium Aevum

MLQ	Modern Language Quarterly
MLR	Modern Language Review
MP	Modern Philology
NMS	Nottingham Medieval Studies
PBA	Proceedings of the British Academy
PMLA	Publications of the Medieval Academy of America
RES	Review of English Studies
RABM	Revista de Archivos, Bibliotecas y Museos
RBPH	Revue Belge de Philologie et d'Histoire
RLM	Revue des Langues Modernes
RP	Romance Philology
R	Romania
RR	Romanic Review
S	Speculum
SH	Speculum Historiale
SC	Studia Celtica
SP	Studia Philologica
SLI	Studies in the Literary Imagination
TS	Tennessee Studies in Literature
THSC	Transactions of the Honourable Society of Cymmrodorion
TRHS	Transactions of the Royal Historical Society
YC	Y Cymmrodor
ZFDA	Zeitschrift für deutches Altertum
ZFSL	Zeitschrift für Französischen Sprachen und Litteratur
ZRP	Zeitschrift für Romanische Philologie

8   OTHER ABBREVIATIONS

AMT	Alt und Mittelenglische Texte
ANTS	Anglo-Norman Texts Society
AoM	Of Arthour and of Merlin
BEHE	Bibliothèque de l'Ecole des Hautes Etudes
BFR	Bibliothèque Française et Romane
CFMA	Classiques Français du Moyen Age
DIAS	Dublin Institute for Advanced Studies
EETS	Early English Texts Society
GGK	Sir Gawain and the Green Knight
GRL	Gesellschaft für Romanische Litteratur
HRB	Historia Regum Britanniae
ITS	Irish Texts Society
LP	Lancelot en Prose
MGH	Monumenta Germaniae Historica, Auctores Antiquissimi
MMW	Modern and Medieval Welsh Series
ODCT	Oxford Dictionary of the Christian Church
PL	Patrologia Latina
PKM	Pedeir Keinc y Mabinogi
PRF	Publications Romanes et Françaises
PSQ	Philologische Studien und Quellen
RG	Romance of the Grail

Bibliography

RS   Rolls Series
SMT   Sammlung Mittellateinischer Texte
STS   Scottish Texts Society
SATF   Société des Anciens Textes Français
TLF   Textes Littéraires Français
TP   Tristan en Prose
TYP   *Trioedd Ynys Pryddein*, ed. R. Bromwich (Cardiff, 1961)
UMPLL   University of Michigan Publications in Language and Literature
VM   Vulgate Merlin

INDEX

171